THIS IS THE YEAR
I PUT MY
FINANCIAL LIFE
IN ORDER

THIS IS THE YEAR

I PUT MY

FINANCIAL LIFE

IN ORDER

JOHN SCHWARTZ

AVERY

an imprint of Penguin Random House
New York

AVERY

an imprint of Penguin Random House LLC
375 Hudson Street
New York, New York 10014

Most Avery books are available at special quantity discounts for bulk purchase for sales promotions,
premiums, fund-raising, and educational needs. Special books or book excerpts also can be created
to fit specific needs. For details, write SpecialMarkets@penguinrandomhouse.com.

ISBN 9780399576812
ebook ISBN 9780399576829

Printed in the United States of America
1   3   5   7   9   10   8   6   4   2

BOOK DESIGN BY TANYA MAIBORODA

To Jeanne

CONTENTS

INTRODUCTION

Annual income twenty pounds, annual expenditure nineteen pounds nineteen and six, result happiness. Annual income twenty pounds, annual expenditure twenty pounds nought and six, result misery.

—CHARLES DICKENS, *DAVID COPPERFIELD*

I AM AN IDIOT.

That, at least, is the impression I get from personal finance websites and magazines and books. They all seem to say I'm doing pretty much everything wrong when it comes to my financial life, basically because I don't pay that much attention to my finances.

As a journalist, I understand that telling people to doubt themselves is part of the game of newsstand sales and, in the digital age, page views. That's why "You're doing it wrong" is such powerful clickbait. None of us spends much time on a website that affirms our choices and tells us we are in good shape. No parenting magazine could last long if it didn't suggest that its advice will make a world of difference. This is especially true when it comes to advice about parenting: "Our seven-step plan will help you raise a future Ivy Leaguer!" "Ignore us, and you will end up with a basement-dwelling angry loner who spends his days playing online games and staring dully at porn."

It's much the same persuasion game when it comes to financial advice: the person giving the advice has to start from the position that you'll go broke without this help. In publishing, sex may sell, but insecurity sells even better.

In my case, they could be right about my being all wrong. I mean, look at me. I had reached my mid-50s and didn't have a will. How dumb is that? I had no idea whether the life insurance that I got through my employer was enough to support my family if I got squashed by a bus during my morning run. And I hadn't given any thought to figuring out whether the money I'd been putting away for retirement had been well invested and would lead my wife, Jeanne, and me to comfort or misery. Living in the now may be great Zen wisdom, but it's a lousy way to go about planning for retirement.

We all *know* we need to do these things: to balance our portfolios, to get a will, to make sure our life insurance policies are generous enough to take care of our loved ones if we meet up with that aforementioned bus. Still, we procrastinate, or don't know what we should do. We're supposed to buy low and sell high. Or is it buy and hold? We're supposed to spring into action and refinance our mortgages the moment interest rates drop below, uh—what was that rule of thumb again? We're supposed to pay down all our loans, except maybe for the loans that have really low rates. Or is it the smallest loans first? And in the middle of all that, we're supposed to finance the kids' college educations and deal adroitly with expensive family emergencies.

So over the last year, Jeanne and I embarked on a project: we took a hard look at what a rather heedless financial existence has left undone. I tried to educate myself about the world of finance and investing. Then, with the help of books, friends, and a few professionals, we worked to get our financial life in order. This book is the story of how we got here, what we did, and what we learned along the way.

I realized it was time to get our financial house in order, not because I'm near retirement (I hope not!), but because this reckoning was overdue. We were surely starting later than we should have, but without a time machine, starting now was as good as it was going to get. Better late, than, you know.

Our financial life has not been a straightforward march toward prosperity. We have struggled; for much of our adult lives, Jeanne and I have lived paycheck to paycheck, and we have veered close to financial disaster more times than I'd like to remember. Our late 30s were a nightmare. Jeanne and I lived through a crisis that started when we moved from New York City to Washington, D.C., so that I could take a great job. But a New York real estate slump kept us from being able to sell our apartment, and deadbeat tenants drove us nearly to bankruptcy. We lost the New York place, and the resulting squeeze kept things tight for years after that.

How tight? When I was working at *The Washington Post*, on the days before payday, my lunch order in the company cafeteria was often french fries with gravy. The mess of carbs, salt, and fat cost less than two bucks, and that filling meal kept me going until I could get home for dinner. And I knew that one solid knock from illness, or a layoff, could have transformed our financial life from tight to devastated.

That didn't happen, thank goodness. But the ups and downs continued. Things would let up for a while, and the squeeze would set in again. About a year after I'd gotten to *The New York Times*, an editor predicted that, financially speaking, I was going to crash and burn. He wasn't my boss, but we both worked for the business section of the paper and had gotten to be friendly. We often rode the same train into the city from Maplewood, New Jersey, and back again.

"I know what you make," he said, "and I don't see how you're going to make it."

He edited personal finance stories and had planned out his own retirement beautifully. He had built up a generous cushion in his retirement plan and could count on a good pension, as well. He lived frugally, driving a beat-up Ford Fiesta that got more than 40 miles per gallon. In the year or so before he retired, he had built a house on Cape Cod and planned to keep up a little freelance editing work for additional income. This cobbler's children did not go barefoot. It was clear from our conversation, however, that he didn't understand how Jeanne and I survived from paycheck to paycheck, much less saved for the future. And he was hinting at something even worse: he didn't think we were going to make it. At all.

And you know what? He wasn't wrong. We were in trouble. Despite our best efforts to stay within our means, we were spending more than we were making, and our debts were once again adding up.

Result: misery.

So I might seem like the last person in the world you'd want to take financial advice from. After all, we had made bad decisions, and they put us in a hole. It was very hard to climb out.

But we did climb out.

How did we do it? Some of it was luck. Some of it was good choices we made in our 20s. Some of it was, in our confusion and fear, finding people who knew much more than we did and following their advice. And some of it was learning new things and acting on that hard-earned wisdom.

You have probably made some bad decisions, as well. But you can climb out, too. You can find your guides. You can make your own luck.

Sid Richardson, the legendary Texas oilman, liked to say, "I'd rather be lucky than smart."[1] In his business, he had seen booms and busts, enriched wildcatters and humbled titans. He knew that it wasn't necessarily the smartest who thrived. Of course, Richardson was aw-shucks-ing a little; he had enjoyed a share of luck, but he was also damned smart.

That resonates with me. A large portion of my good fortune has been getting jobs and keeping them at companies that had old-fashioned pension plans. I've also made some of my luck; keeping those jobs is no small trick, and anyone with sense knows that you can improve your situation through preparation and hard work. If you succeed, good fortune is always part of the picture. Yet fortune favors the prepared mind, as Louis Pasteur is supposed to have said.

So this story is also not just about us. (Jeanne and I aren't *that* interesting.) Yes, it involves our experiences, and also the process of exploration I've gone through in trying to understand and fix our financial situation. That information becomes, for you, the reader, a sort of guide to the financial world and planning for retirement. What I taught myself also turns out to be what you might need to know. What are the foundations of a good retirement account? What the heck is an exchange-traded fund? Should you ever go to one of those free dinners that retirement consultants send invitations for in the mail? And why does money make so many of us so very, very crazy?

The things Jeanne and I did over the course of the year to take charge of our financial life—figuring out life insurance, drawing up our wills, and the rest—I've written up in a way that will show you how it's done. That's the part where my being a reporter, someone who can take complicated information and make sense of it for readers, comes in handy.

So this is not your standard personal finance guide. It's more of a hybrid. If you would rather be reading one of those other kinds of financial books on financial planning or getting rich by 40, your local bookstore has long, heavy shelves of them. Many are written by people who have real financial expertise, or at least talk a good game.

Let me admit that I find most of those books impenetrable, teachy, and preachy. Worse, too many of them suffer from their authors' need to dress up what is, generally, a short list of common-sense investing ideas with gobbledygook and big promises.

This book, by contrast, keeps the advice simple, throws away the cloak of mystery, and blends in our story in ways that we hope can be useful. Without whining.

I wrote *This Is the Year* for people like us: a little money-phobic, maybe, but willing to learn before it's too late. There are a lot of us out there. While more than half of Americans fret about whether they will have enough money for retirement, just 39 percent have ever tried to figure out how much they will need, according to the Financial Industry Regulatory Authority (FINRA) Investor Education Foundation, an organization that tracks our money sense.[2]

So if we're idiots, we're not alone. Many people don't save enough for retirement, or don't save at all: According to a report by the National Institute on Retirement Security, some 45 percent of working-age households have no retirement account assets, while the overall national median retirement account balance is just $2,500. As the institute put it, "the average U.S. working-age household has virtually no retirement savings."[3]

And that's preparing for the future; many of us can't even handle the present! A 2016 report from the Federal Reserve found that 46 percent of Americans couldn't cover an emergency expense of $400 without borrowing the money (which includes putting it on a credit card) or selling something.[4]

Ideally, anyone reading this book might want to look at what we did and decide to do the smart things—only better, and earlier. I hope that people younger than us will take the lessons directed at them to heart, and end up not having to eat as many lunches of fries and gravy. Or whatever affordable staple millennials eat. Quinoa? Okay, quinoa.

Quinoa is, apparently, a seed and not a grain.

That's everything I know about quinoa.

==

The idea that became this book started with a piece I wrote for *The New York Times* about retirement planning.[5] It walked readers through our efforts to figure out where we stood with regard to our financial endgame: how much we'd have to live on once we retired.

The process of writing, I figured, would help me get over my money phobia. After all, I tackle tough topics all the time in the course of my work, especially in my science journalism. So, I thought, why not make it an assignment? If it's part of my job to learn about my finances, I'm likelier to get over the hump and figure things out.

That led me to pitch the story. I would have a deadline, an obligation to an editor, and (because special sections are considered freelance work at the *Times*), I'd get paid. All that would provide me with the incentive I'd previously lacked.

This is the way my mind works. I won't defend it.

The story described my own nervousness when it comes to thinking about finances. The response from readers was surprising—apparently, there are many, many people out there who share my anxiety. One colleague called it "frighteningly familiar," and my inbox became a digital confessional for readers who found themselves, uncomfortably, in the same boat. Other readers offered advice: Buy more bonds! Buy fewer bonds! Go jump in a lake! One helpful fellow told me that the answer was to buy a house in a small town in rural France. He had done this, and things were going great for him. I congratulated him. I write back to almost everyone who isn't really insulting.

That story got passed around. A neighbor, a great guy in his 30s with a couple of kids, told me his father sent him a three-by-five index card, his usual epistolary medium, lauding the piece. "Take it to heart," he wrote. "Before you know it, you are looking at your ability to keep paying for things during the 2nd half of your life." The neighbor, Brian, noted in an email to me, "I have to say, this is one of the longer written notes I have received from my father in the past several years, or maybe ever."

Had we struck a chord? Could we be the wake-up call for other people, whether in their 50s, or 30s, or just about any age this side of retirement? How could we purport to be teachers, after having done so many things wrong? I was drawn to the idea that we might be useful fools, teaching by good choices and by our flawed example.

This is not a unique idea: we all learn from failure as well as success. As poor Jude Fawley, the epic loser of Hardy's *Jude the Obscure,* put it, "I may do some good before I am dead—be a sort of success as a frightful example of what not to do; and so illustrate a moral story." Our disasters are good for something, if we know enough not to let them go to waste.

This book opens with that first step in the project to get our financial lives in order: taking a hard look at our progress toward funding our retirement. The other chapters present broader areas of personal finance that most of us face—saving for kids' college, buying and selling homes, dealing with a medical disaster, bankruptcy, debt, getting insurance, and writing a will—along with the experiences that Jeanne and I have had, for better or worse, in facing them.

So, hello, reader! Welcome to the secrets of our failures. (And, yes, our successes.) Jeanne and I, in telling our story, are trying to walk a line here between self-revelation and self-flagellation. I won't call this story a "journey," because the word is overused. But what a long, strange trip it's been. If we entertain you, that's great. If you get something useful out of it, even better.

And if our story at times gives you a soul-warming rush of schadenfreude, we don't mind one bit.

1
THE PROJECT

THIS PROJECT BEGAN with my realization that it was time to finally figure out whether we were going to be comfortable in retirement or miserable.

Going into it, I knew that we were pretty fortunate compared with many Americans. As I've said, I have always worked for companies that pay reasonably well and that provide pensions. Those pensions have been fully funded, at least within the legal definition. Those companies have also sponsored retirement plans for employees and encouraged them to build 401(k) accounts with matching contributions, and I have done that. Also, I've been able to hold on to jobs over the years in a business that's seen plenty of layoffs. Our household budgets have been tight, but aside from that ill-fated apartment purchase in our 30s, our family hasn't suffered the kind of financial setback or catastrophic illness that destroy many a family's nest egg.

We knew we had something tucked away. But was that something enough? Thanks to the recent sale of a house we had lived in for 15 years, we had some financial breathing room, at least for a while. But I had no idea where we stood in terms of being able to retire someday. I'd all but stopped looking at the envelopes from Vanguard after 2007, when my funds lost about 40 percent of their value—not an outrageous dip in the context of the broader economic crisis and recession, but a searing one for me. As a sometime financial reporter, I knew enough to not sell stocks during a sell-off, so I didn't compound the damage with a panic sale. Besides, I've always found it easy not to do anything; sloth comes naturally to me.

I figured that the accounts had bounced back to some extent, but hadn't been tracking them closely. And I had no idea how long such funds would last once I stopped getting a paycheck. A gnawing feeling in my gut convinced me at last that this was the year to get our finances together. Maybe past time, if the numbers didn't come out right. And while I hope to have good years of productive work ahead, I also have to think about retirement and plan for it—to look at whether I'm on the right track, and to begin addressing some of the other issues that I'd been avoiding all these years.

Where to start? With an industry built around retirement planning, I was faced with the paralysis of too much choice and too little knowledge. How do I find a retirement consultant? Those who work on commission might be tempted to sell financial products that increase their incomes, not mine. And those who charge a flat fee might try to keep things quick and easy (for them) to ensure that their time is efficiently used. I had no intention of being a quick hit on somebody's conveyor belt.

As it happens, the 401(k) accounts I built up at the three publications I have worked for over the last 30 years are all under the same roof, the mutual funds giant Vanguard. That promised to make things relatively easy, and the company offers free counseling from a certified financial planner to clients of employer-sponsored plans who are over 55.

So one evening in January, I made the call to Vanguard's 800 number. After navigating the voice-command system, I ended up talking to an upbeat guy named Jeff, who told me that I could either set up an appointment for a phone session with one of their certified financial planners, or I could get a more thorough counseling session by first filling out an online questionnaire that would give the planner a "more holistic view" of my financial picture before our conversation. The result, he said, would be a "personalized financial plan."

Filling out the document "takes about 45 minutes," he said.

As I hung up, Jeanne, sitting across the living room on the couch, asked, "Any luck?"

I told her about the 45-minute questionnaire and said, "We can fill it out together."

"Thrilling," she said.

The very first question stumped me. It asked the age I plan to retire.

Well, see, this is part of the problem. That is precisely the kind of question I've been avoiding all these years. Jeanne and I had never discussed it. I love my job—journalism is a career that calls for hard work, but it rarely feels like work. So we were starting with a big, big question. (Jeanne has worked part-time for years, so her decision would have less impact on our retirement picture.)

We knew that Social Security has traditionally kicked in at 62, but that you could earn more if you hold out longer—say, until 66. Medicare begins at 65. And after hunting around online, it appeared that sticking with gainful employment until 70 would lead to the biggest Social Security benefit. Jeanne, a pragmatist, noted ominously, "Your retirement isn't under your control, entirely." My employer has a lot to say about it. But we could project a best case, and decided that sticking it out to 70 would be the likeliest course to set us up in terms of our investments, Social Security, and pensions. Besides, even if I got booted out of one job, I could probably still find a way to keep earning; many of my friends at the *Times* had moved on to fulfilling careers on the outside. Seventy it would be.

Okay. So we had an answer! Success!

"So that was question number one?" Jeanne asked. Yes, I said.

She laughed. "That was more than 45 minutes."

Okay, it was going to be a long night. The first answer had taken so long that the Vanguard website had logged me out for inactivity. I went back in, entered the answer. And soon came to an ever more difficult question: How long do you expect to live?

Well, holy guacamole. Let me check my appointment book! We had moved abruptly from economics to metaphysics, or at least actuarial science.

Here, too, however, we decided to plan for a good outcome while understanding that the slings and arrows of outrageous fortune could make best estimates meaningless. Our four parents were still going strong in their 80s and 90s. My father, at 91, was still working as a lobbyist in the 2016 session of the Texas legislature. He'd laugh at the idea of quitting at 70. So we again filled in some rather optimistic estimates and then marched on through questions that were pretty obviously intended to measure my tolerance for investment risk: whether I was likely to sell stocks in a market downturn (no), whether I would invest in a fund based on a casual conversation or tip (heck, no), and suchlike.

Then came another stumper: What percentage of our income would we hope to receive in retirement? Searching through financial websites, I found that many people look for about 70 or 80 percent of their working income in retirement. The assumption is that retirees will live less expensively than they did in their more active years. So once again, I plugged in yet another guess, based on yet another rule of thumb that I hadn't known moments before.

As Jeanne and I discussed these things, I realized we had never really talked about whatever passed for my investment strategy. I offered to describe mine, such as it is. But she cut me off, saying, "My strategy is not to know your strategy."

I was gratified by her level of trust in me but wondered whether it was justified. And whether she was just trying to shut me up. Still, I did my best to express my amorphous thoughts on investing. I explained that I'd been skeptical of financial advice programs about hardcore investing by gurus like Jim Cramer. I never felt that I was the kind of guy who could beat the market. That's how I came up with my laissez-faire approach. I had a hard time remembering how much of my income I had assigned to the funds 14 years before, when I came to the *Times*. (After doing some research, I discovered that it was 10 percent, the same portion of my income I'd maintained during my years at *Newsweek* and *The Washington Post*.)

Jeanne said, "I approve." Which, after more than 40 years together, is nice to hear.

Proceeding through the questionnaire, I then had to track down what we could expect to receive from Social Security each month at age 70—a pretty easy figure to find from ssa.gov—and what my various pensions might bring in. That process could not be handled from my easy chair, as I had to ask former employers to come up with estimates. One would answer during the course of a single phone call; the other took weeks to calculate an estimate and send it by mail. Anticipating a slog, I decided I'd had enough for the night.

When I shut my laptop, four hours had passed from the time I had started the survey, and I was far from done. But we were thinking about the right questions at last.

The next day, Jeanne sent me an email mentioning a conversation she'd had with a coworker who had asked "a quality-of-life question." If you wait until you are 70 to retire, you might get a bigger payout, but will you be in any condition to enjoy it?

I responded: "An excellent question. If 70 is the new 50, yes. If 70 is the old 70, no."

Our parents, as I said, had been very young 70-year-olds. It seemed like a safe bet. But I decided to ask the counselor to look at the numbers under a couple of different retirement ages.

Over the next few days, I gathered the final bits of information about what my pensions from various employers would amount to and finished the form. Soon after that, Vanguard came back with a report generated from my answers. It said I should be more heavily invested in bonds; considering my age, the report stated, I had too much money in stocks. Vanguard's quarterly mailings had been telling me that for a while, so this advice was no surprise. But then I saw words that seemed to levitate off the page:

You're on track to meet your retirement goals.

It was a beautiful thing. If we continued the way we were going, if the financial markets didn't collapse, if the magical fairies that govern employment and health were good to us, we would make it. I was, frankly, surprised. Jeanne was exultant. She said, "We won't be eating cat food!"

But, of course, there were uncertainties. The document from

Vanguard presented three scenarios for my portfolio over time, based on past U.S. market performance: best, average, and worst. The worst-case scenario left us with $800,000, well below what we'd need for a comfortable draw-down from our 401(k) in retirement. The best-case was ridiculously high: nearly $4 million. The average scenario put us at about $2 million, which should make for a comfortable retirement. But which will it be? There's no way to tell. It's still a game of if, if, if.

A week later, I had the conversation with the financial adviser, an upbeat guy named Greg. We discussed how to get on what he somewhat ominously called the "glide path" to a more balanced portfolio for retirement.

He explained that the allocation between stocks and bonds mentioned in the report was actually a big deal—"the most important one you make as an investor," even bigger than deciding what funds we invest in, since bonds help cushion your investments against stock market drops. "When things are bad, your drops are not as extreme. So your recovery doesn't have to be as extreme," he said. I didn't have a lot of my money in bonds; the recommended percentage at my age (and considering my aptitude for risk from the questions I'd answered) was about 35 percent in bonds and 65 percent in stocks. I told him that I'd take a hard look at shifting the balance toward more bonds.

He also wanted to talk about some of the mutual funds I'd been invested in since starting to save 30 years before, and noted that several of them were funds run by fund managers and based on research in the markets, with higher rates than I would pay if I put more of my assets into so-called index funds, which are based on market indexes like the Standard & Poor 500. While much of my portfolio was already in such an index fund, he explained that I could make more money by putting more of my assets into lower-fee index funds. The report from Vanguard had recommended a number of index funds the company offers that focus on large companies, midsize companies, and international companies. It all went by pretty fast, but I caught most of it.

He didn't push me on any of these proposed changes—he told me that I could shift the assets myself, when I was ready, from my home computer. The report that Vanguard had generated recommended some of those funds, and I could use those or find others, he said. Most important, changing funds within Vanguard would cost me nothing—"no asset-transfer fees," he said. Sweet!

He also explained what we could expect if I wanted to shorten my time working and retire in my 60s. His estimates put us a little closer to the margins—less travel, buying cheaper cuts of meat—but he suggested that our current portfolio could, barring ill fortune, deliver us to comfort if not prosperity.

It felt good to be done.

But we weren't, of course. This was only the beginning. We plugged a bunch of hypothetical numbers into a model and got a nice picture back. Much was still left to chance. Every decision led to others, and opening one door led to even more doors. I would have to make decisions about whether to buy more bonds and whether to move more of our assets into index funds. And beyond our retirement planning, we still had so much to do to be able to say we'd gotten our financial life in order. We still did not have a will. I still needed to look at my level of life insurance to make sure the family would be covered if that bus found me. And there were things like medical directives: if either of us became incapacitated, under what circumstances would we want someone to pull the plug, and then what to do with our potentially useful organs? And more and more. Answering the next questions wasn't going to give us control over the future, either, but it might offer a buffer against misfortune.

The project wasn't over. But then nothing ever is, until everything is.

INTERLUDE

Why money makes us crazy

What is it that makes money so hard to deal with and to think about?

When my commuting buddy, the editor with the good retirement plan, told me that he expected me to go down in flames, he was comparing the cost of living in our area of New Jersey with what he knew we were earning. He figured that we were spending more than we made. Financial journalism was his trade, and he had us pegged for losers.

PUNCH LIST

NOW IT'S YOUR TURN TO TAKE A LOOK AT YOURSELF

If you're like us, you've been putting off assessing your retirement plans. It's time to figure out what assets you have and where you're likely to end up financially. Take the first step.

1) **Open the envelope.** If you have a retirement plan, whether a 401(k) provided by your employer or an individual retirement account (IRA), rip open the damned envelope (or, if you have more than one plan, envelopes) and take a look. You can also check it out online; you'll find more information on that after you actually open the envelope.

2) **Check your pension.** If you're vested for any pension income, find out what to expect by contacting the employers you should have a pension with.

3) **Have a talk with Uncle Sam.** Find out what kind of Social Security income to expect. Go to ssa.gov/myaccount to see where you stand. If you don't have an account yet, it's easy to sign up for one, and it will provide your employment records going back, well, forever. (The $135 I earned in the summer of 1968 as an 11-year-old page in the Texas House of Representatives was there.)

4) **Add up the rest.** Tote up your other assets, including the value of your home and any other investments you might have picked up along the way.

5) **Get the picture.** As a preliminary check—we'll be talking more about how to structure a portfolio at any age, and finding good financial advisers in a while—plug your figures into any of a number of good retirement calculators out there. You can find them at the websites of the Financial Industry Regulatory Authority, Fidelity, Vanguard, Schwab, Bankrate, and the AARP, for starters.[1]

This will take longer than 45 minutes. But, like us, once you've gone through the process, you will have gotten a start on figuring out your financial future.

There's a journalism cliché, almost a verbal tic, that you might have noticed in your years of reading the news. A writer starts the story with an example of a person—in distress because, say, he is going through a harrowing experience with the health care system or airline baggage fees, or dealing with frustrating automated telephone menus, or, well, just about anything. End paragraph. The next paragraph begins:

"He is not alone."

Then begins the part of the story that explains that this is, in fact, a surprisingly common problem, with statistics to back up the thesis. (If no such statistics exist, you'll see some version of the hoary "statistics are hard to come by, but . . ." and some reference to experts saying that they see the troubling trend of people being frustrated by baggage fees or automated telephone menus more and more frequently.)

So here goes:

We are not alone.

Half of Americans either break even or spend more than they make, according to the 2016 National Financial Capability Study from FINRA, which collects statistics like these. Statistics are, in fact, pretty easy to come by on topics like this. About 20 percent of people admit to spending more than they earn. (I also assume that many of the rest of these people are lying. Only 20 percent? COME ON!)

In 2012, 26 percent of those surveyed said they had overdue medical bills; in the improved economy (and health insurance) market of 2015, that percentage was down to 21 percent. About a third of Americans found themselves paying the minimum on credit card balances instead of paying off their cards each month; that's down from 40 percent in 2009.[2] In 2015, 34 percent of those surveyed said they either probably or definitely could not come up with $2,000 within a month if a sudden need arose; another 23 percent said they "probably" could come up with the money, and probably gave that answer nervously.[3]

If you're not already well off, in other words, it's likely that you are feeling squeezed and certainly at some financial risk. A different report from the Federal Reserve in 2016 found that 31 percent of Americans—about 76 million people—were either "struggling to get by" or "just getting by." (The fact that 56 percent of people in the survey, taken in

2015, said they were "living comfortably" or "doing okay" was good news.) This was the report I mentioned earlier, the one with the startling statistic that 46 percent of Americans couldn't even cover an emergency expense of $400 without borrowing the money or selling something; they had that little ready money.[4]

We've all seen this financial fragility around us: friends or family members who have hit hard times, and the rise of stores with names like Dollar Tree and Dollar General.[5] Jeanne saw the credit crunch firsthand during the years she worked at our local Target store: customers would get to her checkout line and pull out a wallet stuffed with credit cards. The first would be rejected, so the customer would fish out a second. Rejected. This would go on until a piece of plastic could be found that wasn't over its limit. The sum of all those debts was enormous.

Jeanne and I didn't end up with a wallet full of burning credit cards. But life still has a way of messing with your best intentions.

And money makes us crazy.

I don't mean that poverty makes us crazy. Poverty makes us miserable. I'm talking about the ways that people think about money, fret about it, pursue it, and lose it—and wonder why everybody else seems to have more of it than we do.

Why has it taken Jeanne and me so long even to take a hard look at our finances? My excuse is simple: numbers scare me. As a reporter, I can be motivated to learn what I need to know in order to cover numbers in science, business, and other topics. I study up, I talk to experts, and I produce skull sweat until I understand what I'm writing about. If I don't, somebody will fire me. (Incentive!) For the most part, however, I put off thinking about retirement and largely kept out of my own business.

In this, again, I am not alone. Scientists who study math anxiety say that the anticipation of crunching numbers can lead to the kind of agitation that, on a brain scan, looks a lot like the perception of physical pain.[6] One study by Sian Beilock, a University of Chicago professor of psychology, said that the brain reaction can be similar to that produced by "burning one's hand on a hot stove."[7]

We've been there.

Math isn't my only problem. I'm uncomfortable thinking about money. And, let's face it, the future scares me silly. Actually, I find it difficult to make choices of any kind; I agonize over buying a new pair of boots or a coffeemaker. My opinion shifts endlessly, and then after the purchase I suffer buyer's remorse in a way that exasperates Jeanne.

That fear of money is probably part of the reason so few people save for retirement. According to the American Psychological Association's "Stress in America" survey, money is the top source of stress in our lives. Nearly three-quarters of Americans reported feeling stressed about money in the previous month, with higher levels of anxiety for the younger generations and those living in low-income households, according to the survey, which is conducted for the APA by the Harris Poll.[8]

So what is it about money that puts us under all that stress—besides simply not having enough? This is a question that Lindsay Goldwert, a journalist and stand-up comic, asks in her money-oriented podcast *Spent*, in a way that is both profane and profound:

"Why are we so fucked up about money?"[9]

It's a big, important question, however you ask it. I decided to seek out some experts. You may not know this, but there is actually a thing known as "financial therapy." Some of the practitioners are therapists who find that many of their clients need to talk about money, and so they specialize; others have training in both therapy and financial planning and advice.

Here's a revelation that probably will not shock you: money is one of the things that can drive couples apart. It is a point of conflict that is both difficult to talk about and hard to fix. Joan D. Atwood, a marriage and family therapist in Rockville Centre, New York, has written that "speaking about money in marriage is the last taboo. Couples would prefer to talk about sex or infidelities rather than how they handle family finances or how much money they earn.[10]

I called her, and she told me that "money is not a happy thing, for most people." In fact, "it's really a metaphor for feelings of being loved and cared for." Among her patients, she said, "if they're getting money, they feel cared for and happy. If they are not getting money, they are feeling deprived and unhappy," she said. "It's the meaning of money that just triggers deep-seated 'whatevers' in people."

As a therapist, she said, she sees every kind of conflict, and money is often at the bottom of things. "There are different types of couples and different ways that they handle money—and very often, it's a metaphor for the way they manage their relationship." Young couples might come to the marriage with separate finances, but older couples tend to have much more complicated and intertwined financial relationships, she said. Remarried families, with the rivalries and jealousies and financial intrigue, are especially challenging.

Many of us, she told me, unknowingly see money as a surrogate for love. Metaphors abound. Is your husband, your father, your mother, your wife, giving enough? Withholding too much? We are all called to account. With this much going on, resentments can run deep.

After talking with Atwood, I wanted to know more about financial therapy. So I checked in with an organization called the Financial Therapy Association.[11] Their members have training in various blends of disciplines that include marriage therapy, family therapy, and social work, but also financial counseling. Kristy Archuleta, an associate professor in the Department of Family Studies and Human Services at Kansas State University, is a cofounder of the group. The members have different skills, she said, but they work at understanding "behavior, emotions, relations, and how all of those aspects impact money—and how money impacts all of those aspects." This can be a very effective mix, she explained. She told me about a conventional therapist who asked for her help with a troubled undergraduate. The student hoped to enroll in graduate school but had a poor credit rating and was deeply anxious about whether he would be able to get a college loan. The therapist had been working with the student on techniques to handle anxiety and attain a calmer state, but nothing was helping. The therapist then brought in a colleague who was a financial planner. The planner explained that the student's credit score should not affect his ability to get a federal student loan, short of problems like foreclosure or bankruptcy. The reason for the anxiety went away. "The problem was cured," Archuleta said.

In her own practice, she says, she does a good deal of premarital counseling to ensure that a couple's views on money are compatible, and to work through ways to communicate and handle conflict and the many ups and downs of marriage. "You can't handle money without having addressed those other issues," she said.

Among married couples, "not only is it one of the most fought-about topics; it's fought about differently," she said. "It's fought about in ways that make it more intense than other arguments."

Agreeing with Atwood, she said that "it's an emotionally charged topic that hits deep inside of people—people react to it." The fact that they argue about money "can actually be a sign that there's something much deeper going on in the relationship," she said.

Since people don't like to talk about money, the tensions fester, she said, so that by the time she sees them, the conflict has been going on for a long time. "It's almost, at that point, become a habit—it's how they interact with each other." That makes it hard for the couple to reflect on how they got to this point of intense conflict, and, worse, they don't know another way to deal with it.

Secrecy and lack of trust are big parts of money conflicts. Archuleta told me that she has encountered couples on the verge of bankruptcy, but one spouse had no clue because the other spouse had taken out secret charge cards and concealed bills.

As I was talking with Archuleta, I remembered a friend who divorced her husband after discovering that he had emptied their bank accounts through his compulsive visits to topless bars. Another friend, after getting married, discovered that her husband had not paid taxes for years. She was a responsible person, and that was one of her first clues that her husband saw money issues fundamentally incompatibly. She is much happier with her second husband.

"So how does anyone come back from a betrayal like that?" I asked. Archuleta told me about the techniques she uses to help couples regain the trust they once had, and the stability and security. The couples she has worked with have been able to bridge that gap, "but it wasn't until after a lot of time working through grief," she said. They had to learn to communicate differently, and to understand what money meant to them, and what their goals were for each other.

But wait, I thought. "Aren't those the same techniques a therapist would use to help people get past an extramarital affair?"

"You are exactly right," she said. "It would be very similar." But with a difference of degree: In her experience, "it would be easier to talk about them having an affair with someone else than to talk about financial infidelity."

═══

Money occupies such a big part of our consciousness that it's only natural it would be tied into our neuroses. Norm Forman, a psychologist who has studied our fraught relationship with our bank accounts and assets, developed techniques to determine the degree of what he calls people's "money sanity." He came up with a questionnaire that he included in his book *Mind Over Money*, published in 1987.[12]

The book is little known today, but it lays out a pretty cool way to look at the issue. In it, Forman identifies five types of people with money neuroses. He calls them the miser, spendthrift, tycoon, bargain hunter, and gambler.

The misers obsess over gathering money and hoarding it, but don't seem to enjoy having it. They fear losing their money and trust no one. Dickens's curmudgeonly Ebenezer Scrooge from *A Christmas Carol* is one of literature's great misers, though Noddy Boffin of *Our Mutual Friend* gives him a run for his money. (However, Boffin's case is more complicated than it initially seems.)

Then comes the spendthrift, who can't help throwing money around, especially when feeling worthless or depressed. Novelist Don DeLillo captured that experience in his epic novel of consumerism, *White Noise*. His narrator, the pompous professor and pioneering Hitler scholar Jack Gladney, has a peak shopping experience after a distressing social encounter with another faculty member, who tells him that outside his campus domain, Jack looks "harmless." Jack meets up with his family at the mall and finds himself compelled to spend. "I shopped with reckless abandon. I shopped for immediate needs and distant contingencies. I shopped for its own sake, looking and touching, inspecting merchandise I had no intention of buying, then buying it." The effect is like a powerful drug. "I began to grow in value and self-regard. I filled myself out, found new aspects of myself, located a person I'd forgotten existed. Brightness settled around me."[13]

In real life, however, Forman's spendthrifts find that the thrill fades quickly. What's left is often guilt, and an empty bank account.

The third Forman neurotic, the tycoon, is all about the Benjamins, baby. Making money is, for the tycoon, a path to power and influence and to absolute control over his environment. The fourth type, the bargain hunter, is fulfilled only when spending less for goods than the next guy. Nothing angers or depresses him as much as paying retail; the haggling and coupon clipping are compulsive. Finally, Forman's last money neurotic, the gambler, gets off on risk itself and on the adrenaline rush of winning.

Forman's categories are eerily familiar; it's uncanny to see how well he captured the ways that neuroses play out. But taken too literally, they are also a little narrow: pigeonholes for behavior that is often complex and blended. What if I'm a spendthrift gambler? (I'm not; I'm more of a bargain hunter with occasional bouts of reckless spending. Or something.)

Still, some of his descriptions resonate within the broader psychological literature. Some recognition of a compulsive shopping disorder, for example, has been part of medical literature for more than 100 years, and even has a cool Greek name, oniomania.[14] Psychiatric authorities debate whether it should be considered a subset of addictive behavior or something more like obsessive-compulsive behavior, while others argue that the need to classify our problems as diseases—"medicalizing" unwise behavior—is itself a bad trend. Compulsive shopping is not part of the current bible of the psychiatric field, the *DSM-V.* The most recent edition also left out compulsive buying[15] and other addiction-like behaviors such as compulsive sex and kleptomania.[16] The guide, however, does include compulsive gambling, Forman's fifth money neurosis, within its set of "substance-related and addictive disorders" such as drug abuse.

Go figure.

The field is developing, and arguments over the psychology of money will continue. Maybe we should think of it this way: money might not make us all crazy, but it can be one way that we focus and express our craziness.

For my last stop on my tour of our mental money trauma, I called Adrian Furnham, a psychologist and professor at University College London. He worked with Forman and has written an updated version, *The New Psychology of Money*.[17] Furnham told me that he took up the field because he and his supervisor "were both interested in subjects that psychology forgot." Money, they decided, fit the bill: it was everywhere, and was a favorite topic in pop psychology, but most books on the subject were written by therapists; the subject had not been deeply explored as a subject for rigorous empirical research.

Money, then, was like water in David Foster Wallace's famous joke from his 2005 commencement speech at Kenyon College.

> There are these two young fish swimming along, and they happen to meet an older fish swimming the other way, who nods at them and says, "Morning, boys, how's the water?" And the two young fish swim on for a bit, and then eventually one of them looks over at the other and goes, "What the hell is water?"[18]

Money issues, Furnham said, had already come into his life as a student. "I had a girlfriend who was a great spender and I was a great saver." They were divided, he said, by "what I saw as her utter irrationality with money, and what she saw as my utter irrationality with regard to money." The relationship did not last. "I'm very happy to say I'm married to a woman who exactly matches my money beliefs and behaviors—we've never had an argument about money," he said. "I was a lucky boy."

That brought us around to discussing a study he did comparing attitudes of men and women when it comes to money.

He and colleagues gave the Forman "money sanity" questionnaire to more than 100,000 subjects, most of them British. They found notable differences. "For men, more than women, money represented Power and Security. Men were more likely to be Hoarders while women did more emotional regulatory purchasing," which they referred to as "retail therapy." Men, they wrote, were likelier to take risks with money when investing, while "compared to males, females were Worried Spenders; they shopped as a form of therapy; and they worried more about money. Overall, females exhibited a higher 'Money Insanity' score."[19]

What he found, he said, is that "men see money instrumentally— they see it as a way of getting what they want, to influence others. Women see it more emotionally, as an expressions of love."

I suggested that seemed like the language of stereotype, not science, but he repeated that this was derived from the Forman questionnaires, not preconceptions. "The findings weren't strong, but they went in the right direction," he said. I wasn't fully convinced; it seems to me that men and women have come far enough in terms of gender equity to be equally neurotic. But his findings might help explain why money can be such an enormous source of stress for couples.

With these insights, the explanation grew clearer. Suddenly, I was seeing the problem from 30,000 feet: Money makes us crazy because it's important, and not just because of food and mortgages. It's important because it runs deep, way below the conscious level. It runs so deep that it connects with some of our most primal feelings and strongest fears (except for spiders).

Money is also one of the strongest defenses we employ against an unquiet mind, the bit of Jack Gladney within us all. Our buying sprees and accumulated wealth become proxies for love, balm for the distance of faded friends, a crutch to prop up our inadequate supplies of serotonin. Buying ourselves a treat lifts us; having money can comfort us. We use money, whether we know it or not, as a defense against the existential terror that is baked into all our lives, that one piece of knowledge that is uniquely human: someday, we all will die.

Whoa, that got dark fast.

Still! No less true.

2

STARTING OUT

TODAY, TOO MANY families operate uncomfortably close to the financial edge. And, like everything else, that fact has become politicized. Many conservatives like to blame people in financial trouble for causing their problems, and accuse them of profligacy and overspending.

Others look beyond moralistic sensibilities and see built-in problems in rising costs for housing, health insurance, transportation, taxes, and child care. Elizabeth Warren and Amelia Warren Tiyagi tackled the question of why so many people are under financial strain in an article published in 2005, well before the Great Recession (when things got even worse). The article, "What's Hurting the Middle Class," stated that covering the basics of family life—things that have to be paid whether or not someone loses a job or gets sick, and which they call the "nut"—has gotten much more expensive than it used to be. A generation ago, those expenses took up about half of a single-income family's pay. Today the figure is more like 75 percent.

With 75 percent of income earmarked for fixed expenses, today's family has no margin for error. There is no way to cut back if one person's working hours are cut or if the other gets laid off. There is no room in the budget if someone needs to take a few months off to care for Grandma, or if someone hurts his back and can't work. The modern American family is walking on a high wire without a net; they pray there won't be any wind. If all goes well, they will make it across safely: their children will grow up and finish college, and they will move on to retirement. But if anything—anything at all—goes wrong, they are in big, big trouble.[1]

And where are many of us? In big, big trouble. For many of us, the trouble begins early, when we're just starting out in life. That is also the time, however, when making some smart moves and building the right habits can set us up for a stable financial life, maybe even a prosperous one. That's what this chapter is about—and our own experiences help show how certain decisions, bad and good, can shape your financial future.

Here's your preview: there's only one real piece of advice in this chapter, and that is to start saving early. The corollary to that piece of advice is to develop a simple investment strategy that focuses on long-term gains with low costs—but we'll get into that later. First, I'll give you a little of our own financial history.

HOW WE STARTED OUT

To understand how Jeanne and I got into the financial troubles that dogged us for so much of our adult lives, it helps to know our early days together.

We met on a boiling August day in Austin, Texas. It was 1975, and classes at the University of Texas would begin in a week. We had both chosen UT largely because it was a great school in a wonderful town, and neither of us flattered ourselves with the pretension that we were Ivy League material. Besides, it was cheap as rocks, and many of our friends were also going there. We had found our way into a liberal arts honors program that suited our desire to read important books and learn big things. Most important, we met each other.

We were eerily well matched: fast talking, word crazed, and excited about everything around us. She had red hair and freckles and, in the hot months, didn't bother putting on a lot of clothes. I'm not sure what she saw in me, but more than 40 years later, I remain grateful.

Within a few weeks, we were dating; by the end of the semester, we were living together. My roommate in those cramped quarters, who was a saint, tolerated the arrangement. (Hi, Vincent!)

My folks, who are also saints, put several hundred dollars in my bank account each month to cover rent, gas, and our forays to second-hand bookstores—something they might not have been able to do if I'd attended a fancy school in the Northeast. And we did well. I got a variety of jobs: dorm resident assistant, library clerk, projectionist for CinemaTexas, the campus organization that filled the auditoriums each weekend with fans of horror movies and other fare. I even had a brief career as a deliverer of singing telegrams. Jeanne worked at, among other places, Mad Dog & Beans, a burger place just west of campus where the day's best employee got to take a rack of emptied whipped cream canisters and suck in the last whiffs of nitrous oxide for a brief buzz. Life was, in other words, splendid.

Back in the 1970s, Austin was a place where we could live on love and sofa change. I mean this literally: when we were broke, Jeanne and I dug around behind the sofa cushions and found enough quarters, dimes, and pennies to buy an avocado. Los Tacos, a dumpy little place down the street from Mad Dog's, had a 50-cent bean-and-rice burrito that was nearly as big as my head. My parents had also handed me a single, very specialized credit card. It worked only at the Night Hawk, a local chain of steak houses with a location on the Drag, next to campus. So when we were too broke for even a scrounged-change avocado or a trip to Los Tacos, we could get a steak and a loaded baked potato.

The town, still pretty sleepy back then, nonetheless had a burgeoning live music scene with everything from cosmic cowboy to punk. It was a place full of opportunities for "Findin' things to do that we could do for free," as the singer Robert Earl Keen put it in his perfect song about slackerdom, "Dreadful Selfish Crime."[2]

And tuition? That's the cheap-as-rocks part: thanks to oil riches under the lands that the University of Texas owned, tuition in those days was ludicrously low. Each semester cost less than $200. I was able to graduate without college debt.

We had very little. We have never felt richer.

Even so, those Austin days were filled with lessons about money. The world around us seemed to be saying one word over and over: Spend. Spend. SPEND.

The first automated teller machines made their appearance in the United States several years before we got to college; by the mid-1970s, when we were undergraduates, our local Austin National Bank had them. The change was monumental: the bank didn't need to be open for you to make a withdrawal; no standing in line, no fretting about whether you could get a check cashed late at night before heading out to hear some music. The brand name on the teller machines was appealing and apt: "Anytime." Jeanne saw the downside risk of the robot tellers right away. Whenever we stopped by one of the machines, she'd say in a cheery announcer voice, "Now you can go broke . . . *Anytime!*"

We had little income, but already, come-ons from credit card companies were arriving in the mail. The form letters were seductive: Start building your credit record now, with us! What they didn't say was: you can ruin your credit record now, with us—before you even really get started in life! We avoided disaster by not getting a card until we were both employed full-time. The risk was there from the start, but how bad could it be? Even if we built up a balance on the card, the minimum charge was easy enough to pay. We had found our first slippery slope.

Back then, some of the people around us were, in their own laid-back Austin way, starting to think about their financial future. My friend Will van Overbeek, a brilliant photographer, had already become successful enough with freelance work that he was able to buy a small gem of a house north of campus. A friend at Mad Dog's solemnly told Jeanne, "I'm trying to get my money trip together," though it was unclear what he meant by that.

Another friend, Clay, always seemed to have plenty of money. He dated a roommate of ours and took her out to the best restaurants in town, places where we couldn't have afforded the appetizers. They went on romantic sailboat rides. It didn't take long to figure out where the cash came from: Clay sold cocaine. We got a glimpse of what a lot of money could get you at our age, and also a good lesson in risk and reward. One day Clay turned up dead, beaten to death with what the police report referred to as a blunt object. His business associates, we later heard, decided he had snitched.

We graduated from college with our liberal arts degrees. It was time to start thinking about how I would make my money—preferably with less risk than Clay had made his.

So I prepared for a career. I got into UT's law school, largely for lack of a plan. My father and two of my brothers are lawyers, and it seemed like a good idea at the time. Law school tuition was also less than $200 per semester; my textbooks cost more. I had a decent first year, making unspectacular grades but keeping up with my fellow students, learning how to read judicial opinions and sparring with the professors over points of law.

But life intervened. In my second year at the school, I began writing for the university's magazine and its award-winning newspaper, *The Daily Texan*. It wasn't my first foray into journalism; the bug bit me early. In sixth grade I created and ran a paper for Mrs. Henslee's class, typing the *Henslee Herald* up on mimeograph paper on an enormous IBM Executive typewriter my folks kept in the front room. The typewriter hummed; it radiated heat and smelled like machine oil. I fell in love with that beast. I kept writing, helping start a newspaper in high school as well.

So it was natural for me to gravitate toward journalism in college, and it made for a nice sideline to my legal training. But during my second year of law school, and the first year I was working at the *Texan*, the staff walked out on the editor, throwing the publication into crisis. The board that governed the paper put me in charge for the rest of the school year. That watershed moment set up a bifurcated life. My days were spent at the law school, and my evenings at the *Texan*. It didn't take me long to figure out which part of the day felt more natural to me—to know where I fit in best. The student journalists were just as smart as the future lawyers, and equally ambitious. But they didn't take themselves as seriously, and their parties were way more fun. I had more in common with the wisecracking kids putting the paper together in the basement of the communications building than with the serious young legal eagles up 26th Street.

The law students also seemed much more interested in practicing law than I was. I hadn't been deluding myself about my skills or interests: I saw in myself no emerging knack for the law. Yet I figured that while I wasn't likely to have a blazing career as a rich partner in a big firm, I could still end up comfortably doing divorces or personal injury cases, and running loud ads that hawked my services on late-night television. That probably would have been enough. I could hold a cigar, wear a cowboy hat. Yell at the camera. That's how other lawyers on late-night TV commercials did it, and they looked successful. But after I finished my year as *Texan* editor, I started doing a fair amount of freelance writing. Most of the pieces brought in very little money. After finishing my first story for the *Texas Observer*, the legendary progressive "Journal of Free Voices" based in Austin, the editor told me he couldn't pay me but urged me to "just go out in the hall and grab a couple of books off of the shelf." Other publications, though, were starting to pay me a dollar a word or more. Things began looking up. I saw another way to make a living outside of lawyering.

When law school was done, I was still undecided about my future. It was 1984, the nation was climbing out of a recession, and either career looked pretty good. People got out of college and, for the most part, got jobs. With no debt hanging over my head, I was inclined to follow my dreams, as all commencement speakers advise us to do, and try to be a journalist.

My folks were not convinced. They had been thrilled when I had gotten into law school—especially since it was the same law school that Dad had graduated from. He knew plenty of reporters, having served for two decades in the state legislature and become a senior member of the Texas Senate. Reporters loved him—he is preternaturally quotable—but he didn't think much of journalists. My folks saw a stable and bright future for me in the law, and the prospect of my throwing in with the ink-stained kvetchers was not a happy one.

On one visit back to our home in Galveston, Dad handed me a book he'd picked up. The title was *You Can Make $20,000 a Year Writing*. My, how he laughed.

By then, Jeanne and I had gotten married, so now we were partners in big decisions. It was time to make one. I asked her what she thought: Would it be all right with her if I tried journalism as a career? "If, at the end of five years, I've got a real job with a dental plan, I'll stick with it," I told her. "If not, I'll be a lawyer and do divorces. What do you think?"

She didn't take long to answer. She wanted an adventure, and also wanted to get out of Austin and live someplace like New York City. She took the deal.

I'd also gotten a gentle shove from my boss at the time, an editor at *Texas Monthly*. "Johnny, you know your world very well," he said. "But it starts at the river and ends at 29th Street," which described the area from downtown Austin to the north border of the campus. He suggested that I expand my horizons.

Both Jeanne and I had come from comfortable families, but not from wealth. We'd joke that each of us thought the other was rich. "Your dad was a state senator!" she'd say. I'd reply, "Your granddad was an oilman!"

"An oil *service* man," she'd explain. He didn't strike it rich on gushers; he poured the concrete for drilling platforms that made the drillers rich (or poor—you never knew). Anyway, neither of us had, as the characters in the old British novels put it, "married money." But we were fundamentally Texan, which means believing in self-reliance and being willing to work hard and take risks, and in being guided by a kind of optimism that everything will work out if you work at it. So we held hands and took a leap.

Getting a job in journalism, though, was not easy. I applied to a number of publications in New York without immediate success. I didn't have the experience at local newspapers, or the journalism prizes, that big-city publications like to see. I did have a possible in, though, at *Newsweek*, a magazine I'd been freelancing for since I'd ended my term as *Texan* editor.

In my trips to New York to meet with *Newsweek* editors, I would always see Jerry, the guy who headed *Newsweek on Campus*, which was the college edition of the magazine. I'd been doing most of my stringing for him. He bemoaned a hiring freeze imposed on the magazine by upper management and assured me, if the freeze were ever lifted, "You're high on my list."

This sounded promising! What I did not understand about fancy New York editors is that lines like "You're high on my list" are sweet nothings that provide hope without substance, intended to get you out of their offices and on your way in time for them to have a nice long lunch and then come back to get through the rest of the day's work— after a nap on their very comfortable couches, because lunches in those days tended to include adult beverages. That "high on my list" thing was a way to keep me available but at bay. (In the years since that *Newsweek* job, I would meet more than one resentful journalist who told me that the same editor had told him that he was high on his list, and who felt I had taken the job that had been promised to him. How long was Jerry's list, anyway?)

I'd see other *Newsweek* editors during those trips. One, tilted back in his chair with his feet up on the desk, told me that he'd like to hire me but that the magazine was in the middle of, yes, again, a hiring freeze. I blurted out that I could wait a long time in Austin, since my share of the rent on the big house Jeanne and I shared with some buddies was just $150 a month.

His eyes narrowed. He growled, "I despise you."

I waited. A year later I had the job.

It happened through a combination of dumb luck and perseverance. After finishing law school and passing the bar exam—why not?—I called the editor whose list I was so proudly on. "Jerry," I said, "since I'm high on your list, why don't you just hire me? My wife and I have decided to move to New York. I'll be there the last week in April, so you won't have to pay any relocation expenses."

Then an amazing thing happened. He told me to show up for work the first week in May.

What I did not know was that one of his small cadre of writers had just left *Newsweek on Campus* and he had a hole to fill. He was a lawyer, too, and liked the fact that I'd taken the bar. "It shows you finish what you start," he told me. What about that hiring freeze? Still there, but he'd figured a clever workaround: he would pay me a full-time salary out of his freelance budget. He said he could offer me $26,000 a year. (Those 1985 dollars would be close to $60,000 today.) He named the sum, and I did some quick mental math to find that this would cover the rent I expected to pay and other living expenses. In fact, it sounded like wealth. I said yes, without a moment of negotiation.

I came up and slept on a friend's floor for several weeks while starting work and finding an apartment for Jeanne and me. Every evening after work, I'd walk from Midtown to the Upper West Side to get to know my new city. Along the Central Park Reservoir, I bumped into a friend from Texas. (This actually happens in New York; it has something to do with the population density.) We chatted a bit; he'd been living here for a few years, he said, and was working at Salomon Brothers. He had one piece of advice that he delivered with a chilling edge.

"New York is great," he said. *"Don't run out of money."*

Thanks to another *Newsweek* boss, Lynn Povich, I snagged a one-year sublet on an apartment on the Upper West Side for $1,000 a month. Jeanne got to town a few weeks later, and we were on our way. My mental math that said we'd be rolling in money turned out to be faulty—New York was expensive!—but by the time I realized that, it didn't matter. I was launched. And if we were going to be squeezed, well, there are a lot of sofa cushions and avocados in the world. Finding things to do that you can do for free in New York wasn't that difficult, and the free things were grand: watching Shakespeare in the Park, sneaking onto the roof of our building to watch the Fourth of July fireworks, and using my *Newsweek* ID to get complimentary access to great museums. Just walking around the city is a free show daily. We ate inexpensive burgers—you could still find them in New York then—and watched movies for next to nothing at the Thalia, an art house whose aisles, weirdly, sloped upward toward the screen. One day we sat in the dark and watched a Roger Corman horror triple feature. Jeanne got her master's degree in history from NYU and worked as a secretary, and later in the archives of Trinity Church and the New York Public Library theater collection. Life was damn good.

My job was hard. My job was fun. I did the job. At the end of that year, one of the top editors of *Newsweek* called me into his office. He wanted me to know that they had defrosted the hiring freeze slightly, or at least enough to actually hire me. It didn't hurt that the union that represented *Newsweek*'s rank and file had started making noises that hiring somebody out of a freelance budget and not paying benefits looked like a violation of the union contract. If they had filed a grievance—or, to use the labor jargon, "grieved" me—I'd probably have lost the job. Instead, I was finally really hired.

At the end of our conversation, the editor, a natty gentleman who wore hand-tailored shirts with those fancy white collars, told me that my new salary would be substantially more than what I had been earning. He explained drily, "We don't have anyone writing here who makes . . . what you've been making." He was letting me know without saying it out loud that I'd been played for a rube by the guy who had hired me.

Was I mad? Nah. Jerry had gotten me in the door. And the editor who had just finished telling me what a dope I'd been softened the blow by telling me that writers at the magazine made at least $40,000 a year, and so that would be my new salary. He had just raised my pay by 50 percent.

In 2017 dollars, the new salary came to more than $88,000 a year. It still wasn't enough to live high in such an expensive city, but it was a great bump and a great start. Even being brought into *Newsweek* at a bargain salary was, in a strange way, a favor. It meant Jeanne and I had to learn to stretch our paychecks. And for the time being, it was enough.

Enough. The word is resonant.

John C. Bogle, the personal investing trailblazer and author, loves to tell the story of the writers Kurt Vonnegut and Joseph Heller at a billionaire's party out on Shelter Island, New York. Vonnegut told Heller that their host made more in a single day than Heller made off every copy of *Catch-22* ever sold.

Heller responded, "Yes, but I have something he'll never have . . . enough."

Bogle used that story for the title and introduction of his 2008 book, *Enough: True Measures of Money, Business, and Life.*[3]

And it's profound. What is enough? Enough to live on? Enough to retire on?

Which gets us back to our little family and our story.

So there we were. I had gotten a job at an internationally recognized magazine—as the giveaway pencils said in engraved letters, *Newsweek* was "America's most-quoted newsweekly." And I had a decent salary, higher than the $20,000 a year promised by the the book Dad had handed me as a joke.

"ENOUGH"

Was it enough? Well, is any amount enough? When you hear "money can't buy happiness," do you get irked? I always want to respond, "Well, let me test that hypothesis." No less an authority on the perils of wealth than the late rapper known as the Notorious B.I.G. put it simply: "Mo Money Mo Problems." Again, while I respect your expertise, sir, let me find out for myself. I will try out the aforesaid Mo Money, and I'll judge the scale and scope of the resultant problems.

There has actually been some well-regarded research into the amount of money it takes to make people happy, and whether there is a point of diminishing returns. The psychologist Daniel Kahneman and the economist Angus Deaton of Princeton University published a famous paper in 2010 showing that while people's level of happiness does rise with the amount of money they have, that correlation ends after income rises beyond $75,000.[4]

Both Professors Kahneman and Deaton, who are winners of the Nobel Memorial Prize in Economic Science, analyzed nearly half a million responses to Gallup polling on well-being. What they found about poverty was obvious: The pain of misfortunes like divorce or being alone is significantly greater for people making less than $1,000 a month.

The authors stated, "More money does not necessarily buy more happiness, but less money is associated with emotional pain."

In trying to decide why things did not get significantly better for people who made more than $75,000, they wrote, "Perhaps $75,000 is a threshold beyond which further increases in income no longer improve individuals' ability to do what matters most to their emotional well-being, such as spending time with people they like, avoiding pain and disease, and enjoying leisure."

Of course, most people still believe that more money will mean more happiness. It's just that it doesn't always turn out that way. The researchers Elizabeth W. Dunn and Michael Norton—she is an associate professor of psychology at the University of British Columbia, and he is an associate professor of business at Harvard Business School—found that Americans surveyed predicted that someone making $55,000 would find twice the satisfaction in life of someone making just $25,000. When the researchers actually compared the satisfaction levels of people making $55,000 and those making $25,000, however, they found a jump of just 9 percent.[5]

I got the job at *Newsweek* before any of this amazing research had gotten out there. All we knew was that we had a lot more money than we'd had when Jeanne was making milkshakes and I was delivering singing telegrams. But in light of Kahneman's work, it turned out that with my first job out of college, we were (in inflation-adjusted dollars) beating the happiness line, at least initially. True, we were living in a very expensive city, and that makes a difference. In many parts of Texas, $40,000 could have made me feel rich, but not in New York City. Yet Kahneman has said that the $75,000 threshold is the same in expensive cities as in inexpensive ones.[6]

While some of my colleagues were struggling financially and came from working-class roots, a surprising number, it seemed to me, were swimming in cash. Jeanne and I were still looking for things that we could do for free, but they weekended in the Hamptons, or on Shelter Island, or up at the family's summer house—it's really pretty basic, they'd say almost dismissively, and not much to look at. One editor spent an evening dinner telling the rest of us about how damned expensive it was to properly maintain the large pond on his property. Many of my coworkers had degrees from Ivy League colleges, and I learned from them the snippy things that Ivy grads said about other Ivy grads. They love to make fun of those Harvard people. A Brown grad joked, "Question: How can you tell if someone went to Harvard? Answer: They'll tell you!" These were not jokes I heard in Austin; for a land-grant university boy, it was eye-opening.

These were people who had never had to dig in their sofa cushions to be able to pay for an avocado. Some had substantial double incomes, thanks to a spouse who was a doctor or lawyer, or Wall Street shark. Whatever their income level, I found my colleagues smart, talented, and fun to be around. I wasn't like Josiah Crawley, the impoverished reverend in Anthony Trollope's *Framley Parsonage* who rejected the fellowship of his well-off college classmate: "His poverty had been so terrible to himself that it was not in his heart to love a rich friend." I didn't resent their vacations, though I could have stood to hear a bit less about them.

That first step

That pay bump at *Newsweek* allowed me to make a decision that affected every other financial decision we'd ever make. As a real employee, I'd be eligible to enroll in a retirement savings plan—a 401(k). *Newsweek* also offered a pension plan, which I'd be enrolled in automatically, but my friends told me that I'd be nuts to pass up the 401(k). The pension would not pay for much of a retirement, they explained. And the Washington Post Company, which owned *Newsweek*, sweetened the savings by kicking in extra money to match a portion of what you contributed. So I signed up, picking some Vanguard mutual funds from *Newsweek*'s offerings that looked good to me. One was the popular Vanguard Wellington Fund, which has been around since the 1920s and which offers a diversified mix of stocks and bonds. I had no sophisticated method of choosing the fund, no theory of investing.

I assigned 10 percent of my income to the account—money I'd

probably never miss, because it was money I hadn't been getting before. Jumping from $26,000 a year to $40,000 a year let me make the move without feeling a pinch.

And then I basically forgot about it.

This is important. Even when we got squeezed financially as time went by, we never considered dropping the weekly contribution to the 401(k). We were able to treat it as one more of those mysterious, untouchable lines on the pay stub, down in there with the Social Security withholding and my part of the health insurance and the union dues.

About the same time, Jeanne and I were feeling so good about our money sense that we made a financial mistake as well. It was still in those early days after the big pay hike, and I'd been reading about the need to save for retirement. If one account is smart, two would be smarter! So I opened a Roth IRA, a retirement account independent of the 401(k) at work, and plunked down $6,000 as the initial contribution. I fully expected to put in a similar amount every year after that. We were on our way to financial independence—trips to Hawaii in retirement!

Dreams are nice. Then you wake up. By the next year, our credit card was groaning with a high balance. I mentioned New York City was expensive, right? We realized that we'd have to make do with the 401(k) alone; we couldn't afford to put thousands of additional dollars away every year. So we liquidated the account. That's no simple thing, however, since there were penalties for withdrawing the money before retirement, and fees to pay. We ended up getting back about $3,500, which a financial expert would call a negative return on investment. It was irksome and embarrassing, but we needed the cash.

It turned out to be as expensive a way to pay down the cards as going to a loan shark. Thinking about it today, I realize that we could have put the money away with an automatic payroll deduction, which would have required paying $115 a week to reach that $6,000. But putting that on top of the 10 percent of my income we were already contributing to the 401(k) would have pinched us. So we kept our retirement contribution to 10 percent of my income and focused on the other pressing financial issues before us.

After all, we were starting a family. Jeanne and I had decided to have kids.

Actually, the conversation went something like this. When we talked about getting married back in our Austin days, Jeanne wanted to talk about having kids as well. I asked her to promise that we wouldn't even talk about having children for two years. We were already making one enormous decision, and I didn't want to have to deal with any others right away. There would be too much else going on in our lives; I wanted to get a job, have insurance, have a sense that my career was on track. She agreed.

Toward the end of two years, she said, "You know, it's coming up on two years."

"Okay," I said.

On our second anniversary, she said, "It's been two years."

I said, "So we can start talking about it."

"No," she explained. "We're done talking."

See how easy that was?

We had already been together, from our dating into marriage, for 10 years. We'd found ways to accommodate each other. There was some give and take, but also a recognition of when one of us had reached an unbudgeable position. We had friends who would battle any disagreement to the end of time; neither of us felt it was more important to win an argument than to move on.

That's how money discussions go with us, too. We might argue over how much to spend on this or that, but we generally agree on what we really need to spend our money on, what is most important. Over time, we have developed a division of labor, of sorts: Jeanne deals with the bills, and I pay what attention I can to our long-term financial goals. It's a good division of labor, especially for me, since the bills require constant fretting while our approach to our investments is not to think about them at all.

We have other divisions of labor that work well for us: I'm computer tech support, and worry about things like making sure the water level in the boiler is right. That makes me the home handyman; Jeanne's the one who recognizes when I'm trying to fix something that is beyond my abilities. Then she calls an actual repair person, who inevitably looks at the way I've, say, wired a light switch, shakes his head, and exclaims, "It's a good thing you called me. This place coulda gone up any second!" Then she pays the bill.

And that's the way it's been, for richer and for poorer. There would be tight times, but we'd never quite gotten past that cheapo, college-waif way of doing things. So we've been lucky in love, especially when it comes to our ability to agree on money stuff.

MILLENNIALS, AMIRITE? STARTING OUT TODAY IS WAY HARDER

I came into the employment world on the tail of the recession of the early 1980s—and while the economy was recovering, the advertising that supports print publications is often late to respond to shifts. Jobs were tight, but I still got in.

Now think about what lies ahead for the next generation—those starting out in the past decade. Compared with them, baby boomers like Jeanne and me, for all our problems and mistakes, had it easy when it comes to economic opportunity and the ability to build a secure financial future. Many of today's young people emerged from college in the middle of one of the most ruinous economic downturns in U.S. history, and with the kind of college debt that past generations didn't have to deal with, into a world of narrowed possibilities.

The thought hit me hard in mid-2016 when I was listening to a talk by Patti Smith, the singer and punk poet, for staffers of *The New York Times*. Her passionate music was an important part of my 20s (and 30s, and 40s, and 50s, to be honest), and it was wonderful to hear her speak. But one thing she said left me sad and troubled.

She said that kids write to her today and they want to do what she did: they want to head up to New York with five dollars in their pockets, find a cheap apartment, and live the life of an artist and poet. She said that she has to tell them You Can't Do That Anymore. New York has changed. If she were starting out today, she couldn't do what she had done back then.

She's right. It's now a city for those with money to burn. And New York is not the only city that's become a playground for the richest. San Francisco? Good luck. Heck, even Austin is too expensive for the slacker lifestyle I loved in the '70s. Los Tacos is long gone.

Do today's young people starting out have the same opportunities we had? Of course not. Jeanne and I feel fortunate to have grown up when we did, when we could live on our own in dirt-cheap apartments and buy that avocado with sofa-cushion change. When we moved to New York City, we weren't living Patti Smith's Bohemian lifestyle, thanks to my having gotten that job at *Newsweek*. But we had friends who were scraping by with low-paying jobs and living in ratty old apartments in Alphabet City and played in rock and roll bands. It was harder, but still possible.

We didn't have as much economic opportunity as our parents did. But we seem to have dodged a bullet, compared with the millennials, the large population of young people born between about 1980 and 2000, and the Generation X (and Y) that came after our baby boomer generation.

The prospects for the younger generations to outstrip their parents in earning power has diminished greatly over time. According to the economist Raj Chetty and his colleagues, if you were born in 1940, you had a 92 percent chance of earning more than your parents had. Born in 1960? You're down to 62 percent. If you were born in 1980, the odds that you are outearning your folks are just 50-50.[7] These figures are not guesswork: they are drawn from millions of tax records over the decades. You can only wonder how the numbers will look for millennials.

David Leonhardt, who won a Pulitzer Prize for his economics columns in *The New York Times*, called the data "deeply alarming," and said, "It's a portrait of an economy that disappoints a huge number of people who have heard that they live in a country where life gets better, only to experience something quite different." He rightly tied these grim figures to Americans' distrust of so many institutions—the federal government, corporations, the news media, and others—as well as the roiling election season and the victory of Donald Trump.

Leonhardt calls for steps to address the fundamental issue here, which is income inequality: improved access to a good education, a tax policy that is more fair to the middle class and less servile to the richest Americans, a reduction in corporate power and the strengthening of labor unions, as well as steps to address income inequality. All of it is beyond the scope of this book, and my expertise, and is the subject of great books by stupendously smart people: Joseph Stieglitz's *The Price of Inequality* and Thomas Piketty's *Capital in the Twenty-First Century* and Timothy Noah's *The Great Divergence*.

Leonhardt closes his excellent article with optimism: "If the American dream could survive the Depression, and then thrive in a way few people imagined, it can survive our current troubles."[8]

I hope he's right. In the meantime, the kids are not all right. One-fifth of young people in their 20s and early 30s live with their parents, writes Adam Davidson in the terrifying 2014 article "It's Official: The Boomerang Kids Won't Leave."[9] A generation ago, that number was closer to one in ten. By 2016, the numbers looked even worse: The real estate website Trulia estimated in 2016 that 40 percent of young Americans between the ages of 18 and 34 were living with their parents—the highest percentage in 75 years. It's as if the postwar boom never happened. Young people are more likely to be living with the folks than with a romantic partner, according to the Pew Research Center.[10]

Of course, it's wrong to assume that a young person living with parents has failed: many of them are making a sound financial decision about how to save money while starting a career, especially if they are also burdened with student debt. Stiff rents and lagging income growth make the old bedroom a rational option, once the soccer trophies have been boxed up and moved to the attic. But the boomerang trend also means that some of the better engines of the economy, including home construction and sales, are weakened. And the sheer size of these numbers is troubling.

The media is no help

The media obsesses over millennials because there are so many of them. They are a demographic segment and a market. So the stories abound, with their endless questions. What are millennials buying? What are they reading? What are they killing?[11] Who will they vote for? And what is their problem?

We seem, as we so often do, to be asking the wrong questions.

Before I go further, let me acknowledge that lumping all millennials together is ridiculous. The attempts by journalists and others to corral a broad and diverse population of Americans by age is an exercise in marketing, pop sociology, and the worst of a trend journalism that is likely to produce shallow generalizations rather than insights. My favorite example: *Time* magazine tried to capture the millennial stereotype with a cover image in 2013 that showed a good-looking redhead in butt-hugging lime-colored jeans taking a selfie, with language that would become infamous:

The ME ME ME Generation
Millennials are lazy, entitled narcissists who still live with
  their parents
Why they'll save us all[12]

That "ME ME ME" was a twist on the phrase made famous in Tom Wolfe's 1976 cover story for *New York* magazine, "The Me Decade," so the *Time* cover is journalistic archaeology, too.[13] The last line, "Why they'll save us all," is a classic newsmagazine hedge, but it did nothing to balance the lazy insult added to a generation's economic injuries. These young people never asked to have their prospects harmed by a sludgy economy and college debt even higher than the fancy climbing wall at their university gyms; little wonder that many of them end up living with their parents—and also resonating with the economic message of fundamental unfairness in the economy that Bernie Sanders was sending.

That's why the *Time* cover was such a mess, despite its ending on an attempt at a positive note. Millennials responded with glorious snark, creating instant parodies of that cover. They held on to the redhead, but changed the words. One took on the entitled Boomers and Gen Xers who were looking down their noses at these kids:

The UNEMPLOYED Generation

We Derailed the Economy. We Destroyed the Environment.
  We Allowed and Praised Corporate Greed. We Elected
  Crooked Politicians. We Started Wars we won't be
  Fighting in. We are Racist. We are Sexist. We are
  Homophobic.

Yet, Damn those Unemployed Social Media obsessed
  Millennials.

THEY ARE THE PROBLEM![14]

Jeanne and I share the anger. We have ourselves made three millennials, basically out of materials lying around the house. Each of them is great, and their differences show the absurdity of lumping people together by age cohort and expecting them to fall into patterns. Our oldest, Elizabeth, crammed her undergraduate work at the University of Michigan into three years and got a law degree from the University of Texas with her husband, Matt. They both practice law in Texas, where they own a great house outside Austin and have a delightful baby girl. They sound like baby boomers! But with one enormous exception: they got out of law school with $200,000 in debt between them, which is as much as a house. They will pay it off, and we are helping where we can, but it's hard, and it's a hell of a boulder to be chained to while trying to start your career climb. I wonder how anyone can build retirement savings while simultaneously trying to chip away at that rock.

When our middle child, Sam, was 10 years old, he got very serious and asked me, "Dad, is there a job where you don't have to do a lot of work but make a lot of money?"

I told him I was still looking.

He's 27 now and recently told me, "I'm still looking for that niche in life where I'm getting rich without having to work too hard." He is our adventurer, has traveled the world, working long enough to get the money for another trip; along the way, he met an Australian woman, Courtney, who has as much global wanderlust as he does. He likes Elizabeth and Matt's lifestyle, but decided not to go to law school after seeing the debt they had built up on the way to entering a shrinking profession. He'd rather make a living on his terms and without the burdens that his sister faces. He briefly lived with us between jobs and before his marriage, but he was eager to get moving again. At the moment, Sam and Courtney are getting ready to travel to China, where they'll be teaching English. I have no idea where they'll end up next—he's recently talked about law school again—but I have no worries about their independence or resourcefulness.

Our youngest, Joseph, is still college age; it's too soon to say how he will turn out. But he's anything but a millennial narcissist stereotype, and I believe he'll find his way.

Each of these three homegrown millennials is unique; none of them fits any easy stereotype. Though, selfishly, I wish they'd pick up a newspaper every once in a while.

And though, sure, I love to brag on our kids, I see plenty of determined, dedicated millennials all around me. Some of the most hard-charging journalists at the *Times* are in their 20s. They are smart, terrific, and the opposite of spoiled.

That's why it pained me to see the reaction among some younger readers to my *Times* essay about my retirement worries.

Doree Shafrir, a thirtysomething novelist and writer at the news and entertainment website BuzzFeed, issued a scorching critique on (where else?) Twitter: "58-y.o. NYT writer worries about retirement, learns he's totally fine bc pensions. How nice for him & his generation!"[15]

We've never met, but I love Shafrir's work: she wrote a wonderfully honest and smart piece a while ago about freezing her eggs.[16] She tweets with insight and a scalpel's edge.[17] Her response to the story—she said she found it "grating" on many levels, including what she saw as underplaying my own privilege—set off a bit of intergenerational conflict on Twitter, where doing battle is as easy as coming up with 280 characters.[18] Some people stood up for me, noting, as my colleague Nicholas Confessore did, that I'd acknowledged that my generation had it better in terms of pensions; she was still unhappy, characterizing my argument as "I'm healthy enough to work 'til 70 so I'll keep collecting my high salary while 20somethings struggle to find work."

Okay, I thought, so I'm supposed to die. While I try my best to be obliging, there are limits. As a sign on a colleague's desk reads, "I can't make everyone happy. I'm not pizza."

I tried to explain myself. I wrote a follow-up piece for Times Insider, a part of the *NYT* website where reporters talk about their work, and pointed out something that had been missing from the Twitter discussion: that, as I said in the piece, I'd been saving since my 20s, though I had not paid much attention to the way the 401(k) was behaving. And it's true that conventional pensions are going the way of the coelacanth. Still, I concluded in the Insider essay, "there's no doubt that some of the things I've got going for me are getting harder to find. So you know what? She's right. And that stinks."[19]

It doesn't help that even when journalists try to figure millennials out, they can't help taking an accusatory tone. *The Atlantic* had a good story about the fact that some studies show that millennials may not be saving money to the same extent that older people are, but its title seemed to wag a finger: "Why Aren't Millennials Saving Money?"[20] When that title went out as a tweet, millennials reacted with scornful and self-aware responses. "We're broke as hell," tweeted one. "Buying too many selfie sticks," joked another.

The Atlantic piece was, in fact, a well-documented riff on a Moody's Analytics report (cited in *The Wall Street Journal*) that found that those under 35 have a savings rate of negative 2 percent, compared with a positive savings rate of 3 percent for those between the ages of 35 and 44.[21] The savings rate for the under-35 group in 2009 had been 5.2 percent, so the rate had dropped substantially.

The author of *The Atlantic* piece, Bourree Lam, gave some good reasons for the lack of savings in her age group, including the millennials' staggering college debt and distrust of banks.[22] The piece did not deal with contrary evidence that these young people may, in fact, be saving pretty well. A survey by the Transamerica for Retirement Studies released earlier that year suggested that 70 percent of millennials are, in fact, saving for retirement through employer-sponsored plans or self-funded plans like 401(k)s, and that they started saving at the age of

22—much earlier than older folks.[23] That study is based on telephone surveys, and people tend to lie to pollsters, but it's still a counterweight for all that hand wringing.

And what if the doom and gloom turns out to be wrong? Catherine Rampell, a columnist at *The Washington Post* who writes on economic issues, said that the Moody's data was not so dire: "young people almost always have had a negative savings rate, with 'dissavings' for earlier generations of youth far worse than that among today's supposedly irresponsible millennials."[24]

There are signs that things might be looking up for this young crowd. The Federal Reserve of New York published a report in January 2016 showing that the average annual income of recent college graduates has jumped to $43,000, the highest in more than a decade.[25]

So who knows? After this long period of pain, and if the economy holds, the kids could turn out all right after all. Let's all root for them, even if they think I'm in the way.

PUNCH LIST

――――――●――――――

STARTING OUT IN YOUR 20s

Whether or not you have a job with a pension, you can do what we did, but smarter. These three deceptively simple steps will set 20somethings on the path to financial stability.

1) **Save more; spend less.** I don't want to sound like a scold, but these are the years to develop strong habits of saving. This will help you avoid debt and interest charges on purchases, and will provide you with a cushion against emergencies. Financial writers offer plenty of tips intended to help you save, but the best way is simply to begin. Set up automatic deposits from each paycheck in a savings account separate from whatever retirement funds you build. There are many, many books and websites offering tips and tricks about living within your means, but the bottom line is common sense: avoid extravagance. Think about the things you buy, and why you are buying them. Ask yourself if you need them. Don't deprive yourself, but a little mindfulness goes a long way.

2) **If you have credit cards, pay them down.** If you don't, you'll be spending money to pay off interest, and you could probably rack up late-payment fees as well. It's like having a big hole in your pocket. If you have cards with benefits like airline miles and rebates, keeping a zero balance means you get the benefits without giving the credit card company so much money that it makes the benefits no bargain. As the Federal Reserve Bank of Boston put it, "Paying off credit card debt has a riskless return that averages around 14 percent, which no other asset class can match."[26]

3) **Set up a 401(k) or an IRA.** Saving is a habit that you can build. So start saving for retirement just as soon as you can, especially if you have an employer that matches your 401(k) plan. Free money! Find out about your payroll plan at work. If you are self-employed, look into the options offered by your state government. A few years of savings early on can add hundreds of thousands of dollars to your retirement fund over the decades. You don't have to start with 10 percent; you can open your 401(k) with a smaller percentage of

your income and add a percentage point a year until you build up to 10 percent, or better. When you get a raise, put part of it toward retirement; if you never see the money, you'll never miss it.

4) **Pick your funds wisely.** There's no need to get fancy starting out. Make simple mutual fund choices, and don't invest in more complex financial instruments like annuities or exchange-traded funds until you've given yourself time to study up.

But which investments? How are you supposed to make sense of them? That is what the next chapter is about, whether you are in your 20s, in your 30s, or older.

3

YOUR INVESTING PRIMER

A man who loves money is a bastard, someone to be hated. A man who can't take care of it is a fool. You don't hate him, but you got to pity him.
—STEPHEN KING, *THE STAND*

JEANNE AND I had come out of our retirement review feeling pretty encouraged. But let's face it: our good fortune basically came down to that one smart decision in 1986 to siphon off 10 percent of my income into a 401(k) built on set of hastily chosen mutual funds. From there was the happy circumstance of staying employed, and working at companies that had decent pension plans.

In setting my financial course, I had no strategy, no deep understanding of what I was trying to accomplish. I might as well have been throwing darts at a list of mutual funds. Starting early meant it has worked out well enough, but if I'd known more at the start, I could have done better.

So in this time of reassessment, I wanted to make sure I fully understood what the guy from Vanguard was advising me to do about my 401(k). I needed to learn more—to find out whether we could do better with the time we have left to build that retirement nest egg. Could we be more comfortable, more able to travel, and, when we shuffle off this mortal coil, to leave something to the kids? I dove into research mode, trawling the websites of government agencies, financial organizations, and the incredibly rich and contradictory world of personal finance journalism. I did this not just so that I could better understand what I'd been through on my retirement odyssey, but also to provide information that you, the reader, might be able to benefit from.

Here's what I learned:

We are the lucky ones. As I've mentioned, many Americans haven't saved at all, or haven't saved enough. The most common reason for that is, predictably, not having enough left over in the paycheck to put much aside. Remember that National Institute on Retirement Security study that showed 45 percent of households have no retirement accounts at all? It also found an enormous income split between the savers and the save-nots. Households that do have retirement accounts have more than 2.4 times the annual income of those that don't, a median income of $86,235 compared with $35,509.[1] So nearly nine in ten families in the top fifth of income had retirement savings in 2013, and fewer than one in ten in the bottom fifth did.[2]

There's an age difference, too, according to the group: while the typical working-class household has $2,500 in retirement-account assets, those closer to retirement age, 55 to 64, have an average of $14,500—still not enough by a long shot. In that older group, 62 percent have retirement savings of less than one year of income, which won't get anyone very far.

Of course, those are averages that lump in the grasshoppers with the ants, those people who have saved nothing with those who are saving well. Averages that include half of those in it at zero will naturally end up very low. But what about the average savings among those who have been putting something away? Still not great: the Economic Policy Institute, a progressive think tank in Washington, found that the median retirement-savings figure among families with retirement accounts is $60,000.[3] With numbers like that, no wonder the Center for Retirement Research at Boston College has warned that more than half of American households won't have enough retirement income to maintain the standard of living from their working years.[4]

Americans aren't doing so well compared with those in other nations, either: despite our high per-capita income, the United States ranks 14th in retirement security globally, according to Natixis Global Asset Management, which compares 150 countries on factors like material well-being, health care, and quality of life.[5]

It's a mess. Or as the satirists at *The Onion* put it, "Nazi Treasure Hunters Following More Realistic Retirement Plan Than 86% of Country."[6]

We—you, me, the rest of us—can do better.

For many Americans, retirement used to rest on three legs, like a stool: on savings, on Social Security, and on pensions. A big part of the current problem comes down to the squeeze on pensions across the country. In 1975, nearly half of private nonfarm wage and salary workers took part in the classic defined-benefit pension plan; by 2004, that number had ducked under 17 percent.[7] The loss of pensions removes one of the legs of the stool, and makes saving for retirement more dependent on a wage earner's decision to put money away in a retirement savings account and to keep contributing—a voluntary act, and one that is in competition with many other demands on our cash. Pensions don't make people as much money as a well-funded, well-invested 401(k) or IRA can, but they can provide a dependable income in retirement.

While saving money for retirement has become more important, many of us don't feel that we know what to do or how to do it. Even among those who do plan, honest people tend to admit they—we, okay, I—don't really know what they are doing. According to a 2016 survey from the Federal Reserve, nearly one-half of non-retirees with retirement accounts admitted that they were "not confident" or only "slightly confident" about being able to make good investment decisions.[8]

So don't feel like a dope! Half of us don't think we know what we're doing. We're right: most Americans really don't know that much about money. The FINRA Investment Education Foundation has been studying our money sense for years, and the results don't look great.

Part of its work involves a five-question quiz (with a bonus) that it gives to more than 25,000 people.[9] Most Americans get only about half the answers right. (The national average is 3.16; those in Montana did much better, with a score of 3.78, while my home state of Texas came in with a low-low 2.81.)

The trend is not good; since FINRA started asking the questions in 2009, the percentage of right answers has dropped, from 42 percent in 2009 to 39 percent in 2012 to 37 percent in 2015. The question with the fewest right answers, just 28 percent nationwide, asks how bond prices move compared with rising interest rates. (They tend to drop.)

What's worse, we tend to think we know more about money than we actually do. FINRA surveys show that more than three-quarters of people they asked to assess their own financial knowledge gave themselves a nice high score: five to seven on a seven-point scale. While their actual financial knowledge was dropping from 2009 to 2015, their self-confidence was growing, with high self-assessments up from 67 percent in 2009.

This plays out pretty clearly in FINRA's surveys. Of the 42 percent of Americans who gave themselves the highest score on dealing with day-to-day financial matters like tracking their expenses and managing bank accounts and credit cards, nearly a third made expensive credit card mistakes such as paying only the minimum amount due (which builds up interest debt), getting stuck with late fees, and using cards for cash advances. More than one in ten of the people giving themselves the highest marks nonetheless overdrew their checking accounts.

So what we have here, nationally, is the financial version of what social scientists call the Dunning-Kruger effect, which tells us that people who are not competent tend to have greater confidence in their abilities than people who are good at what they do.[10] As David Dunning and Justin Kruger put it in a paper, "Not only do they reach erroneous conclusions and make unfortunate choices, but their incompetence robs them of the ability to realize it."[11]

Sounds familiar! We see this kind of aggressive ignorance all around us. And no, I am not making a political comment here, at least explicitly. You could consider it a subtweet, though.

In any case, there's no financial overconfidence in our little house, I can tell you that.

I took the FINRA quiz. It asks things like *"Suppose you have $100 in a savings account earning 2 percent interest a year. After five years, how much would you have?"* It then offers a range of answers: "More than $102" or "Exactly $102" or "Less than $102."

This is about compound interest, I thought, and picked "More than $102," though I would have broken a couple of pencils before coming up with exactly how much the account would have in it after five years ($110.41). As for the question *"True or false: Buying a single company's stock usually provides a safer return than a stock mutual fund,"* well, the value of baskets of funds over stock picking in the long term is such a basic fact of financial life that even I understand it—and you should, too. (More on that later. Much more.)

I ended up getting all six right, which made me feel great.

I asked Jeanne if she wanted to take the test. Sure, she said.

"Oh," Jeanne groused when I sent her the link. "I don't like numbers." Which is funny, since she's the one running our bills and initiating some of our bigger decisions in the financial world.

Still, she groaned as she took the quiz. Repeatedly. It's not that long a quiz! But she sighed at each question, and said, "I'm going to do really badly." She missed the bond question, but got three right, coming in at the national average and beating out half of Americans.

HERE WE GO: THE BASICS

We—and I mean the big "we" here, as in "all of us"—don't have to remain ignorant about money. We can learn.

The easiest way to save is the way we did it: through an employer-based savings plan known as a 401(k). Most retirement saving still takes place at work. There is much to be said for shunting dollars automatically from your paycheck into an account that you don't have to think about. You don't have to be strong, don't have to be good. You just have to stay employed. And many employers kick in a little extra to boost what you are saving, which is an even greater incentive for you to put money away. Free stuff!

Along with the automatic savings involved with 401(k) plans, the additional beauty of them is this: you don't pay taxes on the money you put in during the years you are building your savings. You get taxed only when you take the money out again. Since most people can expect to be in a somewhat lower tax bracket after they are not drawing a regular paycheck, the taxes on the money you take out at retirement are smaller. (There can be expensive penalties, however, if you pull money out early.)

There is another kind of 401(k) offered by many employers that's known as a Roth 401(k). The main difference between a plain-vanilla 401(k) and a Roth plan is that you pay the taxes up front, as the money goes into the savings plan, and so the money coming out at the other end is tax-free. The Roth is a popular option for younger employees whose income and tax rate may be relatively low; they expect to be paying a higher tax rate down the line, so want to take the smaller sting up front. It's also a tactic used by people who are trying to set up an inheritance plan so survivors won't be burdened with income taxes. If your employer offers both, you can split your contributions between a traditional 401(k) and a Roth.[12] (You can find online calculators that help determine whether a traditional or a Roth is better for you at sites like betterment.com.)

So employer-sponsored savings plans are great! But while that kind of employment used to be the way of the American economy, not everyone has access to a plan these days. A study by the Pew Charitable Trusts found that 58 percent of workers today have access to a savings plan sponsored by their employer. (Because not everyone who could use the plans does, an even smaller percentage of workers, just 49 percent, takes advantage of them.) The shifting world of employment plays a part. Many of us are working differently than our parents did. Maybe you are self-employed or working for a small company that doesn't go to the trouble and expense to set one up. That's pretty common: Just 22 percent of companies with fewer than 10 employees have access to a workplace retirement plan. At companies with at least 500 employees, it's 74 percent.

A nation divided in so many ways is also divided when it comes to retirement savings. The folks at Pew found that participation in plans varied because of factors like geography, income level, and race. In Wisconsin, 61 percent of workers have access to an employer-based pension or retirement savings plan; in Florida the figure is just 38 percent. Workers in New England and the Midwest are likelier to take part than those in the South and West. As for income level, only a third of workers making less than $25,000 a year have access to one; for people making more than $100,000, it's three out of four. And Hispanic workers are 25 percent less likely than non-Hispanic workers to have access to a plan.[13]

So how do you save if your employer doesn't help you save?

The main retirement savings plan for self-employed people and those who don't like their employer's 401(k) plan (some companies offer a limited range of investment options) is the IRA, Individual Retirement Account. You set it up through financial institutions like banks, mutual fund companies, and brokerage firms. As with 401(k) plans, they come in two flavors, traditional and Roth, with the same differences in tax treatment. That is, you can make contributions to traditional IRAs tax-free and pay the taxes during retirement—presumably at a lower tax rate than during your working life. With the Roth IRA, you pay the taxes up front and make the withdrawals tax-free later.

IRA plans have contribution limits set by Congress. For 2017, the limit for either kind of IRA plan is $5,500, though people older than 50 have a higher "catch-up limit" of $6,500. You can have both a 401(k) and an IRA, but you might not be able to deduct all your contribution if you have both.[14]

If you need to tap either a 401(k) or an IRA, you will find that the money is expensive: pulling out funds before the age of 59½ will bring on a 10 percent penalty, along with whatever taxes you have to pay on the money. There are also penalties if you don't take out enough of your money once you pass 70½; there is a "required minimum distribution."

Small-business owners and freelancers can also take part in what are known as a simplified employee pension (SEP) IRAs.

In recent years, other savings plans have emerged. Some states have retirement programs of their own, including California, Connecticut, and Maryland, according to the Georgetown University Center for Retirement Initiatives.[15] Illinois has introduced the Secure Choice Savings Program for small businesses, with a pilot program scheduled to begin in 2018.[16]

Even if your employer does offer a 401(k) plan, it's worth checking to see what fees might be hidden in the plan. I looked at a plan being offered to our younger son through his employer. He would be charged a 3 percent "annual third-party administrative service fee" and a 1.5 percent "annual asset charge." So these folks were going to take 4.5 percent of his 401(k) deposits—not counting additional fees that he'd be paying if he signed up for so-called advisory services that cost $25 annually and an additional 0.65 percent of assets. That's obscene.

The company BrightScope, which rates 401(k) plans, says that large plans with more than $100 million in assets "almost uniformly have fees below 1%." Smaller plans tend to have higher fees, since their operational costs are higher, but the company warns that "paying north of 2% a year in fees makes investing prohibitively expensive and eats a big hole in participant retirement balances, regardless of the services that are offered at that fee level."[17] I suggested to my son that, unless the employer is offering a very big match to his contribution, he might do better to start with a personal IRA with automatic payroll deductions.

Some funds now: common investment vehicles

Whether you have a 401(k) or an IRA or some other form of retirement plan, you'll be making choices among many kinds of investments. Most common are the mutual funds, which spread your buying power by giving you a portion of a more diversified package of investments than you could afford if you had to buy each stock or bond in the fund.

The largest group of mutual funds are equity funds, made up of stocks—that is, shares in companies. Within the world of stock funds, some focus on big companies (known as large cap, for "large capitalization"), with at least $5 billion in market value. Others focus on small ones (small cap), which generally have a market value of less than $2 billion. There are also funds focusing on what's in between, known as the mid-cap stocks, and myriad others, including some that give you the opportunity to invest in foreign stocks. Some funds focus on so-called growth stocks, which appear to be on the rise—companies in hot technologies like renewable energy and biotech, for example. Others focus on what are called value stocks, which are seen as trading below what they are actually worth. And many, many funds blend the categories. Generally, buying into the stock market is the way to make money in the long term.

Going beyond the world of stocks, there are funds based on bonds (debt of businesses or governments), which tend to not provide as much investment growth over time but do tend to be more stable, with a lower risk of loss through market ups and down. On the even more financially conservative end of the spectrum are money market funds, which are built from extremely stable investments like U.S. Treasury bills.

Because nothing is simple in this world, there are also all kinds of funds that blend stocks, bonds, and other investments, as well.

What's the right balance between stocks, bonds, and money market funds? It depends on how old you are. Investment advisers generally suggest being heavy into stocks early in life and shifting more toward bonds as retirement nears, when a downturn could leave you substantially less to live on. There's an old rule of thumb for asset allocation: subtract your age from 100, and the resulting number is the percentage of your investments you should have in stocks. Because people live longer than they used to, and because investments like Treasury bonds don't pay as much as they used to, rule-of-thumb watchers have revised the number to subtract from to 110 or even 120.

Let's go back to the discussion I had with the guy from Vanguard about stock funds versus bonds: he told me that I should, at my age, have about 35 percent of my investments in bonds and about 65 percent in stocks. That was a little aggressive on Vanguard's part, compared with the revised rule of thumb, but they were working with my own questionnaire that said I was willing to take on a fair amount of risk.

If you want to balance your portfolio to include more bonds and fewer stocks as you get closer to retirement, there are funds that adjust the balance automatically. These are called target-date funds, or TDFs.

You decide when you think you'll be retiring—there's that big question again!—and pick a fund with a matching date.

Not only are there different kinds of investments such as stocks and bonds; there are also different kinds of funds you can use to invest in those stocks and bonds. The most important difference: actively managed funds versus index funds.

In a managed fund, financial people do research and figure out what stocks, bonds, and other instruments should be in their mix of investments and buy and sell them. The idea is that a smart manager will help you beat the market and make more money—a debatable proposition, as we'll see. In any case, that management infrastructure costs money, and you, the investor, pay it in the fund's fees. You can expect to pay 1 to 1.5 percent of your investment each year for these funds. It may not sound like much, but it adds up.

Index funds were created partly in reaction to the relatively high fees of managed funds; they are based on a simple grouping of stocks—say, all the companies in the popular S&P 500. We'll be talking a lot more about index funds later in this chapter, but for the moment know that they generally cost less than 1 percent per year, and can cost just 0.03 percent.

There's another kind of fund out there that you should know about for this primer: an exchange-traded fund, or ETF. An ETF looks like a mutual fund in a lot of ways but can be traded like a stock, so they are easier to get in and out of than mutual funds. ETFs can combine stocks, bonds, and other financial instruments, and a lot of them are created as index funds. (The best known of these is the Spider, which goes by the symbol SP.) ETFs have been around since the early 1990s, but boomed in the 2000s, with some $3 trillion in assets worldwide.[18] Now, the ability to easily trade ETFs goes against my personal set-it-and-forget-it philosophy, but they are enormously popular. And who am I to argue with people who, at least, are saving?

What an alphabet soup this all is. And I haven't even mentioned REITs, real estate investment trusts.

And I won't.

There's more. For example, annuities, which are an investment—

often, a form of insurance—that is designed to pay out a certain amount of money each year. Essentially, you are paying for peace of mind. They can be complex, but they can also be useful under some circumstances, and a deep dive into what they do is beyond the scope of this book. But I will give an example showing how they can serve as an add-on to your retirement plan. If you've saved plenty, you can take a largish chunk out of your 401(k) and roll it into what is known as an "immediate annuity," essentially a contract from an insurance company to begin paying you a set amount based on the money you have put down. That sets up a system to pay you a certain amount a year, no matter what happens to the market. With the annuity, your risk has been reduced. The money won't run out, as could happen with a drawn-down IRA if you lived to a Methuselahan age, and that investment, at least, won't lose value if the market takes a hit.[19]

There are plenty of nonfinancial investments as well: things we buy thinking they will go up in value, like collectibles, art, even comic books. If you've got the cash, and a gift for spotting a vintage Gibson Les Paul in a pawnshop or a Richard Diebenkorn painting on the wall at Goodwill, go ahead and indulge. I have a friend who paid his kids' college tuitions from the profits he made selling indigenous art objects from around the world.

For the rest of us, though, that kind of investment is a risky business. Art as an investment is tricky. In our house, we have two large canvases. One shows Venice by day, and the other Paris at dusk. The Paris painting is a view of Place Pigalle; the rain-washed streets, filled with pedestrians and horse-drawn carriages, reflect the light pouring from the shops and clubs. The Venice one, by contrast, shows a pale sky over a drowsy assortment of boats sitting moored just beyond Piazza San Marco. Those big paintings had hung in my parents' house. Dad and Mom bought them on their honeymoon in New Orleans; I figure they found them in one of those great old shops on Royal Street. For years, the name on the paintings was unknown to me: A. DeVity. When my parents sold the house I grew up in and asked if any of us kids wanted anything from the old place, I asked for Paris and Venice.

They are treasures—or, at least, so says Dad. At various times when he's been worried about our financial squeezes, he has suggested we sell the paintings. "They're probably worth a couple of hundred thousand dollars now!" he'd say.

I'd asked for the paintings because I loved them; they reminded me of home. We had no interest in starting an art collection. We have some pieces we like, including works by artist friends that we bought in galleries, and a painting of a tiger that Jeanne's dad painted on boards joined at a 90-degree angle so that it could hang in the corner of a room. But no overarching personal aesthetic guides us. Some of our friends' homes look like galleries. Our homes have looked like us—comfortable and familiar, if a bit of a mess. And our art, we've always been pretty sure, isn't valuable.

Dad was insistent, though, that Paris and Venice would set us on our feet financially. So I did some research, and discovered that works by DeVity—there are two generations, father and son, and there are thousands of paintings out there, including forgeries—are not highly valued today. Their paintings fetch anywhere from a few hundred dollars to $1,500. Not worth selling, in other words. And that's fine. I love looking at them. The research helped me confirm, for my own sake, that I don't come from a line of savvy art collectors.

There's another problem with collecting: fraud. The main reason I know that works by the abstract painter Richard Diebenkorn are valuable is that in 2001 I worked with another reporter, Judith H. Dobrzynski, on stories about a scam involving crooked bidding on eBay. The ring of art fraudsters made it look like an auction for what appeared to be a Diebenkorn was legitimate and drove up the price on a single painting to $135,805. Bogus artworks from the crew, who also auctioned works purported to be created by Edward Hopper, Alberto Giacometti, and Clyfford Still, cost buyers $450,000. So caveat emptor and all that.[20]

Getting to know yourself—and your tolerance for financial risk

There's still more to say about investing—so much more. But it's a start; if this is an intellectual battle, consider yourself lightly armed. At the end of this chapter, I'll be saying more about the simplest way through the maze. But with these basics, you are at least ready to read more, or to talk with a financial adviser to figure out your next moves. (I've got a lot more to say about investment advisers, as well, in the next chapter.)

Even before you put money into investments, though, it's best to know yourself. What kind of investor are you? How much risk can you tolerate?

Risk is part of every investment decision. Where you strike the balance between stocks and bonds in your own investment portfolio has a lot to do with your attitude about risk.

The questionnaire I filled out for the Vanguard retirement evaluation tried to get at my attitudes toward risk, but in a fairly superficial way.

Ron Lieber, who writes about personal finance for *The New York Times*, wrote a great column about quizzes that help you understand your willingness to take on financial risk.[21] He pointed people to quizzes they could take at websites like riskprofiling.com and riskalyze.com, as well as tests at Betterment.com, Wealthfront.com, and Finmason. com.

It's important to know your risk tolerance, he explained, because finding the kinds of investments that fit your emotional makeup can help avoid making market mistakes. He said, "Too many people don't know their tolerance well enough and take on too much risk. This can result in getting greedy and buying more investments while stock prices are high and selling when stocks have plunged, thus locking in losses. The result of such moves is too often a portfolio that earns many percentage points less over the years than it may have if you had just left things alone." If you're going to meet your financial goals and be able to deal with emergencies, you're going to have to take some financial risks with your investments; knowing how much you'll be comfortable with can help you reach your goals.

I took one of the tests, a one-pager based on research by Ruth Lytton at Virginia Tech and John Grable at the University of Georgia.[22] It said, "There are no 'right' or 'wrong' answers. Just have fun!"

The quiz asked 13 questions, including this one:

> **In addition to whatever you own, you have been given $2,000.**
> **You are now asked to choose between:**
> - *A sure loss of $500*
> - *A 50% chance to lose $1,000 and a 50% chance to lose nothing*

The thing made my palms sweat a little, but at least it didn't take long. And when I was done, it gave me a number. My score was 24: "average/moderate tolerance for risk." A little lower than I expected, but it probably wasn't far wrong.

I asked Jeanne to take the test, and she scored 22, which is considered a below-average tolerance for risk, which we kind of knew already.

The results page led to another page that listed investments grouped by their relative risks and rewards.[23] The high-risk category included investments like aggressive growth funds and cheap, volatile "penny stocks" and precious metals funds. In the moderate range were things like the stock index funds that make up most of our 401(k). At the very bottom of the scale were the investment equivalents of stuffing money in the mattress: certificates of deposit and savings accounts.

If we were just starting out, tests like this could possibly help us figure out what kinds of investments best suited us, maybe with the help of a kindly financial professional. The tests can be abused, however, by brokers, as the financial planner and *New York Times* columnist Carl Richards has written, "to plug investors into a prepackaged blend of mutual funds without really considering the specifics of annoying, messy things like values and goals. In other words, it's a lazy way of making a basic diagnosis and then writing you a prescription."[24]

Quizzes take you only so far, especially when our attitudes can be shaped by events. In hot markets, people love risk. If it looks like it's hard to lose, we tell ourselves, "Go big or go home." When markets go south, we become risk averse.

You can gain some insight into the kind of investment strategy you'd like by thinking about the kinds of risks you take in your own life.

In my personal life, I've taken plenty of risks, but I don't consider myself foolhardy. I have gone skydiving, but just once, in my 20s. That was enough. For work, I've done things like riding in military helicopters with open cargo doors into disaster areas, and herding cattle away from Hurricane Harvey's floodwaters in a two-seater helicopter with a 22-year-old daredevil. (As we were about to climb in for that wild ride, the young man's father soberly asked, "Ryan, did you get him to sign the waiver?")[25] I've experienced zero gravity in a NASA plane and worn a metal suit while being zapped with a million volts from a big Tesla coil.[26] But I didn't do anything I thought was truly unsafe, even the million-volts thing. Just google "Faraday cage" and you'll see why. I've been in greater danger just driving on icy streets to my morning commuter train.

Evaluating risk is something that each of us does every day, though we might not think of it as such. We decide whether to eat healthy food, and try to make sense of the newspaper stories about whether coffee is good or bad for you—and then probably drink coffee anyway.

Part of our tolerance for risk comes from how we were raised. I grew up in the distant past, before the emergence of overanxious parenting. There's no doubt our folks loved us, but they weren't what you'd call fretful. Trucks that sprayed DDT lumbered through the streets of Galveston on summer nights; we ran behind the trucks to feel the cooling mist from the sprayer and to breathe in the weird, sweetish fog. We survived; DDT is far tougher on bugs and birds' eggs than on people. But I'd have never let my own kids do it.

That was not our only toxic exposure. Natural oil seepage from the floor of the Gulf of Mexico and oil shipping sent hard little tar balls onto Galveston's beaches. After the BP oil disaster in 2010, tar balls were a source of anger and worry for coastal communities and tourist parents. When I was a kid, our parents simply pointed at tar balls and said, "Don't eat 'em." We kept some turpentine by the back door to wash the gunk off our feet when we came back to the house, because that stuff was never going to come off the terrazzo. For all the environmental damage associated with disasters like the Deepwater Horizon oil spill, my parents, apparently, were right about tar balls; studies suggest the risk from mere skin exposure is low.[27] The turpentine might not have been a great idea, though.[28]

These days, I have to think through questions of risk more than most people, because I learn about new ones all the time as a science reporter. Take plastics. In *The Graduate*, they were the future. Now they are a big problem for the planet. Tiny shredded bits of the stuff can be found in the world's oceans and other bodies of water; people throw away trash, and much of it ends up deteriorating in the sea. Not just plastic bags and bottles but also toys and even the tiny microbeads that have been used in some exfoliants, shampoos, and cosmetics. There are even shredded plastic fibers that come from washing clothes made with some blends of polyester. Anyway, this stuff is pretty much everywhere now, and the pieces of plastic attract nasty chemicals like PCBs. Tiny marine animals and fish eat the plastic, which means that by the time you work across the marine food web and up the food chain, creatures that eat a lot of fish, like herons, end up having a lot of plastic in their gullets, and, potentially, the toxins, too. The science is still being worked out, but basically, this means that the fish that's supposed to be healthy for you also contains new additional risks. As with mercury in tuna, the question of whether to eat fish in light of ocean plastics is a risk-balancing act.

So what do I do about fish? I eat it. I'm a product of my upbringing: by nature, I'm not a nervous person, and I balance the risks against the possible rewards. I don't change much of my behavior if the extent of the problem is still poorly understood. Gulf Coast oysters were a big part of my childhood, as were those Gulf brown shrimp as big as my fist. We can't eliminate all risks from our lives, and most foods are a mixture of upside and downside, and so I tend to eat what makes me happy, and not to eat too much of any of it.

That doesn't mean I'm stupid about risk. I did stop smoking. There's nothing good about using tobacco, except that it made me feel good and I miss it *so much.*

But I also still grill meat, which may increase my risk of cancer slightly.[29] Eating meat entails other risks, including an elevated risk of heart disease. I eat less of it than I used to, both for my health and for environmental reasons. And, so far as I can tell, the health benefits of eating a hunk of salmon still outweigh the risks of grilling it.

Still, I floss every night. I didn't always, but I needed periodontal surgery in my late 20s and started flossing soon after that. Never stopped, and never had the problem again. Recent much-hyped research suggests that the benefits of flossing are not proven.[30] Like a lot of people who have looked at the evidence, I don't buy it.[31] Or, as I put it in a passionate tweet, "I don't care what the small, poorly done studies don't prove. I'm flossing, baby. Now and forever."

What does all this mean about how I invest? By standard measures, as the Vanguard guy told me, I have stayed in stocks to a greater extent longer than I probably should have. Partly, of course, that's because I wasn't paying attention and hadn't changed the mix much since I bought into my current funds when I started out at *Newsweek* and then the *Times*. But it also means that I'm inclined to continue staying heavily invested in stocks a while longer.

After the article about our retirement plans came out, several people wrote to warn me about bonds. With interest rates at historic lows, they pointed out, bonds aren't actually a great investment right now, and their protective value might be overstated by conventional wisdom. And when was I actually going to retire? If I kept working until 70, it might make sense to stomach a greater amount of risk until I was closer to the send-off.

I may have come to planning late in the game, but if my dad is any indication, I've got a good 20 years or more left. I'm healthier at this age than my dad was, thanks to things like getting more exercise, having quit smoking earlier in life, and eating less barbecue.

So I'm putting off that rebalancing for a while longer. Because, as far as I can tell, I've got longer. And you probably do, too.

So how about you? Do you floss? Would you jump out of an airplane? How does any of this translate into your own personal tolerance for risk, especially when it comes to investing?

My fretting about all this, and my worry that I might be making irrational choices, puts me in good company.

In his fine book *Your Money and Your Brain*, *The Wall Street Journal* "Intelligent Investor" columnist Jason Zweig told the story of Harry M. Markowitz, who developed a theory of portfolio selection that balanced risk and return so effectively that it won him the Nobel Memorial Prize in Economic Sciences.

But Markowitz, in his investing life, found that he couldn't follow his own plan. Zweig quoted him as saying, "I should have computed the historical co-variances of the asset classes and drawn an efficient frontier. Instead, I visualized my grief if the stock market went way up and I wasn't in it—or if it went way down and I was completely in it. My intention was to minimize my future regret. So I split my contributions 50/50 between bonds and equities."[32]

If a certified genius couldn't do it, I'm not going to feel as bad about myself.

AGING PEOPLE, CHANGING INVESTMENT STRATEGIES

As I mentioned earlier, your investment needs to change as you age. Planning for retirement in your our 20s and 30s is largely all about getting started with a savings plan and building those funds aggressively. One strategy: start small, with a contribution that is just a few percent of your income. Preferably, you'd want to channel enough into an investment account to make sure that you take advantage of any match that your employer provides, if there is one. Many employers will match a portion of your contribution up to, say, 5 percent of your income. Don't give up free money! Once you've started, you can increase your contribution by 1 percentage point a year—not enough to hurt, but enough to be putting away 10 percent or more of your income before long. At this writing, the federal government allows you to put as much as $18,000 into retirement accounts each year.

By your 50s, it's more about disentangling yourself from debt and figuring out what your retirement income might look like and taking the steps you can to address it. After you reach the age of 50, the federal government allows a $6,000 bump up to the maximum contribution you can make to a 401(k), which means your total can be as much as $24,000. But you can put money into IRAs as well—and if you haven't put away savings by your 50s, you need to push yourself to address that problem while you still can. Carrie Schwab-Pomerantz, the coauthor of *The Charles Schwab Guide to Finances After Fifty*, writes that if you reach your sixth decade and haven't started saving yet, you'll need to siphon off at least 40 percent of your income each year until retirement to catch up.[33]

By your 60s, it's about making sure that your mix of assets is balanced in a way to protect you from market volatility during the years you'll be drawing money out of your plans. And, more and more, we're being advised to expect that period of drawing down these funds to be longer than we'd expected.

But then what? The biggest change in the world of retirement is that Americans are living longer. According to the Society of Actuaries, a 65-year-old man can expect to live, on average, to 85.8. A woman will live longer still: 87.8 years.[34] In 2000, life expectancy at 65 was 84.6 for men and 86.4 for women.[35] Longer life is good—it sure beats the alternative—but financially speaking, it introduces complications. For one thing, it puts pressure on the Social Security program, which was designed for an America with a shorter lifespan. The program now has to pay out benefits to people who will be spending more of their lives in retirement.[36] (It was also designed for families that had more children than we have today, so the built-in assumptions called for more wage earners putting money into the system. A 2010 report from the Social Security Administration suggested that by 2035, taxes will be enough to pay for only 75 percent of scheduled benefits.)[37]

For people like you and me, those additional years spent in retirement could mean needing a greater amount of money in the ol' retirement account—remember the question from Vanguard about how long I expected to live? So that calls for more retirement planning than our parents' generations needed, especially since more of that older generation had jobs with decent pensions. A 401(k) or an IRA offers you the opportunity to earn more than you might have from a straight pension, but the obligation and risk are on you to build that fortune through perseverance and smart investing. Those pensions kept going as long as the former employee kept breathing.

That trend has led many employers that provide pensions to their employees to now offer retirees a lump sum. If you have worked for an employer that provides a pension, you will probably hear from them with the prospect of being paid a large chunk all at once. These really took off after the Great Recession, and save employers from the obligation of a lifetime payout. They get to dump you off their pension plan, and you get money up front. The lump is usually big and attractive. The Government Accountability Office found 22 plan sponsors that offered lump-sum windows in 2012 along with 498,000 employees involved and lump sums totaling $9.25 billion.[38] If you think you might not need the pension to live on, you can invest the lump sum and pass it on to the kids. But if you'll need the money throughout your old age, holding on to the pension is the better idea.

INTERLUDE

I try to become a financial genius by reading a shelf of books

Even though I don't generally like personal finance books—particularly the ones that are teachy and preachy and that try to make their rather pedestrian advice sound like a secret code for success, as you'll see, I found something to like in almost all these books. But they are not enough.

For real insight into how people deal with money, for powerful warnings and examples that stick with me, I turn to novels. You might have noticed that I've been quoting more Dickens and Trollope than Dave Ramsey or Suze Orman. The novelists don't tell us how to properly balance our portfolios, but they do tell us how to balance our lives. Many of the financial guides are trying to sell us something; the best novels teach us something.

Why, yes, I did major in liberal arts in college. What's your point?

Take it from Friedrich Engels, no slouch in the economics realm. In a letter describing Balzac's *La Comédie humaine*, Engels said, thanks to that work, with its detailed description of French society down to its economic details, "I have learned more than from all the professed historians, economists, and statisticians of the period together."[39]

I have read some Balzac. I have tried to read Engels. I know who I'd rather have with me at the beach.

So as I have worked my way through the finance books, I have also read some amazing novels. (I get most of my reading done using audiobooks during my morning run and my commute.) Some of our greatest writers have obsessed over money—its getting and spending, and what the want of it does to our lives. When Jane Austen's characters talk about being "distressed for money," you know exactly what she means.[40]

Dickens shows us the pain of grinding poverty and the frippery that can come with wealth and position. He gives us literature's famously optimistic spendthrift, Wilkins Micawber of the timeless *David Copperfield*. This book opens with one of Micawber's great and simple statements about money: "Annual income twenty pounds, annual expenditure nineteen pounds nineteen and six, result happiness. Annual income twenty pounds, annual expenditure twenty pounds nought and six, result misery." He's talking about a difference of just sixpence each year between success and failure. That's hyperbole, but the underlying logic is unshakable: spend more than you take in, and you're headed for trouble.

Like Hamlet's Polonius, however, Micawber is the least likely character to look to for advice. He ends up in debtor's prison in the course of the novel, though he eternally believes that "something will turn up" and deliver him and his family from penury. (In the 1935 film based on the novel, you see how W. C. Fields captured that old scoundrel Micawber brilliantly.)[41]

Anthony Trollope, too, gives us many characters who fall into trouble with spending and debt—most spectacularly, his George Vavasor, a young man in *Can You Forgive Her?* Born a gentleman and once elected to Parliament, he is feckless, and his need for money drives him to evil—he even attempts to kill his rival for a well-heeled woman's affections.

You don't have to go back 150 years to find good writing about money, though. Just look at the delightful mess Sue Townsend describes in *Adrian Mole and the Weapons of Mass Destruction*, the sixth book in her series of hilarious novels about a young man's progress in the world.

The 2004 novel is about the continuing misadventures of Adrian Mole. On the world stage is the epic fiasco of the war in Iraq, which Adrian enthusiastically supported. On a private level, it is the fiasco of his finances. A decided lack of planning and foresight underlies each part of the story, of course. Adrian has fallen into ruinous debt, spending money on things like a fancy apartment and a high-tech refrigerator that tells him when the food inside has reached its sell-by date. A friend who is a financial adviser tries to talk Adrian into more sensible, frugal ways, even quoting good old Micawber. And when Adrian asks him what he can do, the friend, Parvez, gives it to him straight.

You could start by living in the world me and Fatima live in. I don't earn much so we live in a small house, and we ain't got a talking fridge. Ours just sits under the worktop and keeps its gob shut. You can't afford a lifestyle, Moley, only a life.

The first time I read that, it gave me chills, and not just because I recognized the bit of Adrian Mole in me. That's what great novels do: they help us experience the lives of others, and get to know ourselves better in the process. Can Robert Kiyosaki (*Rich Dad Poor Dad*) do that?

In any case, I did take on a shelf of personal finance books, both to learn more about finance and to serve you, my patient reader. To be honest, I selected a pretty small shelf. Maybe it's an end table.

Anyone embarking on a course of reading in personal finance should probably start with *The Only Investment Guide You'll Ever Need*, by Andrew Tobias.[42] It first came out in 1978, and Tobias has brought out new editions regularly ever since. This book is a gem: commonsensical, conversational, and fun. He urges frugality in a thousand ways because of a fundamental point: money saved is more valuable than money earned. Tobias put it this way: every nickel you earn has already been pretty costly, because it has come to you after taxes and everything else that makes the gross income number on your tax return so much bigger than the net. Every nickel you spend has already been through the withholding wringer. It is a precious thing.

Tobias writes that Benjamin Franklin had it only half right: that while a penny saved is a penny earned, "the updated adage would read, 'A penny saved is *two* pennies earned.' Or nearly so." So he tells us to buy in bulk and get discounts and weatherize our homes and other actions that can save those earned pennies.

He tells us that the wealthy businessman Charles Revson bought Cepacol mouthwash by the case, saving money on the discount and beating inflation, using this year's mouthwash at last year's price. Buy your wines by the case, he said. Ten percent off a ten-dollar bottle of wine, he wrote, would put about $400 extra in the bank account by the end of the year—what he called "a chickenhearted way to play commodities."

All these savings add up.

His first edition has the Cepacol story in it. It was written before the spread of big box stores like Walmart and Costco, with their discounts on mountainous packages of toilet paper and other necessities. The world caught up with Tobias.

In his 2016 edition, he points out that the 1978 version of the book came out before the existence of 401(k) plans, adjustable-rate mortgages, and . . . the Internet. Even with all the change in the intervening years, he wrote, "the basics of personal finance haven't changed—they never do."

Whew, I thought. His message, true to his word, is simple and entertainingly delivered: live within your means, save a lot, invest over the long haul.

Savings is only the beginning—this broad guide has tips on patient investing, sensible tax planning, and other topics. Even so, Tobias lets you know that he's a little embarrassed by the "immodest" title, which "was the publisher's idea; in a weak moment I went along"—and that it's the "only" guide you'll need mainly because so many of the other guides are so awful. He doesn't promise to make the reader rich, but he promises not to lead you on a chase for get-rich-quick schemes.

Even more important, he dissects what's wrong with most other guides:

> The ones that hold out the promise of riches are frauds. The ones that deal with strategies in commodities or gold are too narrow. They tell you how you might play a particular game, but not whether to be playing the game at all. The ones that are encyclopedic, with a chapter on everything, leave you pretty much where you were to begin with—trying to choose from a myriad of competing alternatives.

How seductive are the ideas that Tobias gives us? Taking all my newly learned financial experience, I decided to do one new thing: to buy my next bottles of wine by the case. For the last year or so, I've been drinking a glass of wine a night before bed; it's good for maintaining a healthy cholesterol level, it helps me get to sleep, and it tastes good. It makes me feel pretty good, too. One glass doesn't give me much of a buzz, but that's not really the point of drinking at this stage of my life, by which I mean I'm not in college anymore.

What do I buy? Mainly Italian reds, mainly Chianti, thanks to a six-month study-abroad program in Siena in my undergraduate days. I'll probably never be able to afford the hearty Brunellos (check them out next time you're in a nice wine shop). I usually spend less than $10 a bottle, and never more than $20.

But one wine, from the Monsanto vineyards in Tuscany, appealed to me especially. It is the wine we bought for our wedding, more than 30 years ago. When I started making the effort to have a bottle of wine around, I remembered the label. (It has no connection to the Monsanto corporation, in case you are wondering.)

I found it at the Wine Library in Short Hills, New Jersey, and bought a bottle for about $17. It was as good as I remembered, and it gave me a great feeling to drink something that brought such sweet memories. It got a decent rating from Robert Parker, depending on the year, but nothing to jump at.

Armed with my financial acumen on my most recent visit, I told the clerk I'd like to buy a case of the Monsanto. They were pushing case price discounts, with big signs explaining the math on selected vintages. The clerk called downstairs for a case of the 2010. When it was hauled up to the checkout, I asked what the case discount was. "There's no case discount with this one," the clerk told me.

Well, damn.

I bought it anyway. Yes, I was a little reluctant to walk away after having put them to the trouble of lugging it up. I'm polite, okay?

But I also figured that I buy plenty of wine from them at $10 and even $4 a bottle (a tasty red table wine that's as good as some of the Chiantis they sell for much more). And if they raised the price later, I'd have beaten inflation.

Jeanne convinced me that I made the right choice; it's a wine I can bring to friends' homes for dinners, and it will be there whenever I want a bottle. It will be nice to have it around. I'll try for a discount next time. Life is long.

At least I hope it is.

After Tobias, I moved on to another classic, *The Money Game* by "Adam Smith," the pen name for George J. W. Goodman.[43] This is another of those revered works that has sent a lot of people down the road to financial independence. He has updated it since the first edition came out in 1967, when its frank recognition of the craziness of markets set it apart from the other go-go guides to wealth. It's been a longtime bestseller for a reason, and not just because the author was the host of *Adam Smith's Money World* on PBS. Lucid explanations of the financial world meet up in these pages with a literary sensibility that can be startlingly effective, as when he explains what happens when a bullish stock market collapses.

We are all at a wonderful party and by the rules of the game we know that at some point in time the Black Horsemen will burst through the great terrace doors to cut down the revelers; those who leave early may be saved, but the music and wines are so seductive that we do not want to leave, but we do ask, "What time is it? What time is it?" Only none of the clocks have any hands.

Good stuff! This book provides real insight about the ways that Wall Street works and market timing and mass psychology. He freely admits that playing the market is a game, and that only a gambler can find it compelling. "If you are a successful Game player, it can be a fascinating, consuming, totally absorbing experience, in fact it has to be," he writes. "If it is not totally absorbing, you are not likely to be among the successful, because you are competing with those who do find it so absorbing." That's an important warning.

The book's a gem. But the latest version came out in 1976, shortly after the birth of index funds and the vast changes they brought to the market. Index funds allow you to do well at the Game without the gambler's instinct. So this one can feel dusty. But for people who do want a better sense of the market, and who do want to develop a strategy for investing, *The Money Game* continues to stand out.

Bonus: another relatively ancient book for those who really want to pursue an active investment path is Benjamin Graham's classic *The Intelligent Investor*, published in 1949. Graham wrote the bible of what is known as "value investing," the method of finding undervalued stocks that has been followed by Warren Buffett to great success. Buffett says it is "by far the best book on investing ever written." And who am I to argue with him?

The next book I tried was from one of the best loved personal finance writers out there, Dave Ramsey. He is an advice machine: you can hear his reassuring, folksy Tennessee accent on radio, or pick up tips on his popular website, or read any of his many books. Wherever you find him, his basic message is super simple: Debt is the enemy. Get out of debt.

That is the message of Ramsey's *Total Money Makeover: A Proven Plan for Financial Fitness*.[44] I find it hard to argue with that basic thought. And many people find his step-by-step plans to reduce debt and build wealth very appealing. His big idea is the "Debt Snowball," a simple and psychologically satisfying way to pay down debt. Many economists will tell you to pay off the debts with the highest interest rate first. Ramsey tells you to list your debts from the smallest to the largest, and start working your way up from the little stuff. The reason has less to do with economics than with psychology: you will see your progress as you knock out the smaller debts, and that will give you the morale boost to keep at it and go after the bigger ones. "When you start the Debt Snowball and in the first few days pay off a couple of little debts, trust me, it lights your fire," he writes. "And getting fired up is super-important." He also offers workbooks and "Financial Peace budgeting software."

The book is friendly but strict, with helpings of scripture and preaching. When Ramsey tells us the Debt Snowball is easy to understand but requires "truckloads of effort," he recalls the words of his pastor, who said that living right "isn't complicated, but it's difficult."

Ramsey has his critics—his blinding success has spawned a mini-industry of Dave doubters who point out that not all debt is bad, and that borrowed money can be used to make money, and that Ramsey's methods are needlessly strict. You can read more of the criticism at sites like the White Coat Investor, where it's argued that when it comes to investing, Ramsey gives "terrible advice."[45] Mr. White Coat, whose real name is James M. Dahle, seems a little dogmatic to me, but I do have problems with Ramsey's stern attitude about making and keeping a family budget, which I'll be talking more about in the chapter on debt.

The next volume on my list: *The Little Book of Common Sense Investing*, by John Bogle, the former chief executive of the Vanguard Group, which he founded in 1974.[46] Over the years, he's achieved well-deserved guru status and has written his own shelf of books. I'll be talking a lot more about Bogle in coming pages, because he revolutionized investing through his development of low-cost index funds. But if you want to know more than this little book will tell you about his investing philosophy, you could do a lot worse than to go to the man himself. It's all here—the admonition to avoid picking individual stocks, or working with brokers who want you to trade and churn and trade your way to riches. He writes: "The way to wealth for those in the business is to persuade their clients, *'Don't just stand there. Do something.'* But the way to wealth for their clients in the aggregate is to follow the opposite maxim: *'Don't do something. Stand there.'*" Buy and hold is his mantra, and index funds, with their low fees, are his tonic.

Bogle is the debunker's debunker, genial on the page but burning with outrage over the ways that the financial industry exploits its customers. He is also taken with certain phrases, like former Supreme Court justice Louis Brandeis's observation that speculative crazes fall to the "relentless rules of humble arithmetic," which comes up in the text more than a dozen times.

His writing style is simple and straightforward; he's a no-bull kind of guy. He writes that his detractors say all he has going for him is "the uncanny ability to recognize the obvious." But don't believe it; often, nothing is less obvious than the obvious, especially when there are whole industries built on trying to make things seem complicated. So when he says that the message of his book "is little more than common sense," it should remind us all how uncommon common sense can be.

Speaking of simplicity and common sense, it would be hard to beat Helaine Olen, a writer on personal finance and other topics. She and Harold Pollack, a public policy professor at the University of Chicago, have written a tremendous book about investing that's hype-free and simple down to its bones: *The Index Card: Why Personal Finance Doesn't Have to Be Complicated.*[47] Their basic point is that you can, and should, boil your financial goals down to a single index card—as Pollack did during a video interview with Olen in 2013, a moment that led to this book. And the advice is good! Pollack's own index card has nine points, including put as much money as you can into low-cost index funds, pay off credit cards, don't buy individual stocks, save hard, and make any financial adviser you deal with commit to the fiduciary standard.[48]

Of course, you might ask, if everything Pollack needed to say could be boiled down to an index card, why read a 240-page book? Pollack explained this, wittily, to the financial journalist Penny Wang, in an article in *Money*: "Even the 10 commandments needed some back-up material."[49] And that back-up material includes a lot of the same basic information about investing that the other folks listed here provide—the stuff like telling you the difference between a mutual fund and an exchange-traded fund. And it adds some things that didn't fit on the original card, including insurance and buying a home. They refuse to follow the convention of the personal finance genre that tries to make the world of money seem like a dark and mysterious thicket that only they can guide you through; they demystify finance.

SO HERE IT IS:

Okay, so I did it. I read a stack of books to see whether there is a trick, a knack, that can help people like us—mere mortals—beat the market.

It led me to a stunning conclusion: no.

A lot of books insist that they offer the secret, but the only real secret is that there is no secret. Many of these books offer common sense and humor, but they will not make you rich. All this means that you will not learn how to pick individual stocks from me, no matter which financial guides I've read.

Here is the not-so-magic formula: don't even try to pick individual stocks, and be wary of mutual funds that try to pick a basket of stocks for you. As I've mentioned, managed funds tend to have high fees. Instead, focus on those index funds that have low fees and track the market.

You could stop reading now—here endeth the lesson. But don't you want to know why index funds are the main investment you want? As Pollack put it, there's back-up material.

First, the caveat: There are, of course, people who do become fabulously wealthy through their investments—people like Warren Buffett.

Buffett, as you surely know, is the Oracle. Just think what you could have done if you had grabbed his coattails early on and bought a share of Berkshire Hathaway. Between 1964 and 2014, the per-share market value of the stock jumped by 1,826,163%.[50] The entry cost is a little high, though: at this writing, a single share costs about $220,000. And while I hope that he and his genius live forever, the actuarial tables suggest that an 86-year-old man is not going to have another 50-year run. His acolytes are, no doubt, very smart, but they aren't Warren Buffett.

What about the rest of us—you and me and all the other mere mortals? Take just a moment and put the book down to look in a mirror. I'll wait.

Welcome back. Did you see Warren Buffett in the mirror?

I thought not.

I didn't see him in mine, either. I long ago realized I'm not the kind of person likely to become a market maven. I can't bear watching financial gurus like Jim Cramer, who shouts and touts across the airwaves. I've visited online investment forums with people who eat, sleep, and breathe trading, but I might as well have dropped into a chat about quantum physics or pro football. (I really *am* an idiot when it comes to sports.)

How long ago did I realize that I was not going to rule Wall Street? It was soon after my thirteenth birthday, in 1970—you know, back when we rode our pet dinosaurs to school. Around that time, I thought that I had a good shot at becoming a financial wizard.

My plan was simple: after my bar mitzvah, I took some of the money that people had handed me in envelopes at the reception and decided to parlay it to riches in the stock market. Investing, I figured, would start me on my road to adulthood. Today I am a man! With a brokerage account! I knew what to invest in: IBM. Computers were the future. My research into the stock tables in *The Galveston Daily News* showed that the computer company, like most tech stocks, had been enjoying a climb like a Saturn V rocket muscling its way toward the moon. The Apollo program was even using IBM computers to get the Apollo astronauts to the moon. How could I go wrong buying IBM?

So I bought a share, or maybe two. Big investor! Each share cost more than a hundred bucks.

Soon after my purchase, that rocketing stock turned around and became a lawn dart. My personal piece of IBM lost 42 percent of its value during that first month. Shares were being squeezed in what would later be known as the "Earth Day crash" of tech stocks, which coincided with the very first Earth Day.[51] I did not understand those larger trends and forces. What I did know was that getting rich in the stock market no longer seemed like a sure thing.

I followed the share price for a while with a sick feeling in my belly. Should I sell? Even at 13, I knew that only fools sell at the bottom; I'd lost money on paper, but it might turn around; selling at the bottom would make the loss official. But was it the bottom? Selling and shifting the money into a hotter stock might get me something, but I was no longer sold on my brilliance as a stock picker. I held on to my chunk of IBM and gradually forgot that I owned it. I had bought it with easy money, and then (as now) I had a pretty short attention span. I got back to schoolwork, playing with my desktop model Tesla coil,[52] and wondering if I was ever going to go on a date. (There is probably a good scientific paper to be written about the inverse relationship between being the kind of kid who owns a Tesla coil and his likelihood of dating anytime soon, but that is a project for another day.) I figured that the stock would recover or it wouldn't. Eventually, the price did rise a bit, and I sold my shares without a big gain or loss. I didn't take another look at stock tables, or put money into the market, until I kicked off my 401(k) nearly 15 years later.

Part of growing up is figuring out which things you are best at, and which you might as well leave to others. Being a financial genius is not one of my gifts. Over time, I realized I was pretty good at other things. Astonishingly, I'm able to make a living out of hammering out words into sentences and sentences into paragraphs—a process that my friend David Carr called "treating my keyboard as an ATM." So my lack of financial acumen is not a source of shame, especially since very few of us are likely to climb to wealth by picking individual stocks.

To put it biblically—and why not?—none of us has the urim and thummim. Those are, the Old Testament tells us, stones that could be consulted for answers to thorny questions.[53] They were connected to a fashion item known as the high priest's breastplate, and it's all pretty complicated and, frankly, a little comic book–y. From the moment I first read about them, I was hooked on the idea. If I had those, I figured, I probably could pick the stocks that could beat the market. Big "if," though. Like the Ark of the Covenant at the end of *Raiders of the Lost Ark*, the urim and thummim are probably sitting in a cavernous federal warehouse somewhere.

A few years ago, I went looking for the magical doodads for my humor column.[54] I figured they would most likely be in the hands of the one person who most often seemed to make the right financial decisions, and who also had the money to buy truly priceless objects: Warren Buffett.

I called Omaha. A woman with a friendly and professional voice answered the phone at Mr. Buffett's office. I explained that I was a reporter from *The New York Times* and that I was searching for the urim and thummim.

"I don't even know what you're referencing," she said.

No problem. Not everybody is up on Old Testament lore, even in Omaha. I tried explaining what the urim and thummim were. This didn't seem to help, and her tone went from confused to cool.

I asked her name. "I don't think I'm going to tell you," she said.

Could she at least let me know if Mr. Buffett might have left the urim and thummim just, you know, lying around?

"I'm going to have to let you go, sir. Thank you." And with that—you might find this hard to believe—she hung up on me.

I didn't even get to ask whether Mr. Buffett's co-oracle, Charles T. Munger, had them.

This oracle business is tougher than it looks.

Let's not kid ourselves about the potential for total human transformation here. The people who do well in the market are very focused on money and investing. They work at techniques like finding bargains in the market valuation of individual stocks and hitting the right timing to buy and sell. They follow procedures laid out by geniuses like Benjamin Graham and his previously mentioned theory of value investing—finding companies that are intrinsically worth more than their stock value would indicate. They are Adam Smith's players of the Game.

These people use a lot of their brain space to play this game, and some of them, I'm sure, do well. More of them do not. Even professional money managers don't beat the market all the time. Nobody's got the urim and thummim.

And so we're back to that biggest, truest secret that I've encountered, underscored by Bogle and Buffett and the rest: the average investor does best by starting early in life, and by buying low-fee funds that reflect the overall market, known as index funds. While beating the market is hard, matching the market is easy. What's more, the market tends to rise over time.

Meanwhile, avoiding the fees associated with buying and selling individual stocks, or investing in managed funds, puts most people in a better position than those who churn and look for the trick that will make them rich. The far lower fees for index funds make a difference.

Standard and Poor's does a report it calls the "Persistence Scorecard," which tracks the performance of mutual funds. Over a five-year period, the company found that fewer than one-third of 1 percent of 664 stock funds stayed in the top quarter of performance. None of the funds for companies with mid-size and small-market capitalization—that is, the value of all their shares—made it through the five years consistently on top.[55]

Wow, right?

The problem is that stock prices are not, in practice, predictable. They follow what financial journalist Burton Malkiel called a "random walk."

I called Malkiel, whose 1973 book *A Random Walk down Wall Street* is an investing classic, and witty, too. Stock picking just plain doesn't work, he told me. "I was the one who sort of jokingly said, 'You might as well throw darts at the stock page, because you'll pick your stocks as well that way as any other way.'"

In fact, you can't even do that anymore, because newspapers don't print all the stock prices. But you get the idea.

Nobody outdoes the market consistently, and if they claim to—well, the person who comes to mind is Bernie Madoff. "If something is too good to be true, it probably is," Malkiel said. He, too, is a fan of index funds. Picking individual stocks as a solo investor, he said, is not likely to do better than an index fund. Some investors accept the idea that they aren't going to be brilliant stock pickers, but that they believe in relying on other smart people, professional fund managers, to make the money for them. Instead of picking the horse (the stock), they pick the jockey (the professional fund manager). But the record of the pros is not consistently great, either.

When I told Malkiel about my choice of index funds based on my lack of confidence as an investor, he scoffed. "In fact, it's not simply for financial idiots," he said. "It's the thing to do for the most advanced investor." And he said the lower fees on index funds make the argument even stronger. "The only thing I can tell you that I am absolutely, 100 percent sure of is the bigger fee I pay to the purveyor for any investment service, the less there will be for me."

We had warmed up, so I asked him the big question that had been hanging over my head like a cloud since my conversation with the Vanguard broker: Did I need to rebalance my portfolio to include more bonds? I told him that it seemed to me that if I were about to retire, that was a good idea, but I expected to be around for a while.

The country, he believes, is headed into a period of poor returns on stocks and on bonds. But even so, he said, the notion that loading up on bonds in your 50s is misguided.

"I think the sort of traditional advice of 'you need a lot of bonds' is wrong," he said, and "it's also wrong for somebody in their 50s, because it isn't the case anymore that you retire at 65 and then you die the next year or two. Life expectancy has increased dramatically."

If you invest in stocks, he explained, you should have "a long horizon, to ride the ups and downs." Which is what somebody in his 50s has, he said: maybe 35 years until the curtain falls.

I told him about having attended my dad's 90th birthday party. I told him about Dad's two heart attacks, two strokes, brain surgery, diabetes, high blood pressure—and how he was preparing to work the next session of the Texas legislature as a lobbyist, something he had been doing since the 1980s, when he left elected politics. "He is the Terminator," I told Mr. Malkiel, "and I believe that he could still kick my ass."

He laughed. "That's wonderful!" He was speaking from the vantage point of being in his 80s himself. "That's why I wouldn't worry about being a little overexposed to equities," he said. "I think it's the right answer."

Validated! By a big market expert! Now that's a good day.

By the way, a few months after I interviewed Mr. Malkiel, he told my colleague James B. Stewart that he had reconsidered the idea that experts and stock pickers can't beat index funds. He had modified his view to accept the idea that sophisticated algorithms running fast computer-based trading and known as "smart beta" can beat index funds, at least modestly, but that he still remains a fan of index investing for the most part, and for most investors.[56]

Not everyone buys the idea that index funds are the way to go. I once interviewed Mark Cuban by email about investing. The star of *Shark Tank*, a billionaire and serial entrepreneur, answers his own email, astonishingly enough. I was writing another one of my columns—and decided to ask him for advice about how to join the 1 percent. His answer was pretty clearly typed in a hurry, probably with his thumbs. But he told me that I was going about things all wrong:

> **easy answer. Stop investing in mutual funds and depending on some kid in a gerbsl cage running and trying to get ahead of his/er peers and instead pay off all of yoru debt , including your credit cards and invest in yourself. No one ever got rich depending on someone who got hired to be fired.**

His suggestion was, unsurprisingly, what made him rich: entrepreneurship. Even his answer was entrepreneurial.

> **invest in yourself and start a business built around something you are great at, and you have a chance to hit the 1pct. Invest in an index fund, you have no chance**

> **and spend the 3 bucks to read this book :)**

> **http://www.amazon.com/How-Win-Sport-Business-ebook/dp /B006AX6ONI/ref=pd_zg_rss_nr_b_2741_1?ie=UTF8&tag =forecomm-20&utm_source=dlvr.it&utm_medium=twitter**

That's right, he pitched me his self-published book on investing. He never stops selling! And, he said, that's the kind of entrepreneurship that could work for writers like me.

whipping together ebooks that you can sell for 3 bucks a pop is quick, easy and a way to build a business that even reporters may be able to excel at

Oof. He's right about the credit cards, of course, and entrepreneurship has worked spectacularly well for him, and it's the message of popular personal finance writers like Kiyosaki. But would it have worked for me? His financial philosophy glosses over the risks of failure in the entrepreneurial path. About half of new businesses go bust within five years; only a third survive to 10 years, according to the Small Business Administration.[57] And if I know me—and you know me pretty well by now—the half I'd end up in isn't really in doubt.

I'm glad I've stuck with index funds. They might not make me rich, but they are likelier to make me comfortable and less likely to make me lose it all on a crap shoot. Thanks to index funds, the nature of the investing game has changed from a casino to something more like a video game: you can run up the points, sure, but the real goal is to survive.

Index funds weren't always with us: a little history

So where did index funds come from? They have a father, and his name is John C. Bogle. Let's go a little deeper into the history.

Bogle recognized early on that we are not soothsayers. Even the very smart people who consider themselves able to beat the market can't do it consistently, and the rest of us don't stand a chance. If we sit down at the poker table, we are the marks, the chumps, the inevitable losers. As the supercomputer says at the end of *WarGames*, the only winning move is not to play.

I called up Mr. Bogle to ask about all this, and he couldn't have been nicer. He no longer runs the Vanguard Group, but at 87 years old—and more than 20 years after a heart transplant—he's still a supersharp, folksy guy.

Bogle told me he came up with the idea of the first index fund in 1974. He had tried the managed fund business, becoming the head of

Wellington Management and trying to beat the market. "It's not easy to do—this is a hard business," he told me. He engineered a merger that turned out badly, and ran after go-go stocks during a hot market, and it all went bad when the market turned bearish. His partners at Wellington fired him.

Out of that failure came one of the great business successes of history, based on a simple fact: a fund that does well for a while will head south when conditions change, and conditions inevitably change. In terms of statistical probability, there's the problem of reversion to the mean: nobody is on top forever, and things tend to drift back toward the center of the pack, and some will dive past the middle toward the bottom. "The last shall be first, and the first shall be last," he said in our interview, deftly paraphrasing the book of Matthew.

In a set of storied decisions that completely reshaped the investing world, Bogle decided to find a way to run a fund that slashed the costs of doing business. Those costs included all that expensive research. He talked the Wellington board into letting him create what would become known as the Vanguard 500 Index Fund, based on a package of stocks that reflected the overall field. Instead of trying to be a stock picker and to outperform the market, Bogle simply wanted to match it—and watch the rest of the fund managers fly high, crash, and then trade places with each other again. The savings in research and management could be passed on to investors, who would see their dollars work even harder.

He started the fund in 1976, and with precious few investors. He had hoped to kick off the fund with $150 million. He initially raised just $11.3 million. "It was a complete flop," he recalled.

The fund got a nickname: "Bogle's folly."

The idea must have seemed crazy at the time. Actually, the financial journalist Jason Zweig recently wrote, "it was close" to being considered just plain nuts. "Swashbuckling fund managers, often called 'gunslingers,' roamed the markets in the late 1960s and early 1970s; in 1968, several 'go-go' funds had earned returns in excess of 100%." They were heroes.

But Bogle has research to back up his belief in index funds. He was emboldened by the writings of the Nobel laureate economist Paul A.

Samuelson, who had called for the creation of something like index funds in a now-famous 1974 essay. Just four pages long, the essay advocated for "a portfolio that tracks the S&P 500 Index."

In a later essay, Bogle said this amazingly feisty article struck him like lightning. His plan for a low-cost fund would go perfectly with a strategy focused on index funds, "even as 'love and marriage go together like a horse and carriage.'"[58]

Samuelson had tough words for fund managers. "Perhaps there really are managers who can outperform the market consistently—logic would suggest that they exist. But they are remarkably well-hidden." He really took the gloves off in that essay, arguing, "But a respect for evidence compels me to incline toward the hypothesis that most portfolio decision makers should go out of business—take up plumbing, teach Greek, or help produce the annual GNP by serving as corporate executives."

Ouch. Get some ointment for that burn, fund managers.

Naturally, the culture of the gunslinger rejected the new index funds with scorn. Stock pickers had a vested interest in running it down, and the companies threatened by the new business model insisted that it enshrined mediocrity. No swagger, no glory!

That argument made intuitive sense to people who thought money managers were geniuses, Bogle said, and so it was easy to see why no one would want to invest in mediocrity. That is, "until they find out the alternative is worse than mediocrity, and in a lot of cases, a lot worse."

One brokerage firm went on a full-scale attack, publishing a poster exhorting Americans to "Help Stamp Out Index Funds" and screaming in all-capital letters, "INDEX FUNDS ARE UNAMERICAN!"

Some writers have suggested the attacks were tongue-in-cheek, but they seem pretty desperate to me. And whether they were serious or not, the logic of index investing became evident. From that initial $11 million in assets in 1975, index investing jumped to $511 million by 1985. Ten years later, it was $868 billion. By 2016, it stood at $4 trillion.[59]

"Index funds," Bogle told me, "are eating up the world."

Vanguard has won. It is the world's largest fund company, with total assets of $3.6 trillion. With a *t*.

And all because he got fired.

The index method still has critics. In August 2016, a research note from Sanford C. Bernstein & Co., the research and brokerage firm, said that the "passive investing" of index funds is "worse than Marxism."[60] Which doesn't sound like sour grapes at all.

But the more common view is that John Bogle has made investing safer, and more profitable, for us all.

It's not just individual investors who can do better with low-cost index funds. In 2016, little Houghton College in western New York State made more than 7½ percent on its investments in the calendar year. Harvard, by comparison, lost 2 percent. The difference? Ivy League schools like Harvard tend to manage their endowments actively, and in fancy ways, with hedge funds and the like. Houghton has been moving more and more into index funds, with lower management costs and better returns. We should all be as smart as Houghton.[61]

Or as smart as Warren Buffett. In his 1996 letter to shareholders, he wrote:

> Let me add a few thoughts about your own investments. Most investors, both institutional and individual, will find that the best way to own common stocks is through an index fund that charges minimal fees. Those following this path are sure to beat the net results (after fees and expenses) delivered by the great majority of investment professionals.[62]

Buffett has even put down an enormous bet on the proposition. As he described the history of the wager in his 2016 letter to stockholders, he offered $500,000 to prove that no investment professional, investing a million dollars in any five hedge funds, would earn more over 10 years than the same amount invested in the S&P 500 basket of stocks.[63] After two years of no takers, a hedge fund guy, Ted Seides, stepped up, and the prize was set at a million dollars to go to a charity of the winner's choosing.[64] In mid-2017, months before the bet came due, Seides admitted defeat and paid up—though he has said that he believes the S&P is somewhat overpriced now and that if he doubled down for another 10 years, he would have "greater-than-even odds victory."[65]

Mmmmmaybe.

Today John Bogle is considered one of the heroes of business, with a fervent following of investors who call themselves Bogleheads. They have discussion forums and everything.[66] (I don't spend much time in financial discussion forums, because they make my brain hurt. But the Bogleheads tend to be knowledgeable and friendly.)

In a 2014 essay, Mr. Bogle estimated that the combination of total cost of managed funds and the better performance of index funds over time translates into a startling 65 percent more money in retirement for the index investors. By 70, someone who had started investing at 30 and stuck with index funds would have $927,000 to show for it. A neighbor who stuck with actively managed funds, Bogle wrote, would end up with a much less comfortable $561,000 to $366,000 less, in fact.[67]

Learning those statistics made me wonder where I'd have been if I'd gone all in with index funds from the beginning of my investment career. While I was writing this chapter, I looked back through my Vanguard portfolio and moved all the shares I'd had in something called the T. Rowe Price Institutional Large Cap Core Growth Fund into a Vanguard index fund. Still learning!

Anyway, back to my conversation with Bogle. I told him about the book project, about shaping up our financial lives at this late date. He asked how old I am. Fifty-nine, I said.

"You're a kid, man!" he responded. That was encouraging.

When I told him that Jeanne and I had been quietly putting away savings since our 30s but rarely looked at the performance of the funds, he approved. "Don't peek! That's one of my most important rules."

I blurted out, "You saved my life."

"You'd be surprised how many people tell me that," he said. "We've had very good markets, and I've made sure you got your fair share of the returns."

But what about people like some of the readers of this book, I asked him—people who haven't been putting much away, if anything, and who now might be in their 50s? A comfortable retirement, even if saving begins now, would be very hard to achieve, no?

Get going anyway, he said. "Even if you can't get all the way there, it would only be a very foolish person who would say, 'I'd have to put half of my salary away every month—I can't do that, so I'll do nothing.'"

Obviously, he acknowledged, some people aren't in a position to save, and "if you can't do it, you can't do it." But if you can put away 15 percent of your income "you'll get part of the way there, and you'll have some kind of nest egg when you get through."

"Doing nothing," he told me, "provides an absolute guarantee that you'll wind up with nothing."

WHAT ABOUT THE FUTURE?

The world keeps throwing ch-ch-changes our way. David Bowie, gone. Prince. And John Glenn, all in the same rotten year, 2016. In 2017, Tom Petty and Fats Domino, Edith Windsor, Jonathan Demme, and Mary Tyler Moore. That kind of change hurts your heart, but not your portfolio. A change in presidencies, however, can cost you, having far-reaching effects on the economy, on the stock and bond markets, and on the safety net that helps the less fortunate weather personal crises. And so, speaking of chaos, what are we to make of Donald Trump?

A friend at work told me that the day after the election, he put his entire pension into cash—that is, stable money-market accounts with almost zero income but tremendous stability. He was expecting a quick economic collapse with the new president. That hasn't happened—so far, at least. And stocks continued to rise. He recently told me he's thinking of putting his money back into stocks.

One of the smartest personal finance writers I know, Penelope Wang, banged out a smart column the day after the presidential election with the headline, "No Matter What Trump Does, Keep Your Hands Off Your 401(k)."[68] In the piece, she pointed out, "When nervous investors respond to the latest news or market twitches, they often get it wrong." But she also warned that anyone nearing retirement should be looking for a portfolio balance that isn't heavily weighted toward stocks; upping the bonds. Worrying about Trump, she wrote, provides a good excuse to check that stock-to-bonds blend.

She isn't the only expert telling investors to keep calm and carry on. In January 2017, just before the inauguration of Donald Trump, Warren Buffett gave an interview to the financial network CNBC. He spoke optimistically about markets and investing, though admitted he did not know what might happen over the next couple of years. "There will be hiccups from time to time in the economy," he said, but "we'll do well over time." Even though he had supported Hillary Clinton for president, he said the United States has the "secret sauce" for long-term success, even though "it doesn't work all the time perfectly." For long-term investing, he said, "Never bet against America."[69]

I really hope that he has the urim and thummim. Guess I'll stick it out with my current asset mix. After all, if the worst fears about Mr. Trump play out, in the resulting economic devastation no amount of money short of private-compound-prepper wealth will do any of us much good. And if they don't, I might as well continue to ride the ride.

PUNCH LIST

TAKING STOCK OF YOUR PORTFOLIO

1) **Know yourself.** Socrates was right. Get ready for your own financial journey by knowing what you know and who you are when it comes to money. Jeanne and I took FINRA's financial literacy quiz. You can, too, at usfinancialcapability.org.[70] Come on, it's only five questions! (There's a sixth bonus question.) Remember, 61 percent of respondents were unable to answer more than three of the five questions correctly, so don't feel bad if you miss a couple. That's why you're reading this book, after all.

2) **Check your risk tolerance.** Now that you know where you stand, check out your own tolerance for financial risk. There are many such quizzes, and they are readily Google-able. I recommend the one developed by Ruth Lytton of Virginia Tech and John Grable at the University of Georgia. It's 13 questions, and your answers help further their research. (No personally identifiable information is recorded.) You can find it at njaes.rutgers.edu/money/riskquiz.[71]

3) **Now check your funds. Enough with the quizzes.** If you have a 401(k) or an IRA, check the funds you are invested in. What's your ratio of stocks to bonds? I think most people would be more receptive to the traditional ratio of stocks to bonds than I am. The basic idea is that younger investors should have an asset mix that's very high in stocks funds, since they tend to grow quickly, and in the long term, the ups and downs of the market smooth out. As we age, the thinking goes, we need more conservative investments so that our portfolios don't take a hit so close to retirement that they can't recover. The old rule of thumb is that the percentage of your portfolio that should be invested in stocks is 100 minus your age. So at the age of 50, the rule goes, half of your investments should be in stocks. Since we're living longer (among other reasons), these days a lot of the retirement mutual funds choose a ratio that's more closely based on 120 or even 125 minus

your age. By that reckoning, at 50 your portfolio should be composed of 75 percent stocks and 25 percent bonds.

So now take what you've learned about yourself from the financial risk quiz and apply it to what you've learned about the market and your portfolio. If you came out as kind of a swashbuckler, you might keep yourself heavy in stocks longer; if you are more averse to risk, you'll have more bonds and even more stable places to park your cash, such as money market funds. Check the costs of fiddling: Vanguard, for example, charges you nothing if you are shifting money from one fund to another within its stable. And, like much of the rest of the investing population, keep your fees low by investing in low-cost index funds.

4) **Up your funds.** If we were perfect in a world of angels, we'd all max out our 401(k) contributions. Few people can afford to start out at that rate. But what you can probably do is up your contribution by just 1 percentage point of your income. Unless you are truly scraping by, it's not a huge sacrifice. But in the long run, it can make an enormous difference in your retirement account. So add that point.

Next year, up it again.

4

GETTING ADVICE

Now THAT YOU'VE read the previous chapter, you know a few things about investing. I'd hope that you're even ready to manage your investments—or, if you are going to not peek, as John Bogle suggests, you'll be able to keep those eyes shut with confidence, after having set up the kind of portfolio that will do a good job of growing over time.

Does that mean you can handle all of this on your own? You might be able to, sure. Or you might want advice. After all, I sought the advice of that nice guy from Vanguard, whose services I enjoyed at no charge. And there are lots of people who would be only too happy to advise you—and to be paid for their services, whether through commissions or fees.

I figure that my Vanguard guy and I have an open relationship. If I wanted to see other advisers, to find out how others might approach my financial future, he would understand. You know, if you love something, set it free and whatnot.

What might those other advisers have to say about how we've structured our retirement plan? Would they say we were on track? Would they try to move us out of our Vanguard walled garden? I started looking around.

To get a sense of the range of options, I sought help from two types of sources: from brokers and from full-fledged financial advisers. I also looked for the different ways they tend to make money: fee-based consulting versus selling on commission. While my visits with these professionals weren't exhaustive, they can give a sense of what you're in for out there.

WHY GETTING ADVICE COULD BE A GOOD IDEA

Let me start out by saying that it makes sense to seek smart financial advice. We have a pro do our taxes. Accountants know the right questions to ask and the pitfalls of tax form preparation. Even though, when we sit with our accountant, he fills in an online form based on a worksheet he's had us fill out, he's asking expert questions the whole way. (Our previous accountant, a great guy who had a poster of Che Guevara on his office wall, would argue with me over the numbers I'd put down. "What, you didn't buy books for research? *Come on,*" he'd say, coaxing me along as he would a slow child. And then he'd put down several hundred dollars in book purchases. He retired, and I miss his avuncular prodding.) Those questions, asked by a human being, make a difference. You might be the kind of person who can do your own taxes— many of my friends do. You have my admiration. Even when I tried to fill out the relatively straightforward tax form for my daughter some years back, before her marriage, I ended up crazed with frustration— and still got the figures wrong. She got a nice note from the IRS, and a refund.

We also looked to professional help to (finally) write a will. We've always hired a Realtor to help buy and sell houses. No FSBO for us! So why not for investments and retirement?

Still, if "buyer beware" means anything, it's especially important in the investing world. There's good and bad advice out there, and the bad stuff can cost you dearly.

My research has led me to be somewhat wary of stockbrokers for investment planning, as opposed to certified financial planners. There are many honorable people in the brokerage profession, but the bad apples are truly bad.

I called up Reed C. Fraasa, a financial planner in New Jersey, to ask about why somebody might want a planner as opposed to the free advice I got from Vanguard. He had gotten in touch with me after my retirement planning story came out in the *Times*, offering to show me the value of working with a certified financial planner.

Not surprisingly, he told me that working with a financial planner, and paying for the advice that you get, is a good idea.

"What Vanguard is making available to people at that price point is certainly valuable," he told me. "Lots of people have been poorly served by Wall Street." The problem is that, while the Vanguard approach is "much better than the traditional transactional type of delivery"—by which he meant the hard sell—"it is a pretty cursory type of planning," which he characterized as "a telephone type of virtual relationship" with an adviser who is working largely from a computer-generated financial evaluation. That made my interactions with the Vanguard adviser seem a little thin, a point that he then pressed. "I'm sure you've interviewed people on the phone and in person. There's so much more nuance and information that you get face-to-face than you get talking on the phone." His work, he said, goes beyond retirement planning to encompass broader discussion of "life and goals and things like that—it's much harder to do from a questionnaire." Writing a will? His colleagues will help you plan ahead for the visit with the lawyer, and even accompany you to the lawyer's office, streamlining the will-writing process and saving the customer money in billed hours.

Yes, he acknowledged, many people do fine investing on their own—but not that many. "I'm a big believer in the 80-20 rule," he said, meaning that probably about 20 percent of the population is capable of learning enough about finance and devoting enough attention to it to do 80 percent as well as they might with a financial adviser. But 80 percent of the population is not going to have the interest or ability to do nearly as well as a financial adviser, and those people can really use somebody who can educate them and help them make financial and life decisions. Many of his clients, he said, shy away from thinking or talking about money—but will do extensive research to plan a vacation.

But it's not cheap. For financial planning, his minimum fee is $5,000 a year. More if you want investment management, as well. He and his staff make no commissions and receive no incentives from financial companies to push their products: they make their money as a percentage of clients' "investable net worth"—that is, excluding real estate. It's an expensive business to run; members of his staff serve between 25 and 30 clients each. Typical brokers, he said, might have 150 clients. They make it work by doing less. His clients, he told me, have an average net worth of $1.8 million.

I liked him. But I did not feel I could afford him.

And now, here come the warnings

At some time or other, if you've ever bought or sold individual stocks or tried to develop an investment plan, you might have dealt with a stockbroker—someone to help you plan your portfolio. And that person might have been smart, and certainly assured you that he or she had your best interests at heart and was working for you.

It wasn't true—or, at least, it was probably not required by law.

At the risk of sounding all Occupy Wall Street here, let me point out that the investment community has never been about making you rich, or even comfortable. Setting aside the actual scoundrels, the idea in the investment community has always been to make themselves rich by making money off you, but without fleecing you so thoroughly that it would reflect poorly on them and hurt business. Michael Lewis wrote about that world in his bestselling *Liar's Poker*, about working as a bond salesman for a Wall Street firm in the go-go '80s. He tells the story of terrible rip-off investments he was told to push onto his own customers in investment houses. He recalls balking at burning a customer with whom he'd built a relationship just to help out a trader in his company; the trader had bought a bond that had gone sour and needed to dump it. Lewis writes that the trader told him "that I needed to be more of a team player. I was tempted to ask, 'Which team?'"[1]

This attitude is even more evident in the retail market, where people like us are less financially knowledgeable than Lewis's corporate clients were.

This is not a new thought. When the writer Fred Schwed published a funny send-up of the financial world six decades ago, he opened with a story—old when he wrote it down!—about a newcomer to New York being shown the wonders of Wall Street. Down at the Battery, his guide showed him the handsome ships at anchor there, saying, "Look, those are the bankers' and brokers' yachts."

The naive visitor asked, "Where are the customers' yachts?"[2]

Where Are the Customers' Yachts is the book's timeless title, and its message, too, is for the ages: the financial industry is not about making investors rich. Stated that way, it sounds a little obvious, and maybe even too cynical. After all, people do tend to make money in the stock market. And most financial advisers and brokers are honest. That's why people like Bernie Madoff make headlines; he was a spectacular exception. Besides, the government protects us.

Right?

Here is an astonishing fact. Serving your needs, until recently, came second under the law. The Obama administration had to create a rule that requires brokers to put your interests first.

Like so many of the regulations passed during the Obama administration, the future of the fiduciary rule is unclear. It is, unsurprisingly, very unpopular with the financial services and insurance industries; several lawsuits were filed as soon as the regulations were issued in April 2016. Efforts to undermine or overturn it continue, but the rule went into partial effect in June 2017.[3] The Trump administration has delayed enforcement of the rule.[4]

So it's too soon to tell what will happen to the rule, but it might survive. And, in any case, you should know what it tried to do, because it shows one of the seamier parts of the investing world.

Until 2016, most brokers were required by law to recommend only "suitable" investments. That loose standard allowed them to, for example, flog a mutual fund that has relatively high fees—and pays them a fat commission—instead of a cheaper alternative that might better serve the needs of the customer. (Investment advisers, who register with the U.S. Securities and Exchange Commission [SEC], with state agencies, or the Financial Industry Regulatory Authority [FINRA], are already held to a higher standard.)

Foisting less helpful financial products on the customer isn't outright fraud, but it's not helpful, either. The Obama administration estimated that these practices cost consumers about $18 billion a year and cut their returns by a full percentage point. (When it comes to retirement funds, a percentage point, over time, is a lot.) So the administration came up with new fiduciary regulations to protect consumers and to help them get the best financial deal for their money.[5]

The rule, which took six years to develop, does not apply to all investments, but only to retirement accounts with tax advantages like 401(k)s and IRAs. It would reshape the way that most brokers are paid, favoring fees over commissions. It is expected to drive more customers toward lower-cost investments like the kind of low-fee index funds that are already dominating the industry.

What does this all mean to you? If you do decide to go with a broker—say, your brother-in-law has someone he thinks is terrific, and your brother-in-law drives a Porsche, just keep in mind that the broker might not have your best interests at heart. (And where are the customers' Porsches?) Look them up on BrokerCheck (brokercheck.finra.org), which is run by FINRA and helps you find out whether a broker has been in trouble before—whether they have had any penalties or prosecutions, been fired for cause, or have other marks on their record. You might be surprised how many do. You can find out about investment advisers at the SEC's Investment Adviser Public Disclosure site (adviser-info.sec.gov).

The listings aren't perfect. Some brokers get complaints expunged, so you don't get a warning. But it's better than nothing, and you also might be surprised by the kinds of complaints that you find on broker reports. While I was casting about for brokers to talk with for this chapter, BrokerCheck showed me one guy with seven "disclosures" since 2000, four of them involving settlements or judgments over claims of being sold "unsuitable" investments, with payouts totaling about $100,000. FINRA, the regulatory group, suspended 727 brokers in 2016 and banned 517.[6]

If you haven't figured it out yet, I'm pretty skeptical of people who get a commission on the financial packages they sell—especially when the industry fought hard against the fiduciary rule. So, unless you find a broker you feel great about, I'd recommend going with a fee-only financial adviser and certified financial planners. Those folks are already required by law to be fiduciaries: they were obligated to serve your best interests before the Obama administration ever tried to apply the standard to brokers.

You can find them through the nonprofit Certified Financial Planner Board of Standards as well as the National Association of Personal Financial Advisors and the Financial Planning Association. Each group makes it easy to search for an adviser online.[7]

The difference between brokers and fiduciaries can be explained as the difference between a butcher and a dietitian—a distinction laid out in an amusing 2012 video from HighTower Advisors. In it, the company explains through a whiteboard animation that a butcher wants to sell you meat. Maybe great meat, but the game is selling you meat. A dietitian is going to recommend a more balanced diet, with your health in mind.[8]

No matter what kind of salesperson or adviser you go with, you need to shop smart. You need to ask tough questions of anyone who wants to take on the job—and the reward—of handling your money. And you might consider getting whoever you decide to go with to sign a fiduciary pledge like the one published by the Committee for the Fiduciary Standard. It could buy you a little peace of mind, puts the adviser on notice that you are paying attention to your rights, and might even help you if you have a dispute that goes to arbitration.[9]

Ron Lieber, the *New York Times* personal finance columnist, recommends asking any would-be broker or adviser 21 questions (!) about themselves and whatever financial product they are suggesting that you buy.[10] The questions are mostly ways of finding out whether the adviser is acting in your best interest and how many ways you might be milked for fees and commissions; they include "How much money will you personally make in cash commission, now, if I select this product?" and "Are you earning more from selling me this product than you might from putting me in a similar product from a different company?"

I really like Ron, but I get the feeling selling anything at all to him—annuities, a house, Girl Scout cookies—could be a nightmare. He's tough. He's also right: asking questions, even uncomfortable questions, is the way to go.

And yet even Ron, for all his advice about vetting advisers, found himself working with a guy who would later be charged with stealing millions of dollars from vulnerable clients. The adviser did not steal anything from Ron, but Ron confessed to being stunned to find that an adviser he trusted could be a thief. "I thought I knew what I was doing," he told his readers in a great column. "So if I can get mixed up in something like this, trust me, it can happen to anyone."[11]

Undeterred, I go looking for financial advice—and a free meal

So here I am, educating myself on these issues at last. Reading, talking to experts. And, bit by bit, I am making progress. In college, though, I always seemed to get more out of the lectures than the reading. I wondered about whether it might be possible to get a boost in my financial knowledge by hearing experts speak on the topic.

But where do you find a financial expert giving a lecture?

As it happens, just about anywhere. I was in luck—and you probably are, too. At our house, we often get cards and flyers in the mail offering free investment seminars, often with the come-on of a free meal. "You are cordially invited . . . JOHN SCHWARTZ . . . to attend a DINNER EVENT in Fairfield." Of course, "No charge or obligation." Or "COMPLIMENTARY GOURMET LUNCH . . . MAKING THE MOST OF SOCIAL SECURITY."

Now, in my experience, no free meal is ever really free. I've passed up many offers of free trips to explore the exciting world of time-share con-dos. Now that I'm actually planning for retirement, however, I thought maybe I should see what an investment adviser has to say.

I sorted through the recent invites and found a flyer for a seminar sponsored by Rightbridge Financial Group. The company offered a "'Ground Breaking' Educational Event" promising "Fundamental Financial Strategies in the New Economy," with the opportunity to learn about retirement planning, reducing taxes, and "why getting a second opinion might be the most important financial decision of your life."

I hadn't heard of the company, but I had heard of the venue for the seminar, Bloomfield Steak and Seafood House. It's got good reviews, and I'd never eaten there before. The use of scare quotes and the two-word "Ground Breaking" irked my inner copyeditor, but I could live with that. I looked up the leader of the seminar, whose first name is Keith, on brokercheck.finra.org, and his record was clean. The site also showed that he had only formed the firm in 2014 after five years at New York Life. So we weren't looking at an investment adviser with decades of experience. But a young gun might have interesting ideas, and it couldn't hurt to listen. Also, I wanted to try that steak house. So I signed up.

The day before the seminar, a representative of the firm called to ask me some questions, because her boss "likes to tailor his presentation to the needs of the guests," she said. Was I retired? Was there anything specific I wanted to learn about?

This made it sound like a one-on-one experience. I asked how many people would be getting steak with me. She told me 45 people had signed up. I explained that I didn't have any specific questions and that I was pretty clueless—all true. "I just want to hear what he's telling people," I said. I would not need special attention.

The night of the seminar, I arrived at the appointed time, 6:30 p.m., and was sent upstairs to a big dining room tucked into the top floor. Six rows of long tables faced a podium and a screen. I was not the youngest person there and certainly not the oldest.

There were pitchers of soda and ice water on the table. The server stopped by to ask what I'd be having. Most of the people around me were ordering prime rib, but I asked her what she liked. "The prime rib is great, but it's just a piece of meat," she said. She suggested the chicken Francaise, or even one of the salmon or pasta dishes. I said yes to the chicken, even though Anthony Bourdain famously wrote that chicken is what chefs put on the menu "for customers who can't decide what they want to eat."[12]

The representative from the firm who had called me, and who had also taken attendance, stepped to the front, welcomed us and introduced Keith, briefly giving his credentials. ("As of today, he has a 100 percent approval rating!") She said he would be speaking for 50 minutes, which turned out to be the first stretched-truth moment of the evening. The presentation would go on for an hour and a half.

And the food would not show up until he was done.

Keith took the mic and launched into his talk. He turned out to be a lively speaker. He opened with a slide of himself in a baseball uniform at the age of eight—cute kid!—which let him tell us about his childhood, his love of baseball, his days as a player in college. He told us about his father, who worked in construction on local projects, including a number of Simon Malls. His father, he told us, was injured on a construction site and was in a coma for three months. His mother, who had been a bond transfer agent for E. F. Hutton, asked a financial adviser what to do; he warned her not to take money out of their investments. "What I learned from that was the impact of money," he said soberly.

Did they come out of it okay? Did they lose their shirts? He didn't say. His life story, long on emotion but short on information, then led to the end of his baseball career in his senior year of college, when he fractured his spine. There's a message in that, he said: "Tonight we're going to talk about the things we can't control."

Well, okay, that's a pretty good moral to the story so far. But what do we do about it? "You thought you would be here tonight and somebody was going to try to sell you some kind of annuity," he said, but "there's not going to be any selling here tonight." Instead, he wanted to talk about "character." Which must have something to do with that slide of the adorable kid in the baseball uniform.

He then ran through a series of slides showing the various levels of a house, and he talked through a complicated metaphor for the kinds of investments he sees on each floor—the steady savings account is the basement, the roof is the most volatile—"anything that can lose value in the stock market." As you age, you need less stuff in that volatile attic and more stuff in the stable lower parts of the house.

He warned that your broker is probably screwing you with hidden fees in mutual funds. He had an older couple stand up and asked the man his age. When the man replied 63, Keith gave a big, emcee's grin and said, "You look *great* for 63! What are you eating? I gotta come over." He had them hold a tape measure between them to show that we're trying to stretch our retirement savings to a longer life than we may be planning for.

It was a lot of metaphors and warnings, but it wasn't easy to see what he was trying to really say, except this: I'm an engaging guy. If you like me, we can structure your retirement funds together. Which, ultimately, is not a bad way to market yourself to people who aren't financial experts.

Keith then introduced a lawyer who talked about the rookie mistakes that people—and even some lawyers—make in setting up wills and the other documents that dictate whether your death will mean a smooth inheritance for your heirs or a legal mess. He gave a quick look at estate taxes at the federal level and in New Jersey. Good with examples, he created entertaining scenarios about the wills of a couple named Tony and Carmela. And so of course we need to protect the inheritance of the kids, Meadow and A.J.

That's right, he led this New Jersey audience through New Jersey estate law using the *Sopranos* as his hypothetical couple. And it worked.

It was nearly 8:00 p.m. by then, and the only food in sight was a basket of rolls—at the far end of my long table, too far too reach. I worried about the rudeness of asking people to pass them down. My stomach rumbled.

The lawyer ended his talk. Keith stepped back up with a handout purporting to show the difference between two portfolios. He noted that one had only a slightly lower return on paper than the other, but he said that it will produce greater returns. The one with a slightly lower rate, he explained, has much lower volatility and risk, so the buyer will end up richer for it.

The guy next to me shook his head with irritation, muttering that these sheets didn't say anything useful. What were these funds? What companies were in them? Were the earnings histories reflected accurately? These might be useful as a hypothetical description of investing issues, but there's no telling whether these sheets were tied to anything in the real world.

Keith finished by 8:11. "We hope we did a good enough job so you decide we should be your advisers," he said. Everyone had been given a form letting us say whether we wanted to be contacted in the coming days. Don't sign if you're not serious, he said. "The calendar is very booked. Your time is very valuable; so is ours."

Tara came by to pick up the sheets and eyed the check mark to see who wanted to follow up. Once she flicked her gaze over my check mark—on the do-not-follow-up side—she stiffened a little and quickly moved on. I was, for Keith & Co., a wasted investment in a meal: what the industry derisively calls a "plate licker."

The entrées came at last. My chicken was not bad. The mashed potatoes were good and garlicky. And by then I was so hungry that it seemed like one of the best meals of my life.

I struck up a conversation with the guy next to me, the one who had disliked the comparison of the two hypothetical funds. He attends a fair number of free seminars, he told me, but not as many as a friend who eats out on investment advisers all the time. Why? I asked.

"He wanted free meals," my neighbor explained. He and his buddy, he said, talk investments recreationally.

My new buddy was named Dan, and he was married. "I dragged my wife to one" other seminar, he told me. That one had the food first. This format, he said, would not have pleased her. "She would have hated waiting for the food," he said.

And when the staffer came around to sign people up for appointments, Dan took one, surprising me a little. Hadn't you been skeptical, I asked? What about the meaningless comparison sheets? "Just to check the asset mix," he said. "It will be good to have an intelligent conversation."

The evening was not a bust. It was not the sleazy hard-sell session I'd been dreading. But it also wasn't terribly helpful, either. The picture of Keith in a baseball uniform was cute, but I still didn't see what that had to do with moving away from retail brokerage firms and into what he referred to as his more personal investing approach, about which I still knew very little.

In the weeks after attending the seminar, I looked around to see what financial regulators and experts had to say about the practice. Most of what I found were warnings against accepting the free meal. FINRA issued a strong warning about the practice in an alert titled "'Free Lunch' Investment Seminars—Avoiding the Heartburn of a Hard Sell," because even financial regulators aren't above bad puns.

"We are issuing this Alert because, in many cases, free-meal investment seminars are not solely about education," the group wrote. "Their ultimate goals are to recruit new clients and sell products—and while some pitches can be easy to swallow, the consequences can be hard to bear."

Cue the spooky music!

The seminars are common, the group found; according to its own 2013 survey, 64 percent of those responding to the survey who were 40 or older had been offered a meal seminar and nearly a third said they had attended one. Just four lost any money because of these seminars, the regulators said. That's apparently not for lack of trying on the part of those putting on the seminars: FINRA found that in half of its examinations of seminars, the materials made claims "that appeared to be exaggerated, misleading or otherwise unwarranted." Worse, "13 percent of the seminars appeared to involve fraud."

FINRA suggested that anyone going for a free dinner and a money talk should understand that even though the company might insist it isn't trying to sell you anything, it is—whether during that meal or during the follow-up personal session that they almost inevitably recommend. The alert also suggested checking out the broker involved, at brokercheck.finra.org—where I had looked up Keith.

The North American Securities Administrators Association also issued a warning, even more sharply worded:

> There's a certain consistency to the invitations enticements: a free gourmet meal, tips on how to earn excellent returns on your investments, eliminate market risk, grow your retirement funds, and, spouses are urged to attend. These words should be red flags for investors.

That alert listed prosecutions in Missouri, Utah, Colorado, and California, in which con artists and unlicensed brokers were ripping off gullible senior citizens by recommending that the customers sell off their holdings to invest in fancy financial products offered by the seller: "These products are often grossly unsuitable for senior citizens."

State securities regulators are seeing a variety of violations associated with many of these seminars, ranging from outright lies and the conversion of investor funds to more sophisticated forms of abuse. "One agent told seniors that due to his skills, one of his clients could now afford to take three vacations a year and had invited him and his family to join the client on vacation. In truth, the client with whom the agent vacationed was his father." They advise anyone who does go for the free meal to hold on to your skepticism, ask tough questions, and don't make rash financial decisions. If you don't understand it, don't buy it. And if you do get taken for a ride, report it.[13]

I felt that Keith was not one of the bad guys. And, like my neighbor that evening, I got the feeling that I could have a decent discussion with him about investment strategies. But I'm not sorry I didn't ask for the follow-up consultation.

Keith got to write off my free meal, and I got to write off Keith. Seems fair.

Speed dating 1: a financial adviser

I decided to talk with more brokers and advisers. First I tried Daniel P. Wiener, the chief executive of Adviser Investments, a company in Newton, Massachusetts, that manages more than $4 billion in assets for individuals. But he also has a popular and rambunctious monthly newsletter, *The Independent Adviser for Vanguard Investors*, which provides information on Vanguard funds. He is not a financial adviser himself, but has them on his staff; "I'm an investment guy," he said. The day that I called, he agreed to wear both hats for a bit.

He told me that the very first thing he asks people when they start talking about retirement is whether they have any sort of illness or serious medical condition. "If you're reasonably healthy," he told me, "you have to plan on living to 100." If you're planning for anything less than that, you're at risk." If I were to plan that way and get sick later, he said—say, prostate cancer at 70—I could adjust the plan. Planning for 100? He'd out-Bogled Bogle!

Making a financial plan, he explained, "is art and not science," as a look at the various investment companies' target retirement funds shows: the ratios of stocks to bonds and cash, not to mention the types of stocks and bonds, is all over the place, he said. And they don't take individual needs into account. Noting that he and I were the same age, he asked why would we expect the Vanguard 2025 target fund would be right for both of us, with our very different lives?

He had blunt words about the trend toward index investing. As he put it, "Don't listen to all this indexing bullshit. I've got some excellent managers to recommend." His advisers help clients beat the indexes, he said, and invest in the same funds and strategies themselves. "We eat our own cooking," he said proudly, and they make their money through fees on the assets under management.

Mr. Wiener then agreed to take an informal look at my Vanguard portfolio. I emailed him my list of funds, and he got back to me within minutes with a thorough—and embarrassing—vetting.

One of the main things that he noticed was that I had a retirement target fund that seemed to violate his advice about pushing off retirement targets to 2025 or even 2030. He wrote, succinctly, "Target 2020? Ewww!"

I couldn't remember why I'd set the target 2020 as my retirement in the fund. I'm not planning to retire in two years! What was I thinking? Well, we know what I was thinking: I was not thinking.

He also noticed that I had a "silly" 1 percent of my portfolio in one fund. "Why?" he asked. Again, I had no idea, though I figured it was something left over from an earlier transaction. Frankly, I couldn't remember buying that fund.

He said I should be putting at least 10 to 15 percent of my allocation into foreign stocks, citing some Vanguard options, and urged me to put 5 percent of my portfolio into health care stocks, suggesting Vanguard's health care fund. Finally, he argued that I should dump my investment in Vanguard's Windsor Fund, a managed fund. He said that I should be going outside Vanguard for my managed stock investing and recommended PRIMECAP's Odyssey Growth Fund for 25 percent of my stock holdings. He puts a lot of his own family's money into that fund, he told me.

"That's a start," he concluded.

Bracing!

Speed dating 2: a broker

Next, I decided to try a retail broker who works on commission. These are the folks whom experts warn investors to be careful with, since they make money by selling you investments. (Remember Ron Lieber's list of 21 questions for any broker?)

I called the investment services branch of a local bank that offers a free initial consultation, and was transferred to a guy named Gary. I told him that I was looking for a checkup on my investments and retirement plans, and he said he could see me that day. Twenty minutes later, we were shaking hands. He was pleasant and easy to talk to, and it turned out we were the same age. He was pleased that I'd started saving in my late 20s, and seemed to think that the $1.2 million that the 401(k) had grown to was a goodly sum, though he said he wouldn't know if it was enough to count on for retirement until we'd gone over our current expenses and what we expected to spend in retirement. He handed me a 10-page "financial planning profile." The form, he said, "will help me get a good idea of where you stand, how much you're going to need in retirement. We can see if you'll have a surplus, or negative." Flipping through it, I saw it asked many of the same questions I'd encountered on the Vanguard website, but with greater detail: they wanted my recent pay stubs, bank and 401(k) statements, cash flow, including cable and Internet bills, medical costs, assets, and debts. It also took on some of the big questions, such as when we planned to retire and how long we expected to live, as well as "Do you want to leave a legacy?" He said I didn't have to fill out every bit of it in detail, and it did not constitute the last word. "Once we plug everything in, we can adjust it," he said, "any time there's an event in your life that requires it."

After handing that to me, he talked about his mother, who needed years of long-term 24-hour care at home. That, he said, was something we'd be talking about once I signed up for an account: whether I'd like to get long-term-care insurance. He had subtly slipped into a pitch: Long-term-care insurance tends to be expensive, but the company offers what he said was a hybrid account called "MoneyGuard," from Lincoln Financial Group. He quickly described it as a kind of insurance policy for long-term health care that I'd pay into with a large upfront chunk— say, $50,000, though he said one of his clients was putting in more than ten times that much. Beyond that would be monthly additions to the fund, which could be leveraged for a much greater amount of money available for long-term care. At the end of my life, if I didn't need to dip into the fund for long-term care, the investment would be available to my heirs, plus a 1 or 1.5 percent investment earnings. "You'd get more money than you'd put into it." In the example of his client putting in $580,000, he said, there would be $1.75 million available for care, or the $580,000 if she died without needing the care. "I think that's a great product," he said. He then handed me a one-page form to assess my health to see if I'd qualify for the insurance.

I asked him if he would take a look at the funds I had with Vanguard to see whether they were good choices, and he gave them a quick once-over and said that they looked good to him. "These are great." I asked him about the 2020 target retirement fund that Wiener had scoffed at, and he said that he had one with the same target date, too. "You're fine. That's conservative," he said. He didn't notice the "silly" 1 percent investment in that T. Rowe Price fund that bothered Wiener, but it was pretty clear that he intended to move me into a different set of investments entirely if I decided to work with him; he said that he would probably recommend some funds offered through his company that would be equivalent to what I had at Vanguard, and that I would benefit because "there would be no 12b-1 charges" on his funds; "we have something about the same, and we could take out the fees." He asked me to complete the financial planning profile so we could get started, and we shook hands and said goodbye. The visit had taken less than an hour. It was a good visit with a pleasant, likable guy.

I got home and looked up some of what we talked about. I started with his record on BrokerCheck. He's been in the business for 22 years with just one potential blemish on his record, from 2001. A customer alleged that Gary had gotten him into an "unsuitable" bond purchase; the claim was denied. In other words, it appeared that his reputation was pretty clean.

Some of the things he said in our conversation, however, did not add up. The hybrid funds might not be as great as he said. There's been plenty written about hybrid funds like MoneyGuard. These hybrids, which act like something between an insurance policy and an annuity, can help you avoid big fee hikes that can come with traditional long-term-care insurance, but they cost a lot up front. If you've got plenty of money to put aside in such funds, they can bring peace of mind—so long as you pump enough in to get a substantial amount of coverage. A $50,000 kick-in might make the broker a nice fee, but it wasn't going to pay for much long-term care. An article in *Kiplinger* suggested that while the hybrids are popular, investors could do better by investing the money and getting market-rate returns, or simply buying both long-term-care insurance and life insurance.[14]

I also looked up 12b-1 fees to find out what they were. They are fees charged on mutual funds of as much as 1 percent a year. They've been around forever and cut into your investment, and so they are unpopular. I checked my Vanguard funds to see if any of them charge 12b-1 fees.

They don't.

Speed dating 3: an hourly-fee financial adviser

Finally, I looked into the world of investment advisers who charge by the hour, not by a percentage of your assets. For that, I sought out Tom Fredrickson. He is a member of the Garrett Planning Network, an organization of hundreds of planners who work on a fee-only basis. Fredrickson works by the hour; setting up a financial plan can cost between $1,200 and $4,000, according to his website, with a percentage paid annually for ongoing asset management. Smaller jobs cost less: College planning can run about $500 per child. Reviewing a portfolio can run anywhere from about $500 to $1,500. You get the idea.

I was drawn to the simplicity of the services that people like Fredrickson offer. I got in touch and we exchanged a few emails discussing his services and what he would do for us if we became clients. He sent me a worksheet that would show our assets and a spreadsheet that could help us see what we spend our money on. "For many people, a crucial first step is getting our heads around what their spending habits are like," he said; with an understanding of income and spending, he can go on to show how much "discretionary income" there is to meet financial goals like saving for college or retirement.

His average client's investable income is about $700,000, with clients at the high end in the "mid-seven figures." I decided not to go for the full $4,000 treatment. I told him about the book project, and asked if he would be willing to look over the same page of investments that the other guys had. He told me that he would give me an informal assessment for the cost of a lunch near his office in Brooklyn. How could I pass up that deal?

We met over a couple of excellent lamb burgers in a place near his office by Prospect Park, and he started off by explaining what he does for a living. "I actually do a full range of planning, from portfolio—if that's what somebody wants or needs—to a holistic plan," which might include college funding, managing cash flow, saving for retirement, the works. "Life is more complicated than just having a portfolio," he told me. "I think people benefit from having a complete look at everything." He said he likes for his clients to have him take an occasional checkup on their investments to make sure that, for example, the balance of stocks and bonds is about right and whether the tax implications of investments are favorable. "These are people who generally don't like to do the trading themselves, who like a real person they can talk to and not an 800 number."

One of the common services he provides is helping figure out where money is supposed to come from when a client wants something fairly big, like a house remodeling. Do you pull it out of a 401(k)? Spend down some investments? Take out a home equity loan? He helps them figure out when to start taking Social Security (delaying is better, because the payout is so much higher). Sometimes, he's almost a therapist, he said; when a client wanted to draw down a substantial amount of money to renovate his brownstone so that he could make money off it through Airbnb, Fredrickson showed him that wasn't a good investment. The client had to admit that, aside from the financial rationalizations, he really just wanted to spiff up the place, and Fredrickson explained that he could help him find a way to pay for that, but the client should be thinking about the day, say, in his 80s, when he would be smart to sell the house.

He is a fee-only financial planner, he said, because he wants to eliminate all possibility of conflict of interest. "I like to describe myself to prospective clients as a consultant," he said. He will, on an hourly basis, determine a client's tolerance for risk and set out financial goals, recommending along the way the lowest-fee funds. He favors index funds and retirement target funds. And he tells clients how to do that part themselves; "I often talk clients out of my being an active investment manager," telling them, "you can do it yourself."

He said that after looking at the worksheet I had completed for him, which he'd brought in a plastic binder, I was "in pretty good shape," especially when so many people have only Social Security to look forward to. Along with our 401(k), "that $30,000 pension is like an ace in the hole," he said. "It's like doubling your Social Security right there." As long as we didn't pull out more than, say, 3 to 4 percent of our 401(k) investments per year, we should do pretty well, getting maybe $90,000 a year. "It's not a luxurious retirement, but it's comfortable." He recommended, still, that we max out our contributions to the 401(k), noting that we could be adding thousands of dollars to it each year beyond our current contribution.

He then took a look at the same investments that the broker and Wiener had looked at, and had suggestions. He smiled a little at my stake in the Vanguard Windsor Fund, the one Wiener had also scoffed at. Windsor was once a high flier, he said, "the performance happens to be not as good lately." We were, he said, too heavily invested in big companies in the United States—the S&P 500—and would do well to get more small-capitalization stocks and beef up the bonds a bit. The easiest way to do that, he suggested, was to move a lot of my current investments into one of the Vanguard target funds set for the year I expect to retire—"a simple, good way to clean up the portfolio." It would do the diversifying and balancing for me, he said. As for the 2020 fund that I had invested in, and which Wiener had ridiculed, he said, "It's okay, if that's when you plan to retire," with the implication that if I expected to hold on more than three additional years in the working world, I could push the target date back by getting into another fund.

After my experiences in the advice world, I was pretty much back where I started. I didn't hand over all my finances to anyone to rework, but I got some good advice—and some questionable advice—on my portfolio.

I'll stick with Vanguard, but will follow Wiener's and Fredrickson's advice to get rid of the Windsor Fund—that fee is comparatively high, and the return historically isn't so great. But I'm not going to go for the outside managed funds that Wiener was describing, nor was I going to switch investment companies because I hired an adviser who works for one.

And I guess I'll side with Warren Buffett on this one, Mr. Wiener. Sorry, but I still believe in that indexing bullshit.

I also realized that I did not want a full-scale takeover of my finances at what felt to me like a high cost, as good as it sounded; having stumbled my way into a reasonably good retirement plan, I didn't see a need to spend that kind of money. That may be penny wise and pound foolish—and you, reader, might want to consider a different path. I could see fee-only advisers as a great way for someone with a good income who is starting out in life to make sure things are in good order, or for someone looking at retirement to get a thorough checkup.

A few hours after getting back from lunch, a friend sent an email around to me and some other friends asking if we knew of a good financial planner, "someone to save me from financial ruin and/or achieve total prosperity."

Without hesitation, I gave him Fredrickson's number.

PUNCH LIST

HOW TO PICK AN INVESTMENT ADVISER

So you want to find someone to help you with your investments. Here's how to do it:

1) **Figure out what kind of help you need and what kind of adviser you're looking for.** If you just want to play the stock market, you can hire a broker. (Or trade online.) Many brokers also offer financial planning and retirement planning. But if you want all-around financial planning—retirement, investing, and other aspects of your money life—go for a certified financial planner, or CFP. You can find them through the websites of organizations like the National Association of Personal Financial Advisors, the Certified Financial Planner Board of Standards, the XY Planning Network, and the Garrett Planning Network.[15] But also get advice from respected family members and friends.

   If you don't need something as extensive as total asset management or comprehensive financial planning, you might not need an actual human. The growing field of so-called robo-advisers from sites like betterment.com and wealthfront.com cost less than flesh-and blood advisers. They also do less, without the personalized service you'd expect from, well, a person; you get what you pay for. But it might be enough. The adviser I worked with at Vanguard was, essentially, acting as a mouthpiece for a robo-adviser.

2) **Figure out how you want to pay your adviser.** Many brokers and advisers make commissions on the products they sell. That can be a recipe for a conflict of interest. Others make their money directly through customer fees: you pay, whether on an hourly basis or an annual basis, or as a percentage of the assets they manage for you. And ask if they've ever been disciplined or prosecuted.

3) **Make sure whoever will be working for you will really be working for you and not for a beach house.** You might get great service from a broker, but you'll want to make sure that professional is acting with your best interests at heart. Be ready to ask a lot of questions along those lines: ask for the names of other

clients who might vouch for him or her, how the firm is compensated, and about any financial incentives to recommend some financial products over others. You can find a good list of such questions at the National Association of Personal Financial Advisors website, or you can work from Ron Lieber's list.[16]

And be explicit about the adviser's fiduciary duty to you. Anyone you work with should be willing to sign an oath to serve your interests, like the one published by the Committee for the Fiduciary Standard.[17]

4) **Check anyway.** Go to BrokerCheck (brokercheck.finra.org) to find out about past infractions by brokers. For a broader search that includes advisers, double-check at the Investment Advisor Public Disclosure site (adviserinfo.sec.gov), run by the U.S. Securities and Exchange Commission.

5

HOUSES

My house is me and I am it. My house is where I like to be and it looks like all of my dreams.

—DANIEL PINKWATER, *THE BIG ORANGE SPLOT*

WHEN OUR KIDS were little, we loved reading the works of Daniel Pinkwater, the off-kilter writer who can be funny, insightful, and magical all at once. A children's book of his that we came back to again and again was *The Big Orange Splot*, which is basically about uptight people on a "neat street" who become agitated when Mr. Plumbeam goes a little wild with a decorating project. (A seagull drops a can of orange paint on the roof, and, well, things get wacky.)

The neighbors complain, one by one, to Mr. Plumbeam, and he replies to each of them, "My house is me and I am it. My house is where I like to be and it looks like all of my dreams."

I could feel Plumbeam's simple self-confidence and pride in his home. I was moved, too, by the infectiousness of his argument: the neighbors who complain to him end up redoing their own houses. By the end, it is no longer a neat street. It is a sweetly wild fantasy of self-expression, and, as the neighbors put it, "it looks like all our dreams."

That ending has always choked me up. Okay, I'm an easy weeper. And don't ask me about Barbara Cooney's lovely little tales of island boys and lupine-strewing adventurers; I couldn't get through those without a good sniffle.

Anyway.

The point here is that I always wanted our own homes to reflect our family's personality, at least up to the point that it interferes with resale value. (I'm sorry, Joseph. I know you wanted your bedroom in Millburn to have purple walls with polka dots. But we ended up having enough trouble selling the place as it was!) That attitude meant that the kids got to choose the colors of their rooms, within reason (that purple room, nope nope nope), and the light fixtures. The furniture tended to be cheap or secondhand, and we made good use of the stuff Sam made in high school wood shop. The delighted teacher even gave us an extra end table when he realized that, unlike many of the parents in our snooty town, we actually wanted the stuff. The art on the walls is, as I've said, eclectic: those big oil paintings my folks picked up in New Orleans, my 50-year-old certificate from Supermen of America, the L-shaped, corner-hugging painting of a tiger by Jeanne's dad. Suspended from the ceiling, a wire sculpture of an owl that Sam created in middle school. The cowboy boots from when I was five years old, bronzed.

So our houses—we've owned four over the years—have, to some extent, looked like all our dreams. But any homeowner knows that they also reflect our nightmares: the endless punch list of repairs, each with its own financial hit. We know the sense of dread that burbles up within us whenever we hear the sound of water dripping, or of squirrels scrabbling in the attic.

And over it all, and tied to it all, is needing to pay for the privilege of staying in the damned place. Like most homeowners, we have found it to be a struggle at times. We've made mistakes and had bad luck, and learned from both. The subsequent choices we made when it came to buying homes were better, and provided us with a tidy profit when selling.

For most of us out there, our houses are our biggest investment. The primary residence makes up 62 percent of the median homeowner's total assets, according to a 2013 report from the National Association of Home Builders.[1] But buying a home is no guarantee of a good return on your investment. Sell profitably and a house can push you into a more comfortable life. But if the value drops—remember the mid-2000s?—you can be ruined.

The hoary rule of thumb says that housing costs should be about 30 percent of your annual income. Many experts say that the rule is not ironclad. For one thing, income amount counts: families making, say, $500,000 a year have more money left over after spending 30 percent of their income on housing than someone who earns $20,000 a year. For another, those higher-priced housing markets might come with job opportunities not available elsewhere. David Bieri, an associate professor of urban affairs at Virginia Tech, told Bloomberg News that despite its long use by the U.S. government as a standard of housing affordability, the 30 percent figure is "essentially an arbitrary number" that "creates more distortions than it actually solves."[2]

But whether it's reasonable or not, the fact is that many of us spend more than that 30 percent, according to surveys conducted by the U.S. Census.[3] Among homeowners, in 2014 more than 34 percent paid more than that magic 30 percent. More than half of renters were spending at least 30 percent—in part, the survey found, because many renters couldn't qualify for mortgages or come up with a down payment on a home.

According to Harvard's Joint Center for Housing Studies, the pressures on renters are fierce, with 21.3 million renters paying more than 30 percent of their income on housing—and 11.4 million of those households paying more than half of their incomes for housing, according to the group's 2016 *State of the Nation's Housing* report, which is based on 2014 survey figures. The center called that "a record high."[4]

Unsurprisingly, among those with the lowest income, $15,000 per household, things are even tougher, whether people rent or own, according to the Harvard study. Eighty-three percent of these folks paid more than 30 percent of their income for housing in the 2014 survey, and a huge portion of those people pay more than half of their income on housing: 72 percent of renters and 66 percent of owners.

Did you catch that seeming bright spot about the benefits of owning a home in the picture portrayed by the Harvard report? A smaller portion of homeowners than renters were paying more than 50 percent of their income—the category referred to as "severely burdened." Even those paying more than 30 percent, known more gently as "cost burdened," seemed to be doing better than the renters, and the rate has been steadily dropping. By 2014 there were 18.5 million cost-burdened owners, down by 4.4 million since 2008.

But in this segment of the economy, even the good news is bad: fewer homeowners are in the severely burdened category because so many people who used to be in that category lost their homes through foreclosure.

The nation's financial collapse is still being felt: mortgage credit is still tight, and foreclosures continue (though not at the torrid rate as in the late aughts); so the Harvard report tells us that the national rate of homeownership dropped from 69 percent at the peak, in 2004, to 63.7 percent in 2015. Housing prices didn't recover from the crash until 2016. Which brings us to the subprime mortgage crisis and Michael Lewis's astonishing book *The Big Short*. The subprime loans boomed so that more people could buy homes and Wall Street could generate more fees and trade more bonds based on the mortgages. As we all have since found out, it was a bubble. It burst in a way that makes the Bikini Atoll nuclear tests look kind of puny.

Lewis talked about the disaster that awaited the subprime mortgage market in the 2000s: borrowers who couldn't afford their homes facing steep mortgage-cost hikes when their "initial" teaser rate that was fixed for two years expired. These borrowers, he wrote, were already "one broken refrigerator away from default," and the teaser rates on the masses of lousy mortgages issued in 2005 were set to expire in 2007. They did, and we're still climbing back from the economic collapse that resulted.

The problem is that it's not just subprime borrowers who are one broken refrigerator away from default. Remember the Federal Reserve report that said 46 percent of Americans say they couldn't come up with an emergency expense costing $400 without borrowing money or selling something?[6] People with less income, predictably, are even more fragile: two-thirds of them would have trouble coming up with that $400.

And, by the way, $400 is getting off easy. The wood in that lovely bay window in the kitchen turns out to have been rotted by leaks? Thousands of dollars to replace it, my friend. A worn-out roof that needs full replacement? Aieeee.

Still, I was haunted by the words of Simcha Kravitz to his grandson Duddy in Mordecai Richler's great novel *The Apprenticeship of Duddy Kravitz*. The old man says, "A man without land is nobody."[7] Richler's Duddy becomes pathological, a greedy hustler who betrays his friends. But even as I shook my head at Duddy, whether in print or played on-screen by an incredibly young Richard Dreyfuss, the idea that owning land makes you somebody tugged at me.

Jeanne and I had rented places since we first started dating in 1975. We found apartments in complexes that were about to be condemned; portions of houses with floors so tilty that a marble placed on the floor by one wall would roll across the room and into another; an apartment upstairs from a hairdresser's shop with ceilings so low that even we could touch them, short as we both are; a room in a creaky turn-of-the-century mansion that we shared with half a dozen friends. In New York, a lovely, small sublet right off Central Park West and a floor-through part of a Brooklyn brownstone. We knew enough about money by then, however, to understand that paying rent was no way to get ahead financially: buying a place means building equity.

In 1987, I had no crystal ball to know the coming ups and downs of real estate. I did not know what replacing a bay window costs. I was, in other words, an idiot. But the herd was buying real estate, and who was I to argue with that? Sometimes the herd is right.

We knew that renters were just pouring money down a hole and that we needed to start building equity. Besides, you can't go wrong in real estate, can you?[8]

After all, why do the British say that something is "safe as houses"?

OUR HOMES AND WHAT THEY TAUGHT US

We started looking for a place to buy in 1988. Our daughter, Elizabeth, had been born while we were living in an apartment in Brooklyn, and we felt that it was time for a place of our own. I had also been working long enough on staff at *Newsweek* to have gotten the sense that they weren't likely to fire me anytime soon.

We learned that buyers were pushing into neighborhoods they might not have considered a few years earlier, earning the label of gentrifiers. Since Jeanne and I hadn't come to New York City accompanied by trust funds, we would join them.

I was talking with colleagues about starting our search, and one of them said, "You have to come see my building. I have the best apartment in Manhattan." We did visit; he lived at 790 Riverside Drive, up at 157th Street at the southern end of Washington Heights.

The building was a Beaux Arts behemoth, 12 stories tall and sitting on a circle; its name was the Riviera. It had a grand, if run-down, marble lobby. My friend's co-op apartment was on a high floor, and it was nearly a city block long, facing out toward the Hudson with a sweeping view of the George Washington Bridge. At street level, the neighborhood seemed vibrant and somewhat sketchy; the drug dealers working the corner near the subway stop at the corner of 157th and Broadway were brazen. Caribbean music was playing on the street, and the mood of the building seemed relaxed.

We loved it. We had been shown one dark, airless Upper West Side apartment after another within our price range. When a Realtor opened the door to one of the available co-ops at 790 RSD, the hallway stretched more than 50 feet ahead of us. To the right was a high-ceilinged living room and a dining room, separated by French doors. There were three bedrooms and two bathrooms. It seemed like an impossible amount of space for Manhattan. And we could have it for a little less than $140,000.

It wasn't on a high floor. Instead of the river and the bridge view my colleague upstairs had, we'd be looking out on the street oval and the surrounding buildings, which were old and stately. Even that view, however, could be glimpsed only from a single window in our bedroom and another one in what would become Elizabeth's. The big windows in the long living and dining rooms faced one of the deep airshafts that gave the building an odd, folded look. Jeanne and I thought about Elizabeth, who would be walking soon; we imagined her running down that long hallway and playing in the enormous (for New York) living room.

We had saved enough to make the down payment, helped by an $8,000 inheritance that Jeanne had received when her grandfather died. But staying there looked as if it could become very expensive. Mortgages were pricey at the time: the average 30-year fixed mortgage rate was more than 10 percent, and the country was in the middle of a brutal spike. We signed up for an adjustable-rate mortgage with an introductory rate that, for the time, seemed reasonable: something around 7 percent for the first five years. Or was it 9? I don't remember; the point was that it got us in the door. We did worry about what might happen after five years. If interest rates kept rising, we could be laddering up by two points each year, with ruinously expensive payments on top of the maintenance fees for the building. We hoped that before the fixed-rate period expired, we would have moved on.

My hands were shaking as Jeanne and I signed the endless succession of closing documents. But I knew that it was time to take our place among grown-ups—that we had to own our home.

Or something like a home. It was unclear: What had we just bought? We had grown up in houses in Texas; this was a co-op, which we hadn't even heard of before coming to New York, where they are common. It wasn't a condominium, which would have been treated by the law as real property. What we had put our life savings and much of my future income into, apparently, were shares in a corporation that owned the building. What the mortgage broker had called a mortgage was actually more like a loan to pick up the shares and what's called the proprietary lease.[9] The building, which was undergoing conversion from rentals to co-ops, was made up partly of renters and partly of owners.

We still didn't own land, so by the Simcha Kravitz standard we had not graduated beyond nobody. And we were so far uptown that people joked we lived in "Upstate Manhattan." To us, though, we had arrived. At home.

Our joy was short-lived. We were on our way to discovering that you actually can go wrong in real estate.

==

The first problem to make itself known was noise; there was a lot of it. Music that is charming in the afternoon tends to lose its appeal after midnight. That airshaft amplified and resonated every note. One especially loud night, I walked up a few flights of stairs to find a party that was blasting dance numbers through the airshaft at a time when bars were required to close up for the night. A young woman I didn't know opened the door. "It's my birthday!" she said by way of explanation. I asked her to turn down the music a little. She looked confused. "It's my *birthday!*"

The neighbors immediately upstairs from us were also loud, with music that pounded through the ceiling. It was odd, though; the music would stop and start; phrases would repeat. Songs did not seem to begin or end. What we did not know when we'd bought the place was that they operated a recording studio in their living room. On our previous visits, the studio had not been active.

When the musicians were working, the bass thudded through the ceiling and up and down the airshaft. It was hard to even talk over the noise. The owner of the apartment was a well-known keyboard artist and vocalist, Tunde' Ra Aleem. He and his twin brother had worked with Jimi Hendrix, Rick James, and others. We'd have been honored to have such a respected musician as a neighbor if he wasn't shaking the fillings out of our teeth day and night. A knock on their door and a request for a little quiet would get a friendly hello at least at first, but would only occasionally produce the desired result, and my suggestion that they could use headphones in the evening went nowhere.

When I told colleagues about the noise, they nodded sagely. When we were considering buying the place, why hadn't I demanded to come back to the apartment after 10:00 p.m. so that we could tell whether there would be a lot of noise? I had no answer for them; unlike my friends, I am neither perfect nor a genius. Besides, the brothers were running the studio at all hours; we had simply not visited while they were working.

Noise wasn't the only problem with our upstairs neighbors. They did not supervise their kids well. When the children got bored, they would throw things into the toilets and flush them, sending water down into our bathroom and ruining the paint that we and a group of friends had so carefully applied when we moved in. We had coated the walls with new latex paint to seal in what could be found underneath: decades of previous coats, dating back before the ban on the use of lead. If you broke off an ancient paint drip, the cross section looked like multicolored tree rings. It was beautiful, but many of those interior layers bore toxic lead. A neighbor used heat guns to strip the paint off every wood surface, but we weren't willing to try that with our growing daughter in the house and more kids on the way.

While we were living in Washington Heights, our boy Sammy came along. Blond, solidly built, and full of life, Sam learned to walk in that apartment. "Walk" isn't the right word. He *ran*, starting out by standing up, lowering his big toddler head until he began to tip over, and blasting forward to stay upright. Setting a pattern of heedless fun that I hope he never outgrows, he would keep going until he slammed into a wall or a piece of furniture, or one of us. Then he'd get up, laughing. We started calling him the Saminator.

So now we had two children in Washington Heights. It was an interesting neighborhood. Yes, the drug dealers worked the corner up at Broadway, and their lookouts, who we learned were called chichi men, tried to get our attention as we crossed the street from the 157th Street subway station. But they were easygoing and didn't mind when I'd wave them off.

Maybe they were why our block got a lot of attention from police. One day Jeanne noticed that the ground-floor window in a building up 157th was papered over, but with a strip missing; she could see men moving back and forth inside. They were clearly staking out a building across the street. We hoped nothing involving arrests and gunplay would happen while we were heading home after picking the kids up at their schools. We'd let them run down the length of the block to our building's door, and what if they stumbled into the middle of a raid? We were spared that, at least.

Even as we grew more comfortable with the neighborhood, others seemed to think we didn't fit in. One evening, coming out of the subway station, a white cop stopped me. He clearly thought I was headed into the neighborhood to score drugs. I explained to the officer that I only wanted to get home to my apartment.

"You *live* here?" he asked, incredulous and scornful. Many of the city's police officers lived a ways upstate in towns like Middletown, and they did not seem very comfortable on the streets of Washington Heights.

The officer had his opinion, and we had ours; Washington Heights was, in many ways, the friendliest neighborhood I've ever lived in. Heavily African American and Dominican, with remnants of old Irish and Jewish communities, it was accepting even of this little family of cracker gentrifiers. On weekends, I'd take the kids up to Coral Donut, a small diner at the corner of 158th and Broadway, for eggs and pancakes and, of course, donuts. It was a treat; just Dad and the guys. On our way back downhill to the oval, Elizabeth loved to stop in to say hi to Gary, who ran the dry-cleaning place. The little fried-chicken stand across Broadway had tasty eats that we loved for a quick snack, at least until we all got food poisoning one time and decided that we could fry our own chicken.

Sometimes things got a little too lively outside. Cars would occasionally pull up around the Riverside Oval in the middle of the night and play their stereos at top volume. It was loud enough to wake us, several floors up—and, more important, wake the kids.

I started keeping an old egg on the windowsill. One night, when a car sat outside too long and too loudly, I opened the window, slid the screen up, tossed the aged egg down the five stories, and slammed the window shut before impact. My aim was decent; we heard the squeal of the tires racing toward Broadway.

It was briefly satisfying, but I didn't try that trick again. Instead, we found ways to cope with the noise. When we bought a window air conditioner, we asked the salesman for the loudest model he had. It wasn't a request he heard often, but he knew what units got the most complaints. Soon we had plenty of white noise that helped us get through the nights. We had settled in.

Then, in the summer of 1992, Washington Heights exploded. A police officer shot and killed Jose Garcia, a 23-year-old immigrant from the Dominican Republic and a father of two.[10] Some 40 square blocks of Washington Heights erupted into rioting, with scores of injuries and arrests, and trash cans and cars set afire.

We had been visiting relatives in Texas for the July 4 weekend when all this started and had missed the news. Jeanne had stayed in Houston an extra day with Elizabeth, and I'd flown back with Sam.

A cab took us home from the airport, coming down Riverside and avoiding the mess on Broadway. The subject of riots didn't come up during the ride; all I noticed was that the streets seemed awfully quiet.

We got home and then came back downstairs at about 10:00 p.m. to run out for milk and groceries for the next day. At the entryway, I encountered a group of residents standing around the lobby, looking grim. I headed past them toward the door and they stopped me: "Hey, hey, HEY! Don't you know what's been going on out there?"

Well, no, I said. I'd been away. They explained, with the patience reserved for explaining things to dim children, that they were standing there to head off any trouble from the rioters who had been rioting and how could I not have heard about the riots? I would be crazy, they continued to explain, to walk outside with my son. Well, I said, I'd rather face rioters than have a hungry boy in the morning. I at least needed some milk.

Bobby, a tall, skinny guy who was always friendly, said he'd take me up to Broadway to find an open bodega. We left Sam with the guardians in the lobby—he was a sound sleeper, that boy—and walked up together. The streets were quiet; the rioters had cleared out by then. But they had left behind trash-scattered streets and burning cars, their flames tinted with blues and oranges and greens from the various plastics used to make them. It was, I have to say, beautiful. But I didn't spend a lot of time admiring the view.

Bobby and I made our way across Broadway, because he'd noticed that a metal shutter on one bodega was not pulled all the way down, or locked. The man had good eyes! He banged on the shutter. The people inside raised it enough for me to see that there were several of them there, behind the Plexiglas panel of the door, and that they had baseball bats. I pleaded for some help in my middling Spanish. *"Necesito leche para mi bebe!"* I shouted. They opened the door, let me in, sold me the milk. I thanked Bobby and offered him a ten, which he took with thanks. "See you, man!" he said, and headed down Broadway, leaving me to make my way back to our building alone.

Note to self: next riot, pay Bobby *after* he walks you back to the apartment building.

I got back without incident and thanked the men for taking on babysitting Sam while guarding the building. He'd slept through my riot. I took him back upstairs and put him in bed.

==

Over our time at 790, our biggest problem turned out to be our next-door neighbors. There was a matriarch and several of her kids and their kids, all living in a four-bedroom apartment. One of the brothers, Arnold, was well over six feet tall and powerfully, if heavily, built. He worked hard and seemed to be supporting the extended family on his income. He could be friendly and had a ready smile, but any complaint about, say, noise—they blasted their stereos and their video games at all hours—turned him cold and, occasionally, threatening. The other brother, Charlie, was small and thin and clearly smart. But he was troubled. Though I have no medical training, and an actual diagnosis is beyond my abilities, it didn't take long to figure out that he suffered from a mental illness. Some days he would dress nattily; at other times he was unwashed and unkempt, moving in a fog. Asked how he was, he might say, "I'd be okay if they didn't keep putting that stuff in the air." I would agree that the stuff in the air was hard to deal with.

On one good day, he hung art posters in the hallway next to our apartments. A couple of weeks later, they were gone. I asked why he had taken them down and he explained, "John, the pictures had started talking to me." I agreed that it could be very difficult when the pictures start talking to you. Even at his most tormented, he was pleasant. Although people in the building told us he exposed himself to women in the elevators, he treated Jeanne with courtesy and respect. Jeanne told me that she figured it was because he always saw her with a child, but we were grateful, whatever the reason.

Their mother lived in the apartment, too. She had friendly days, but, like Charlie, she had moments when sanity seemed to leave her and she'd tell us about black helicopters. One day she poked her head out the door as I was walking by. "Freddy Krueger! Freddy Krueger!" she shouted, wild-eyed. I didn't know why she was saying the name of the killer from the *Nightmare on Elm Street* movies, and didn't ask.

The apartment was taking a toll on Sammy. It was too dark, too confining despite its spaciousness, and too loud. One afternoon, when Arnold and his friends stood out on the elevator landing, laughing and joking at top volume, Sam, with a voice far deeper than a toddler's should be, shouted, "SHUT UP! SHUT UP!" loud enough to be heard through the door. Arnold probably thought it was me. Jeanne had noticed that Sammy was becoming unhappy in New York; she'd ask him what was wrong and he'd simply say, "I'm sad." He'd wanted something more than an air shaft to look out at.

Tensions continued to grow between Arnold and me. One evening we ended up standing together at the elevator landing, waiting for our ride to the lobby. He had a friend with him. Arnold gave me a smile that was anything but friendly. He pulled out a paint scraper—the kind with a razor blade on the business end.

"I'm going to cut ya, John," he said. His eyelids were low; he seemed a little buzzed.

The friend said nervously, "Come on, Arnold. That's not cool."

Trying to keep my voice steady, I asked, "Arnold, are you seriously threatening me?"

"John, naw, you know I'm just messin' with you," he said.

I told him I wasn't so sure. He put the blade away, still smiling that unfriendly smile.

We made good friends in the building as well. Pam, an around-the-corner neighbor on our floor, was a single mom with an adorable daughter. We would sit and drink coffee while the girls played. A couple of floors above us was a young couple raising a daughter in an apartment with the same floor plan as ours. The husband, who worked for the city, was the neighbor who labored every evening to remove old paint with a heat gun and a scraper, so we got a sense of just how beautiful these old apartments could be.

And the neighborhood was adapting to us, at least a little. When crossing Broadway one evening after getting off the subway, one of the drug scouts stepped out to ask if I was looking to score. *"SSsst!"* another lookout said, calling him back. *"He lives here."*

It felt good. Even the dealers knew me! I thanked him and walked on.

MAKING A MOVE, AND FEELING THE SQUEEZE

Then came change. Toward the end of 1992, *The Washington Post* announced an opening for a science writer. A friend from the *Post* told me, that after my eight years at *Newsweek*, "You really know what you're doing. But it seems to me that you're also bored." He was right; I applied. I was clearly unqualified for a science writing job, since many of the science writers I knew had majored in technical fields in college, and some had graduate degrees. But I had gained confidence at *Newsweek*, where I had also been unqualified to work as a business writer. The editor who had hired me for that gig scoffed when I told him I didn't know anything about business: he said, "Read a book." I sold my would-be new bosses on the idea that, since the beat I was applying for was covering the Food and Drug Administration, my background as a business reporter and my legal training made me more qualified for the job than someone who knew only science. As for the science, I promised to read a book. To my astonishment, they bought the argument and hired me.

Going to one of the world's great news organizations—the paper that uncovered Watergate—was exciting. But I'll admit, just between us, that part of what motivated me was the move away from that problematic apartment in New York.

We had learned a few things from living at 790 Riverside Drive. While we had lived in apartments all over Austin and in our early years in New York, the density of the city meant that any problems we encountered were magnified. We had been naive; we hadn't understood the fundamentals of real estate.

Jeanne summed up how we'd screwed up in buying that first home: we'd fallen for what amounted to a real estate Ponzi scheme. She said recently, reminiscing, "Our mistake was letting other people tell us what financial decisions we should make with our money," referring to the colleague who had sold us on the idea of living in his building. "We figured that since they had sunk all of their money into something, it would be safe for us to do the same. We assumed that they had taken the trouble to assess the risks and the likelihood that their investment would pay off in the end—even make them money." In other words, being afraid of money had hurt us, and we'd substituted the judgment of others for our own. But, she said, it was worse than that. She believed that the other buyers who enthusiastically invited us in knew how shaky the building and the neighborhood were. "We thought that we were being advised by trustworthy people when, in fact, they were using us to validate their own choices. They had bought into this building and could recoup their loss only if they convinced other gullible people to buy in as well." They were trying to create a climate of excitement about this neighborhood, but the neighborhood itself was resistant to change, she said. "Ultimately somebody made a lot of money off of our apartment, but it wasn't us and it was never going to be us."

We also hadn't understood ourselves. We now knew that it was essential to get the feel of a place and its neighborhood before buying. We had also realized that we weren't cut out to be, as Jeanne put it, "clueless urban pioneers." Our next place, we decided, would be a stand-alone house; no more shared walls, so that we and our neighbors wouldn't be so much in each other's business. And that our kids needed space.

The stress of living at 790 Riverside stayed with me a long time, too. For years afterward, whenever I saw a loaf of bread with the brand name Arnold—common in the Northeast—I'd feel a flash of resentment toward my old neighbor. As good as that bread looks, I've never been able to bring myself to buy a loaf.

=

What we didn't know when we left Washington Heights was that we weren't escaping our problems; we were digging ourselves in deeper.

My new salary at *The Washington Post* was comparable to the old one, with one sweetener. The *Post* offered me an extra $900 a month for the better part of my first year with them to help defray (but not cover) the cost of the mortgage and maintenance on the New York apartment. The thinking was that would be more than enough time to sell the place.

But in the spring of 1993, New York housing was in the midst of a multiyear slump that made even our bargain apartment look overpriced. Prices had dropped, and the high tide that washed would-be gentrifiers northward into Washington Heights had receded, leaving us with a much smaller number of buyers willing to look as far uptown as 157th Street. So we decided to rent it out. After all, we might come back someday, right? And if we held on to it, prices might turn around.

We hired a broker who would serve as our property manager, and she found somebody for the first year we lived in Washington: a doctor with the city health department, and a good guy. He let us know that the upstairs was still raining into our apartment now and then, but was otherwise unperturbed by anything else going on around him.

After the nine months of supplemental pay from the *Post* ran out, we were losing money every month on the difference between our tenant's rent and the cost of the mortgage. Worse, the broker told me, in the current market our apartment was "almost worthless." The owners of the building had sold only a quarter of the apartments in the building, far less than most banks' threshold for selling a mortgage. Banks didn't want to take a chance on a building whose co-op structure might collapse. "Even if you have somebody who has cash, *they* won't be able to sell it," she explained.

But then—wonder of wonders!—the upstairs neighbors moved out. With that little problem out of the way, our tenant showed an interest in buying the apartment. He had a catch, however. Since getting a new mortgage would be next to impossible, he wanted to assume the current mortgage. We were willing to transfer it without making any profit on the deal, just to be out from under the apartment. But the bank refused; co-op mortgages, they told him, are not assumable. The good doctor moved out.

The next renter looked almost as good as our doctor had, at least on paper. The broker told me that he made $58,000 a year working with a marketing group and that he had a clean credit record and a good job. The credit record showed that he had no credit cards—a quirk, but not necessarily a red flag. Maybe he was just trying to avoid debt, she explained. He was in his 20s and raised in New York. "I feel okay about him," she said. He moved in.

And that's when things went from financially stressful to nightmarish.

Before a year had passed, the tenant—let's call him Mr. V.—fell behind on his rent. I'd call, and he'd give me excuses, but the checks never came. "Anything could happen," he told me. "Maybe it got lost in the mail?"

"Tomorrow I'm going to Federal Express your check for February," he said in March.

"It's in the mail." Jeanne checked the mailbox every day, and day after day she'd give me the report.

"No check from V. As expected," she wrote in an email.

"No letter from V."

"No check from V."

"Call V. and see what's going on."

The February check came at the end of March. By May, there was no check for April. Or May.

I looked at a copy of one of his checks, which had his bank account number on it. In a move that just might have been a teensy bit illegal, I called his bank's automated account line and punched in the numbers to find out his balance.

It was $26.03.

=

Each month, our savings were being drained away to pay off a mortgage on an apartment that we couldn't sell, and which we weren't getting rent money from. In August 1995, I hired a lawyer and terminated the lease. I called V. and told him to get out. He responded that he knew his rights as a New York tenant and that he would be in no rush to leave.

"I'll be hearing fucking Christmas bells before I'm out of here," he said.

He was at least partly right—New York had laws to protect tenants that flowed from horrifying abuses by landlords over the generations. And now I was the landlord. He also told me that he had Mafia connections and that I shouldn't mess with him.

I was 38 and facing financial ruin.

One day, about that time, I was talking with the superintendent of the building, Nica, about my problems with getting the tenant out. He asked me a simple question: "You want me to kill him?"

Nica was a Serb, having emigrated from somewhere in the former Yugoslavia. He gave the impression that this task was not outside his skill set.

Okay, I do have to admit that it was tempting. Briefly! The tenant had taken our always-precarious financial situation and turned it into a dumpster fire. I paused.

Reader, I did not have him killed.

"Nica," I said slowly into the phone. "No." I paused again, whether for emphasis or simply to catch my breath.

"I do *not* want you to kill him. I mean it. *Listen to me.* I am not saying 'no' and hoping you'll kill him, or even break his arm. Don't do anything to him. I mean it."

"Okay," he said, sounding bored.

=

Instead of killing my tenant, I called the lawyer about getting him out. He walked me through the process of eviction, pointing out the many ways that my tenant could get the court to grant delays and more delays, and even if I got through the whole process, "you'll have a judgment for money, but it will be worthless." If I drove from Washington to New York City and attempted what he delicately called "self-help," I could be in for huge damages. "Judges just don't like that at all." So much for rethinking Nica's offer.

The lawyer had straightforward advice: he told me to give up on the money the jerk owed me. "Bite the inside of your cheek and call him and say if you get out by the 14th I will sign a piece of paper saying I will never go against you for the rent."

He got a little fatherly. "You're giving away six grand, but you're not really giving away six grand—you're not going to get it." He was right. I wrote up the letter and called V. He agreed to go.

By then, I was also talking occasionally to the tenant's boss, a guy named Art. He, too, seemed mystified by his employee. "I think he really does come from a Mafia family," he said. He said V. owed him money, too. He offered his wisdom about New York landlord-tenant law: "What the law says is, 'Fuck the landlord, and give the tenant all the rights he does not deserve.'"

When we ended the call, I couldn't help wondering if I hadn't just been talking to V., who was having a good laugh over yet another deception. I was doubting my sanity.

V. was out by the end of August, leaving a mess behind: he had spray-painted graffiti on several walls and left behind piles of clothes, garbage, and debris. But we cleaned up and soon had another tenant, a nice couple whose credit record looked terrific.

Within a few months, however, the couple broke up. The husband left, and the wife told me she could not pay the rent; she agreed to move out.

Our savings account, which had been a point of pride to me, had long been drained. We had no faith in our ability to find another tenant. We had no idea what to do.

We were struggling, but we also needed a place to call our own in the Washington area. When we'd first moved to town, Jeanne and I had found a rental house in Takoma Park, Maryland, on the northeast edge of the District of Columbia. Takoma Park is an environmentally friendly suburb with a historically lefty bent; people joked about it being the "People's Republic of Takoma Park." The racially mixed town had a sweet, relaxed vibe; it had a fun toy store, reasonably decent pizza, and a small place, Mark's Kitchen, that could turn out excellent grilled-cheese sandwiches *and* Korean bulgogi. It was unlike any place we'd ever lived, and it felt like home.

Parts of Takoma Park slopped over into D.C., and part of it overlapped from Montgomery County to Prince George's County. It was hilly and full of trees, with beautiful old buildings and nice homes.

The old wood-frame place we rented there was comfy, with a big sunny bedroom upstairs that looked out over the backyard. We had brought a washer and dryer. There was no room for it on our floor; the landlord let us set them up in the basement, which had once been cut up into three apartments but was now a stripped ruin with floors that flooded with the slightest rain. We elevated the washer and dryer on boards, dropped some more boards on the floor to help us cross over the puddles, and we were in business. The owner also had an apartment in the attic that was vacant, and it ended up being rented by a Texas friend who was no more picky about his accommodations than we were.

As nice as our new life was—and I loved my job as a science writer with *The Washington Post*, and our Takoma Park neighbors were relaxed and fun to talk with—we had no money. We had none of what the economists call discretionary income, anyway. Continuing to pay the mortgage and maintenance on the NYC place had, to use a term I'd heard from a corporate bankruptcy expert I once interviewed about Enron, "bageled" our savings.

Somehow, Jeanne made it work, keeping long lists of sums in a notebook, scribbling down the bills and what we had to pay first and how to make the most of each paycheck. She would wake up on payday, look at the amount for that week (which varied with expense reimbursements, pay for vacation days worked, and the like), and tell me, "I spent all your money," or "We have $115 until next Thursday." We'd plan our grocery shopping accordingly.

That's when I started buying french fries with gravy at the *Post* cafeteria. I could have brought food in from home, but I found that even more depressing; something about soggy sandwiches in a baggie breaks my heart. And with a fair amount of Tabasco, fries with gravy are pretty good. But there were other belt-tightening measures that hurt. One year, when our temple held its Purim carnival, we had only enough cash to buy a few tickets for each of our kids to play the games. Other children were running wild; our guys had to pick their shots and make a few careful choices. It wasn't something I'd wanted my children to have to do. And let's face it, it's not like going hungry. But in a place where the kids around them could do whatever they wanted, buy what they wanted, get what they wanted, my guys knew that in our family, there wasn't quite enough.

We could not go on that way. Our parents, including my father-in-law, a professor of property law, said that it was time to file for bankruptcy and get out from under our NYC burden. The prospect left me desolate. It felt to me as if the idea of being bankrupt would put the stamp of failure on everything Jeanne and I had done and tried until then. Career? Pretty good, but that bankruptcy would overshadow it, I thought, recalling a former boss who suddenly left his job as an editor at *The Wall Street Journal* shortly before filing for bankruptcy. That story had even been in the newspapers. I wasn't working in his league, but the possibility that going bust might cloud my future couldn't be dismissed. Yet there was still no way to sell the apartment, and no way to make enough money to pay for everything we were dealing with.

THE TAKOMA PARK HOUSE: GETTING SMARTER

Before we did something that could have such an enormous impact on our financial record, however, Jeanne and I decided that we needed to make one more try at buying a house. Once burned, twice shy? Sure, but we had to consider a window that was closing on us, and fast. If we did have to file for bankruptcy, it would wreck our credit; it would be a very long time before we could buy a house again. If we were able to buy and then had to declare bankruptcy, we would be protected under homestead exemptions—it would be unlikely that creditors could force us to sell the house to pay off debts.

And, as people in financial trouble go, we were still in surprisingly good shape. We had a decent income and no other debts to speak of, aside from the apartment and the balance of several thousand dollars on our credit card. We were paying our bills on time. So that left a question: Could we swing a house purchase?

It turned out that we could, as long as we kept things cheap. We started looking, but without really pushing.

One day, as I was walking along Elm Avenue about a block from our house, I saw a For Sale sign in front of a 1920s brick bungalow. The yard was overgrown, and the shed at the end of the gravel driveway was rotting away and leaning toward a slow-motion collapse. But the house looked solid, at least from the outside. I wrote down the number of the Realtor, who was from a small local company.

The line separating two Maryland counties crosses Elm. The house was listed as being in Prince George's County, though it seemed to me to be barely within the line for Montgomery County. This was a big deal: Prince George's County schools were not as well regarded as Montgomery County schools, and so a lot of buyers would not be interested in a house on the Prince George's side of the line. Because of that, PG houses also tended to cost less than MoCo homes.

I called the Realtor, and Jeanne and I set up a tour. The visit was not auspicious. Letting us in by way of a side entrance, the Realtor scraped her heel against the bottom edge of the closing screen door and suffered an ugly cut; she was in pain and limping as she showed the place. The previous owners had left the house a mess. It had gone unpainted for years, and there was a deep burn on the dining room floor and peeling linoleum on the kitchen floor. Worse, the owners had pulled a fridge from the wall—an antique model that ran on natural gas—and left it there with rotting food sealed inside. The stench was eye-watering. The basement had a number of larger rooms, but there was evidence of water damage and dislodged floor tiles, and an ancient boiler that looked less like a heating system than a bomb from a 1950s sci-fi movie.

The Realtor, still bleeding, nearly begged us to leave. She insisted that she had plenty of other listings.

But I loved it on sight. What I saw was a home with beautiful wood floors and detailed plasterwork in every downstairs room. We would later learn that the original owner had been a plaster craftsman, and we could find his masterful work in the local bank and elsewhere. The rooms were not large but were cozy; the main bedroom downstairs was barely big enough for our king bed, but we knew we could make it work. The upstairs bedrooms seemed perfect for the kids. The room we knew would be Elizabeth's had sweet curves in the ceiling where the room was framed in under the angles of the roof. The back bedroom looked out directly into trees—a perfect place for Sam, the boy who loved to look out on green things, to make his own.

But Sammy had to be convinced. I showed the house to him and he was upset. "Dad, don't buy this house," he pleaded. "It *stinks!*"

I did some checking and realized that the place really was in Montgomery County after all, which meant that the kids would stay in the Takoma Park schools they had enjoyed for the year we'd been living there. We hired our own broker, Patricia, to represent us.

The sellers were elderly brothers and sisters; their father had lived in the place until he died, and they wanted to be rid of it without doing more work. They had homes of their own. The asking price was more than $200,000—low for the neighborhood, but not for a house in such bad shape. I offered $150,000. "Are you sure?" Patricia asked, questioning whether the offer was insulting and might destroy any chance of negotiation. "Please. Try it," I asked. They came back with a counteroffer: $160,000.

Startled by our success, we scrambled to figure out how to pull together a down payment. Our savings were gone, but we did have money in that 401(k), which had been growing since 1986 and had more than $100,000 in it. The last thing I wanted to do was to break into that piggy bank, but the opportunity was too good to pass up. With a little research, I found out it would be expensive money: the government charges a 10 percent penalty for withdrawing money from your 401(k) account before you reach retirement age. But, we agreed, sitting in our sagging rental house a couple of blocks away, we might never catch a deal like this again. We signed the pieces of paper, got together the down payment of $15,000, and bought the little house on Elm.

People in the neighborhood later told me they were furious with us for lowering the average sale price in the neighborhood by so much. Comparable homes nearby were selling for twice as much.

But our neighbors hadn't smelled that refrigerator.

Before we moved in, we found a handyman who worked with us for several weeks to fix the place up a bit and paint the walls. The old bad smells departed. But some problems persisted. The previous owner had been a smoker, and had spent much of his time smoking in the downstairs bathroom. The walls were stained with yellowish tar residue from all those cigarettes. We cleaned and painted. But for the next five years, anytime somebody took a particularly long, hot shower that steamed up the room, the residue would once again seep through the paint. We painted two more times but it still happened; so that sometimes gave the house a kind of *Amityville Horror* sensibility.

The handyman was the kind of guy who, when he did tree work, would send his assistant, Pedro, scurrying up the tree with a roaring chain saw and little protection. I stayed home to watch the work, staring fretfully out the back window at what I was sure would be a sickening plunge, with midair amputation followed by evisceration and a death-ensuring splat for a grand finale.

"If you're going to get scared," Owen chided me, "don't look."

Nothing tragic happened to Pedro. The two men knew their business. And the house shaped up, bit by bit. There were good surprises, too: The woodwork in the living room turned out to be American chestnut, a wood largely wiped out before the turn of the 20th century by a blight. It is rare today. The handsome slate roof, while old, was still in decent shape. We found 1950s-style Formica for the kitchen counters with a boomerang pattern, which made the room silly and glorious.

This house looked like all our dreams.

I had walked my father through when we first bought it, and again after the cleanup was done. He looked at the chestnut bannister and the amazing plaster, the light coming through the newly cleaned windows, and the comfortable proportions of the rooms. "I knew it was a good house," he told me. "I didn't know it was going to be a beautiful house."

Even beautiful houses have problems, of course. Cracks worked their way up the walls and into that beautiful plaster. Eventually we would discover that the foundation was settling poorly, and we'd have to shore up one corner and patch. And the basement, which was only partly finished, got damp after any heavy rain. Water would spill into the utility room down there in the fall through a side door because an outside drain quickly clogged with leaves. Whenever it rained, I would have to step outside in the cold, soaking wet, often in the middle of the night, often in my underwear, to clear leaves away from that drain and prevent the flooding, or at least keep it from getting worse. Over time we would spend large amounts on new drains and waterproofing, and would learn terms like "French drain" and "parging." It was troublesome, but we dearly loved the place. When we needed new rain gutters to draw rainwater away from the house, I sprang for copper. They cost more, but were bigger than the standard six-inch gutters that are extruded from a truck, which meant that they'd catch more. But really, it's that they looked perfect against the slate.

Other neighborhood dads walked by to watch the shiny half rounds being installed with admiration and a kind of gutter lust. Those snazzy, overpriced gutters were my midlife convertible, an extravagance of vanity.

How did we pay for projects to repair our crumbling personal infrastructure? Much of it was possible because of a book I cowrote that came out in 2000.[11] The advance was tens of thousands of dollars, delivered in three installments. And each installment went straight into one of the kids' mouths for orthodontia, into the ground for the foundation repair and waterproofing, or into those gutters. The money didn't lift us out of debt, but it kept our hole (the financial one, not the one that the very expensive workers dug around the house for the French drain and parging) from getting deeper.

And there we lived, cheerily, for five years. Our youngest child, Joseph, was born during our stay on Elm Avenue. The kids turned the house into their playground. One day, Sam and some friends figured out a game: rolling down the stairs in a wire-frame laundry basket. They left a weird pattern of dings in that lovely wood. This initially enraged me—what is this going to do to the resale value?—and later made me laugh. A house is not a Fabergé egg; it gets used.

In 2000, our stay in Takoma Park came to an end. *The New York Times* came calling with the offer of a job writing about technology. It was time to move again. Patricia, the Realtor who had helped us buy the house for $160,000, sold it for $305,000. The buyer really liked those gutters.

Finally, it seemed, we were doing this house thing right. We nearly doubled our money, and made more selling that house than we'd lost on the New York apartment. Its value is still climbing: I just checked Zillow. That little house on Elm is worth more than $700,000 today.

BACK TO NEW YORK—OR, RATHER, NEW JERSEY

The call from the *Times* came as a shock, but a happy one. The technology editor liked my stuff and, over lunch in Washington's Old Ebbitt Grill, asked if I'd like to come work for him. I could not imagine saying no and flew to New York not long after for a gantlet of job interviews.

At the end of the day, I met Joseph Lelyveld, the executive editor. A quietly brilliant man who won the Pulitzer Prize for his reporting in South Africa, he also had a reputation for personal awkwardness, which, I was warned, would make our conversation difficult.

That was not a problem for us. We had a lively conversation. It turned out we both adored Ann Richards, the former Texas governor. I had written my first cover story for *The Texas Observer* about Richards when she was state treasurer. He had gotten to know her on a days-long Texas rafting trip that sounded raucous and hellaciously fun. Somehow, he told me, they'd ended up wearing each other's T-shirts. I've wanted to ask him about that ever since.

When he asked me the interview question I hate the most—what do you see yourself doing in 10 years?—a question that invites you to talk about your desire to run the place someday, I answered honestly. "If I'm lucky? Writing. It's all I've ever wanted to do, and I'm pretty good at it. I think this is the place that can help me get better."

As we were ending the interview, he asked whether I had any questions. I told him that I had no idea how, if I got the job, I could ever afford to live in the New York area again. He listened politely and then gathered up a few real estate sections with recent editions of the column "If You're Thinking of Living In . . ." with descriptions of towns around New York. He smiled and said, "As you're walking out through the newsroom, look around you. All of these people live here."

It was a great pitch, and cleverly elided the fact that most of those people had come to the city years before. If I got the job, we would be trying to enter a hot real estate market.

Kevin, the editor who was trying to hire me, told me that Mr. Lelyveld had enjoyed the interview as much as I had; he offered me the job at 10 percent more than my *Washington Post* salary, with a small signing bonus as a sweetener.

I was torn, and carefully considered whether I could stretch our already-tight budget to meet our new circumstances.

I'm joking! I took the job. Leapt for the job. How could I not? It was *The New York* freaking *Times*—as good as it gets for people like me.

The *NYT* put us up in a hotel in Morristown, New Jersey, while we took a couple of days to look for houses. A relocation specialist helped me figure out that we were likeliest to settle in New Jersey.

What had we learned from our previous homes? A few things: we had to be able to afford the house we were in. The public schools had to be good. And I needed a manageable commute—say, less than 45 minutes each way.

That created a Venn diagram: commute, schools, affordability. It sorted things out for us very quickly: the most likely towns were Millburn, Maplewood, and South Orange. All three sit near a handy commuter train line called the Midtown Direct, and all have well regarded schools.

The relocation specialist set us up with a high-energy broker who was efficient and insistent. We drove around with her for two days; at the end of the first day, having seen a fair number of houses, I felt that there was a problem with our tour. In setting it up, I had told the broker, Arlene, that we were not going to be able to afford a house that cost more than $400,000. But everything she showed us was $400,000 or more.

"John," she said, "you aren't going to be able to get a house that meets your standards in Millburn for less than $400,000."

"Arlene," I replied, "you have no idea how low my standards are."

I asked her to hand me her stack of pages printed out from the Multiple Listing Service and sorted them from least expensive to most expensive. There were a number of places with an asking price under $400,000, and even under $350,000. Each of the houses in our price range turned out to be close to the railroad track for the Midtown Direct—often enough, adjacent to it. For Jeanne and me, the house hunt became a game: nice house, where's the railroad track? Oh, there it is, just over the backyard fence.

The cheapest place in Arlene's stack was an unlovely 1950s split-level on a busy street. The train tracks weren't in the backyard; this time, they were at the top of the street; this house was, literally, on the wrong side of the tracks.

The MLS listing read, "NOT A DRIVE BY! MUST SEE." Yes, that's how unattractive it was, with its bedrooms on three different landings and ugly metal awnings over the windows. But it had a sunny "Florida room," an enclosed porch with big windows (and, unfortunately, signs of water damage to the wood), and a big backyard.

Did I mention the house was painted pink? Pink like Pepto-Bismol? Kids on the block called it the "Barbie House." In the hottest of hot real estate markets, it had gone unbought for about five months. And it was just $327,000—the least expensive place we'd seen in Millburn.

It was, in other words, perfect.

We bought the house and stayed in a corporate apartment for a few extra weeks while workers did the floors and freshened the paint on the walls. And we painted that pink exterior dark blue.

The neighbors dropped by to thank us for the paint job.

We were offered a 15-year mortgage, which allows you to pay down the debt while paying less interest and building equity in the house more quickly. But our rule on mortgages was simple: we wanted the lowest possible monthly payment. We were buying the most house we could and were always financially squeezed. So the 30-year fixed, with its more comfortable payments was, for us, the way to go.

This was the house that would do the most to change our lives for the better. In 2014, after fourteen years there, we decided to sell. As I've mentioned, the move and its timing were Jeanne's idea. She had gotten a cold call from a real estate agent who said inventory was low and that our house might be worth $700,000, more than double what we paid for it. Our youngest, Joseph, was finishing high school; I had expected to sell the next year, once he was off at college. But this was the first hot-ish market after a long lull.

When the real estate broker came to the house, she immediately dropped her estimate to $600,000. It was a big house, but not a charmer. Still, we decided to go ahead. The mortgage and property taxes on the place were costing us more than $2,200 each month. Interest payments on the college loans for our two older kids was about $1,000 each month. There were car payments and the stubborn balance on our credit card, which had been pressed into service to buy a new boiler, among other big-ticket emergencies that we hadn't had the cash for. And, of course, there were little things like groceries and gas. Jeanne had a part-time job with the police department as a crossing guard; it helped, but it wasn't enough. We were in trouble.

"We're drowning," Jeanne told me. She said that she spent her time on the job running the numbers in her head, figuring out which bills could wait and which had to be paid. And it was getting harder to make the numbers line up at the end of each month. She was the one keeping our books; if she thought we were headed for disaster, it was time.

And it sold, after a false start or two. Not for $700,000. Not for $600,000. The ultimate sale price was $525,000, which meant that we had cleared nearly $200,000 over our purchase.

It was a life-changing amount of money. We were able to pay off our part of the kids' college loans. We were able to zero out that red-hot credit card. We were able to make a down payment on a smaller, less-expensive house in a nearby town. For the first time in more than a decade, we were not under crushing financial pressure.

Do you remember that FINRA quiz we both took recently to measure our money sense? Jeanne had groused, "I don't like numbers."

When she finished the quiz, she said triumphantly, "I knew when to sell the house. *That* math, I could do."

But did we sell too soon? Many financial planners and money

journalists say that selling the family home is a step toward an orderly retirement. Holding on to the place until you're ready to stop working, and the profit from selling the manse and downsizing, puts that final bump into the retirement account, ensuring later comfort.

There are other options. Some older homeowners who don't care to move can take advantage of what are called reverse mortgages, which pay you from the equity built up in your home.[12]

But we needed the bump a little sooner than retirement, and it got us out of our deep hole. We hope that when the time comes to sell our current place, we'll pocket a little something on this one, too.

Over a period of about 30 years and four homes, we seem to have made the transition from real estate disaster to relative success. We are capable of learning. I hope you'll profit from our mistakes.

BUYING A HOUSE IN YOUR 20s: NOT IMPOSSIBLE!

Let's get back to the millennials for a bit.

In mid-2017, a 35-year-old Australian real estate developer, Tim Gurner, told *60 Minutes Australia* that the reason young people today can't afford a house is that they are spending too much on trifles: you can't buy a house, he said, "when you're spending $40 a day on smashed avocados and coffees and not working. Of course."[13]

He's basically preaching the value of hard work and frugality and speaking figuratively about avocado toast as an example of profligacy. But he was being a jerk about it. It adds insult to the injury of coming into adulthood during a time of diminished economic expectations. And buying a house costs so, so much more than any lunch, at least outside New York City. And so the Australian developer became the day's Twitter punching bag, and avocado toast jokes ruled the day. One wealth management firm, SoFi, offered people who took out a mortgage with the company during July 2017 a free month's supply of avocado toast.[14]

Avocado toast or not, some millennials are buying homes. In an uncertain economy, and with so many younger people working in the so-called gig economy of freelance work, it's not easy. But at least some of them are finding that it can be done. Here's how two couples did it.

We'll start with my daughter and son-in-law—not just because I love to brag on them, but because they did a number of things right. Elizabeth and Matt bought a terrific house in Texas a couple of years ago. Jeanne and I have watched their sure-footed progress in the world with no small amount of wonder. They graduated from UT law school with less than half of the law school debt they'd have piled up at similarly ranked schools elsewhere. It's no longer cheap, but it's still a bargain, so they basically got two degrees for the price of one. Matt then got a job with a small firm specializing in education law, and Elizabeth struck out on her own in family law. Elizabeth built her practice by offering low hourly rates and taking on court-appointed work. The Lone Star State appoints lawyers in cases involving the potential termination of child custody rights, so she signed up in two counties for court-appointed work; her language skills put her on additional lists for Spanish speakers, as well.

Their income wasn't at the kind of stratospheric levels that lawyers pull down at those famous white-shoe law firms, but their combined earnings kept them comfortable. They were careful with their money, starting out in cheap apartments (starting at $450 a month for a cracker box so tiny that they couldn't both comfortably stand in the kitchen at the same time) and moving to progressively larger rentals. They limited their debt, saved money, and put off having kids. They needed two cars, but got one of them from us as a hand-me-down, so they were making only one payment. They have one credit card between them, for emergencies; the credit limit is $1,000—"the lowest credit limit they would give me," Matt said.

By 2015, they decided it was time to buy a house, partly because they knew they wanted to have kids. So Matt started studying up, spending what he told me was "some crazy number of hours" using the real estate site Redfin to understand the Austin-area real estate market. They realized pretty quickly that were priced out of central Austin, and Matt focused on communities somewhat north of town. "We knew it was going to be a big purchase, the biggest purchase we've made," Matt told me. "We allowed ourselves to get picky about stuff like that."

They started talking to mortgage brokers about how much house they would be able to afford—and about the fact that banks would take only Matt's income into account, since Elizabeth did not yet have the two years of self-employment that banks want to see before considering her income.

A mortgage officer with a local credit union helped Matt figure out how to restructure his personal debt to make himself a more attractive borrower. "I was right at the line for what they could approve," he said. By lengthening the repayment plan on his student loans from 10 years to 20, Matt lowered his monthly bill, and his income-to-debt ratio came closer to what banks like to see.

One day, Matt told me, he saw a house pop up on Redfin that looked just about perfect: four bedrooms, built in 2003, and not much more than $200,000. He told his boss about it and joked that it would probably be sold by the end of the day. "Why don't you go check it out?" the boss said. "Go ahead, take the rest of the afternoon off."

Matt contacted a Realtor through the site and arranged a visit. He grabbed Elizabeth. And he also emailed the listing to the mortgage officer he'd been dealing with to see if they could get approved for that house. By the time they drove up to the curb, they had his approval in hand.

And they loved the house. It had high ceilings. And storage space! They hired the Realtor who showed them the place on the spot and had her make a bid. Thanks to Elizabeth's savings from work, they were able to make a down payment of 20 percent, which sweetened their offer and reduced the amount they would have to borrow. A few days later, to their shock, the seller chose their bid over several others.

They had worked toward the moment deliberately, Elizabeth told me: "We've been really, really careful every step of the way." The result was that they could move quickly when the time came. Matt said, "Our patience allowed us to pull the trigger when we were where we needed to be."

It's a great house to raise their baby, Robin, in. I only wish we'd been as smart at their age.

==

After talking with Elizabeth and Matt, I checked in with another young couple, Jason Boyle and Leah Spinrad-Boyle, who bought their first house in Portland, Maine, in 2016. Jeanne and I are friends with her parents, and have known Leah since she was a baby.

During most of their years together, neither Leah nor Jason had worked at a traditional job. Like a lot of millennials, they were proud participants in the gig economy: Jason took on lucrative freelance work as a web developer, and Leah as a massage therapist. They were taking part in an enormous realignment of the world economy, with fewer people in conventional full-time jobs and more people working freelance gigs. A 2016 report by the consultancy McKinsey & Company found that what they called "independent workers" make up 20 to 30 percent of the working age population in the United States, with more than half of those under the age of 25 engaged in such jobs.[15]

Jason and Leah were not going to impress a bank as great bets to get a mortgage, they knew. But when they decided that they wanted to start having kids, they realized that they needed two things: health insurance and a house.

Leah studied up on what would make them attractive candidates for a lender, sitting down with a mortgage banker who walked her through the process used to evaluate applicants. She came came to understand that the most direct path to reaching their goal would be to buckle down to straight jobs. Full-time employment, steady paycheck, and all the things that make bankers smile—with employer-provided health insurance as a bonus. "We could have bought a house with our self-employment arrangement," Leah said, "but it would have taken two years of planning and very steady income, and we didn't want to do that." So she got a job as a receptionist at a beauty salon. Jason found a staff job as a web developer that allowed him to work at home. It was not a simple decision, Leah recalled. Instead, it was a tradeoff: "You have to give up some freedom. But you can't get these things that are really hard to accomplish if you don't have a job."

They also tweaked their taxes, declaring fewer deductions so that their combined income would look larger to a mortgage lender taking a cursory look. And it helps that their credit record was flawless. "We have and always have had really amazing credit scores," Leah told me; they pay off their credit card balance every month, and follow the credit card rule of thumb of keeping their "utilization ratio"—the balance of debt to the capacity of the cards at any given time—below 30 percent.[16] She noted with pride that "being a geek about our finances all the time" allowed them to pay for their wedding in cash. Those good financial habits, she said, "set us apart from a lot of the people I know who don't do that, or don't know."

With clean credit and two full-time jobs, they started looking at the end of 2015. "We bought a house, almost immediately," Leah said.

Their daughter, Mae, is ADORABLE.

PUNCH LIST

BUYING A HOME

Don't make the mistakes we made when buying a home! Here's how to get started, whether you're just starting out in life or looking for your next place. Before you even begin looking for your dream house—or condo, or apartment—make sure your financial house is in order. Buying a house and grabbing that part of the American dream is beyond the abilities of an increasing number of Americans. But if you run the numbers and look at what's out there, you might find yourself in a position to buy. How?

1) **Be like Leah and Jason.** Build up your savings for that down payment. The more you can pay up front, the better your mortgage terms.

- Clean up your credit score. You can check your score, also known as FICO, through any of the three major agencies, Experian,[17] Equifax,[18] and TransUnion,[19] or for all three through MyFICO.com.[20] Contact the agencies to correct any inaccurate information that might hold you back.
- Use credit cards sparingly and pay them off each month.
- Don't max out your cards, even if you can pay them off. The utilization rate on credit cards is a big factor in determining your credit score, according to the credit reporting agency Experian. According to the company's explanation, it can affect "up to 30% of a credit score (which makes them among the more influential factors), depending on the scoring model being used.[21]

2) **If you are in your 20s or early 30s,** you might have to make some adjustments to look good to lenders.

- If you don't have a full-time job, do you have two years of provable income to fall back on? If not, you might have to wait or join the ranks of wage slaves.
- Work with a mortgage broker or banker to see what you can do to make yourself more attractive as a borrower, including finding out

whether restructuring the payment schedule on your college loans will help.

3) **Use apps.** You can get a wealth of information on apps and websites like Zillow, Trulia, and Redfin. These sites can help you find the houses, condos, and apartments in the towns and neighborhoods you want and at the price you can afford. The Internet is also full of house affordability calculators—like these at Zillow,[22] Bankrate,[23] and NerdWallet.[24]

4) **Find help.** Seek out an experienced real estate broker who knows the neighborhoods you're looking in. You can take your list of likely prospects to the broker for advice; your broker can deal with the seller's broker, smoothing over problems you might have in getting to an agreement on the sale. Yes, you can save money by working directly with a seller doing a for-sale-by-owner deal, and there are brokers who are pretty useless. So ask around; it pays to use an expert.

5) **Dig!** Do your research. As you begin to focus on neighborhoods, use your apps to check the issues like local crime rates and the quality of the schools if you've got kids. Along with the sketches of schools available on most real estate apps, you can dig deeper at sites like NCES.ed.gov and greatschools.org. Even if you don't have kids, you'll want to know if the neighborhood has the kind of schools that enhance a home's resale value. Most real estate apps provide basic information on both, but there's detailed local crime information at sites like crimereports.com.

6) **See yourself there.** If you think you've found a place, take a moment to try thinking of it as a home—not an investment, though it will be that as well. Get a feel for what it will be like to live there. Anything you notice that seems like it could be a problem—a damp spot on the ceiling, that funky smell in the basement—is a harbinger. Don't let your emotions run away with you or be swayed by a broker's pressure to buy something quickly. Unless the local real estate market is so hot that bidding wars are turning into fistfights, you can afford to be picky. And remember: adorableness is overrated. The least attractive house in a promising neighborhood

is a better bet over time than the best house in an area headed downhill.

7) **Dig even deeper.** Take your research further. Strike up a conversation with the prospective neighbors about how they feel about the neighborhood: What do they think of the schools? How's the commute? Any convenient mass transit out there? More locally, is there a problem house on the block that they wish they could get people out of? It might not be as horrifying as having a drug dealer or meth lab a few doors down—maybe it's just hard partiers or a fraternity chapter. Maybe the neighborhood is prone to flooding. Know the block.

Visit the house at different times, day and night—is the street used as a shortcut for morning traffic? Is there a music studio next door? An endlessly barking dog? If these things will be a problem but you still want the house, at least you're going in with your eyes open.

8) **Insure it.** Once you've bought it, protect it! In theory, it's legal to own a home without insuring it. In practice, your mortgage lender will probably require you to get homeowner's insurance. And it's a good idea. While you're at it, look into flood insurance, as well. Most of it is obtained through the National Flood Insurance Program, though private insurers can sell the policies. You need to know if you are in a floodplain and where flooding has occurred near you in the past. The insurance tends to be cheap: as little as several hundred dollars a year. Even if the house has never flooded, with climate change increasing the intensity of big rain events, and with real estate development making it harder for water to find open land to absorb it, flooding has become a more pressing risk for increasing numbers of homeowners.

6

BANKRUPTCY

IT WAS APRIL 1996, and a friendly lawyer was telling me that I needed to file for bankruptcy. Stop making your mortgage payments, he said. Hide assets by living on cash. "Don't keep any money in your name."

I told you things got bad. We were at the edge of the cliff.

Still, the lawyer told me not to beat myself up over it. He added, "These days, there's no embarrassment" to file. "It's a business decision." All kinds of people, at all levels of income, declare bankruptcy when their debts grow beyond their ability to pay. Even Donald Trump's businesses have done it—six times![1]

Who hasn't considered bankruptcy after getting into a financial squeeze? What if getting your financial life in order means starting over?

There's definitely an allure to bankruptcy: the potential to get out from under seemingly insoluble money woes. Nearly 820,000 people and businesses filed for bankruptcy protection in the 12-month period ending June 2016, down from a peak of 1.6 million in the same reporting period ending in 2010, at the top of the wave of bankruptcies generated by the Great Recession.[2] The reduction is good news—except that 820,000 is still an awfully big number.

If you're in financial trouble, should you look into bankruptcy? It's not for everyone, as the next pages will show. The basic rule for judging whether you are a candidate for bankruptcy is whether it's become impossible to pay the money back. As with so many things in the personal finance world, there's a rule of thumb: if the debts add up to more than half your annual income and you can't see a way to pay those debts down within five years, you should strongly consider filing.

People get overwhelmed with debt for many reasons. The largest single factor is medical bills—and you'll read more about that in the upcoming chapter on medical disasters. In our case, it was that real estate mess we'd gotten ourselves into with the New York apartment.

OUR NEAR BANKRUPTCY

Our own brush with bankruptcy began in the spring of 1996, after we bought the little house in Takoma Park, Maryland. Our mortgage payments were now higher than the rent we'd been paying around the corner. Two of our kids needed braces. And we were still, yes, paying the mortgage and maintenance on the co-op in New York with no rent coming in. The last tenants had left the place a wreck, a broker told me; just getting it into shape to show prospective renters would cost nearly $2,000, with no guarantee that the next tenant wouldn't stiff us. Still, we got it done and continued to show the place for sale. The bank that held the mortgage told me they would be willing to work with a short sale—selling the apartment for somewhat less than the amount owed. The seller gets out of the mortgage squeeze, the buyer gets a bargain, and the bank doesn't have to deal with a default. But we got no takers. Not only was New York City in a housing slump, our broker explained, the problem I've mentioned before—relatively few of the apartments in the building had actually been sold—meant that even if someone was interested in the place, no bank would lend the money to buy it.

So we circled back to our earlier discussion about how to get out from under the apartment in New York. That's when I spoke with that lawyer at a big firm in New York City. Initially, he held out hope that we might convince the bank to take back the apartment. He sent letters

THE ALLURE OF BANKRUPTCY, AND WHY IT MIGHT BE A BAD IDEA

If you think you are headed toward bankruptcy, get professional advice. Unless your situation is very simple (and whose is?), you will want to find a lawyer, at least for an initial consultation. If you are a committed do-it-yourselfer, you can find guides at sites like nolo.com,[3] but filing for bankruptcy is a lot more complicated than simply writing up some paperwork.

For this kind of work, you want someone who really knows the field, so go with a lawyer whose practice is focused on bankruptcy. Get referrals from family, friends, coworkers, or other lawyers you might have hired for other legal issues. Some employers offer legal services as a perk. You can also find bankruptcy attorneys through the National Association of Consumer Bankruptcy Attorneys website, nacba.org,[4] and local legal associations, though the sites don't provide the kind of insight that a personal referral can.

Once you find someone, you'll probably get asked questions to determine whether there are ways to dig yourself out of your financial problems without taking the big step. Trying to talk people out of using their services might sound like a bad business model for the lawyer, but it's based on sound thinking. The repercussions of filing for bankruptcy are enormous, and not just the humiliation you are likely to feel. Beyond that, the black mark of bankruptcy is going to be on your credit report for up to 10 years. Your credit cards will go away, and you won't qualify for new credit for anywhere from one to three years. The new credit cards will probably come with punishingly high interest rates. A new mortgage? Good luck with that. There are also kinds of debt you would not be able to get rid of through bankruptcy. Student loan debt will stay with you, as will any duty to pay child support or alimony. In other words, bankruptcy is no cure-all.

When individuals file for bankruptcy, they have three ways to go: Chapter 7, Chapter 11, or Chapter 13. Chapter 7 is the most common kind of filing, since it really does clean the slate for people under a big debt burden. It doesn't require you to work out a schedule of repayment to your creditors, as Chapter 13 does. Filing under Chapter 7 can mean the liquidation of your assets—and in some cases and in some states, that includes your home. If you are in a truly deep financial mess, of course, you could well lose your home in foreclosure anyway, regardless of what occurs in the bankruptcy, but a lawyer can help you understand issues like the homestead exemption, which can protect your primary residence but which varies from state to state. Chapter 11, more common for businesses than for individuals, applies to people and businesses that have assets but no income.[5] (In the 12-month period ending September 30, 2017, Americans filed about 487,000 Chapter 7 petitions, 297,000 Chapter 13 petitions, and 7,000 Chapter 11 petitions.)[6]

to the bank offering various arrangements. Each letter cost us hundreds of dollars, and each of them got us the same answer: no. The bank, he told me, was dealing with too many bad loans already and was overwhelmed. It was a pattern that would become even more common in the financial crisis that would occur a decade later: banks found it easier to say no and foreclose than to negotiate.

In April, the lawyer and I had a sobering conversation on the phone. He didn't see the negotiations with the bank going anywhere, and so he gave me the bankruptcy talk.

"That's the only way to get rid of this problem," he insisted, and told me it was time for me to find a bankruptcy expert in Maryland. That lawyer, he said, would be able to tell me about the state's homestead exemption and what it would mean for us.

So I did call a local bankruptcy lawyer, someone who came highly recommended from a colleague at the *Post* who covered legal issues. The lawyer told me in the most polite way possible that she specialized in bankruptcies of people with high net worth, and we did not have enough assets for us to meet the threshold for her services.

Now, that stung: *We didn't even have enough money to fail in her league.*

That lawyer did have some good advice for us, however. She said she was not surprised that negotiating with the bank while we were still paying had not worked. But if we walked away from the mortgage and waited until the bank sued us, we might have a better chance of avoiding bankruptcy by getting the bank to take the apartment back and then having us pay the difference between the value of the property and what we still owed on the mortgage. We would execute, in other words, what she told us was a "deed in lieu of foreclosure." The bank would get the apartment; we would get our freedom and negotiate paying the difference between the market value of the apartment and the remaining mortgage. Why would they take a different position then? I asked; what would have changed? "At that point," she said, "you have an intelligent person to talk to: the lawyer."

In any case, she added, if that didn't work, we could file for bankruptcy, "which might ultimately be cheaper."

Going beyond the advice, she offered sympathy. "It's very nerve-wracking having this hanging over your head," she said. "But you should let it ride for now."

She referred me to another attorney, one who was very good and less, um, upscale.

I had my first conversation with the lawyer, Gregory Johnson, over the phone in May, and he tried to talk me down from the state of anxious misery I'd been living in. First of all, he said, the nice lawyer in New York was wrong: there was no reason to seek bankruptcy protection yet. "I don't see any reason to file before the fact." Instead, he, too, advised me, "Just quit paying the debt—see what happens."

We did. And what happened was that by the end of 1996, the bank foreclosed on the apartment. We had lost it.

It wasn't over, but the end had begun. The bank had the apartment, but it could still sue us for what is called a "deficiency judgment" if it sold the apartment for less than we still owed. I called Johnson, who again counseled me to sit tight.

Then, one day in the spring of 1997, Jeanne called with an anxious edge in her voice. A company in Dallas that we'd never heard of had written to say that we owed them $40,634. According to the letter, she said, "We have 30 days to pay up or they will take legal action against us."

It sounded, again, like bankruptcy time. "We don't have that kind of money," she said. "We've got to file now."

In a panic, I called Johnson. And once again, he calmly talked me down. These were debt collectors, he explained, and this is how they work: they buy debts like ours at a steep discount. They could insist that we were legally obligated to pay the full amount, but these agencies were generally willing to make a deal and accept a lower offer—25 cents on the dollar, or even less. "If they buy it for 10 cents on the dollar, all they're trying to do is make sure they get 11 cents on the dollar," he said. "Try finagling."

I called the collection company and bargained as hard as I could, making a counteroffer and trying to sound them out about how much they would accept. The people I spoke with were polite and professional, though I figure I'd have heard a different tone if I'd said we could pay nothing. Within a few weeks, Jeanne called me to read another letter from the debt collectors: they had agreed to accept $12,000 in cash, or more if we wanted to stretch out payments. "It's stupid not to take it," she said.

We didn't have that kind of cash, but my folks agreed to a loan so that we could pay. (Remember? They're saints.)

And it was over.

Well, emotionally, it was not over. My guts had been churning for months over the various ways that this could still go wrong. I had lost sleep, and lost a lot of pride. I also lost the first home I had ever bought. I had learned a lot about shame.

On the other hand, Jeanne and I had not ended up filing for bankruptcy. Johnson had steered us through the process in a way that left us with the default but no other damage.

And here's the truly amazing thing:

He hadn't asked us for a dime.

He and I had handled all these conversations informally, on the phone. We hadn't even met face-to-face. I'd asked him a couple of times when I should pay him, and how much; he'd told me that we'd get to that if we had to file for bankruptcy. At the end of April 1997, after we had wrapped up our business, I asked him again to let me pay him for what seemed to me the most valuable advice I'd ever gotten. Again, Johnson declined. He hadn't done that much, he said, just guided me without getting directly involved or filing any papers on our behalf; he said he didn't charge for just talking on the phone.

To this day, Jeanne calls him "the angel."

A few months ago, I wrote to Gregory Johnson and told him about the book. "Part of telling our story will be our most grim financial moment: losing the apartment and worrying about bankruptcy, and how you helped us shoot the rapids, miss the rocks, and get safely to shore," I wrote. "Most of all, I'd just like to get you on the phone again so that I can thank you."

He wrote back, saying he'd be happy to talk. He also said he had discussed my email with a client "who has been having a pretty rough go at it financially, and he was truly inspired by your comments," he said. The client "relayed a quote from Maya Angelou which said, 'People may not remember what you say, but they will never forget how you made them feel.'

"So you see, even though you have not finished your book, you are already helping others with their finances, not by what you are telling them, but by the way your words are helping to make them feel."

When I got him on the phone, he said that our conversations had not stayed with him as "a major, memorable kind of thing." In fact, I got the impression he didn't remember me at all.

He also explained something that I'd been wondering about for years: why didn't the mortgage default show up as such on our credit reports after losing the apartment? As it turned out, our credit rating barely suffered.

He explained that New York's crazy real estate market saved us. NYC, uniquely, has vast numbers of co-op apartments instead of the condos that are prevalent in other cities. And co-op mortgages are weird. Buying a co-op doesn't mean you own real estate; instead it involves buying shares in a corporation that gives you the right to lease the apartment. A foreclosure on a standard mortgage would have stained our credit record, but this didn't have the same effect. The fact that we satisfied the creditors ended the matter.

What Jeanne and I had gone through, he had seen many times, and he understood our anxiety over those months. "It's like the horror movies," he said; the biggest fear comes from anticipation. "Once you see the monster coming around the corner, it's not so bad." That's why he had told us to get through this calmly; he said: "The worst-case scenarios rarely happen in life."

Still an angel.

PUNCH LIST

IF YOU ARE THINKING IT MIGHT BE TIME TO FILE FOR BANKRUPTCY

Take a deep breath. Whatever you may have heard, it is neither simple nor easy. So here's a (very) brief punch list for figuring out your next steps.

1) **Learn bankruptcy fundamentals.** For a deeper look than this chapter provides, go to the website of the federal courts bankruptcy page.[7] It includes a link to a thorough description of the kinds of bankruptcy and the process involved.[8]

2) **Talk to a bankruptcy lawyer!** There could be alternatives you haven't considered, and you may not have a sense of how hard life after bankruptcy can be. A good bankruptcy lawyer can help you with the process, or talk you away from the ledge. As always, the best legal referrals come from people whose judgment you trust— family, friends, coworkers. You probably know someone who has been through the process; ask about their experience and about whether they would recommend their lawyer.

3) **If you do file, don't be cute.** Don't run up those cards in the belief you won't have to pay. Any unusual spending will be scrutinized by your creditors and the court. You could end up having to pay back all that last-minute spending. Similarly, don't transfer assets to relatives or friends to evade the jurisdiction of the court. Ask your lawyer about what happens if you are found to be committing fraud. It's not good.

4) **Once you have filed, don't go back into the cycle.** If you do go through the bankruptcy process, you'll have been given a fresh chance. Don't mess it up; if your debt was the product of unwise spending, this is the chance to change the habits that got you into financial trouble. A financial planner can help you rebuild.

7

THE KIDS

As he walked across Rockefeller Plaza, he thought wryly of the days when he and Betsy had assured each other that money didn't matter. They had told each other that when they were married before the war, and during the war they had repeated it in long letters. "The important thing is to find a kind of work you really like, and something that is useful," Betsy had written him. "The money doesn't matter."

The hell with that, he thought. The real trouble is that up to now we've been kidding ourselves. We might as well admit that what we want is a big house and a new car and trips to Florida in the winter, and plenty of life insurance. When you come right down to it, a man with three children has no damn right to say that money doesn't matter.

—SLOAN WILSON, *THE MAN IN THE GRAY FLANNEL SUIT*

MONEY DOES MATTER, all right.

And having three children, as we do, does cost money—along with everything else that costs so much in our lives. There's the house, the food. Medical costs. Taxes.

But of these things, children add many costs, expected and unexpected. How could that graphing calculator required for the totally ordinary math class at the high school possibly cost $80? Don't we still have the $80 graphing calculator the last kid used in that same class? What do you mean, they changed the requirements?

Oh, man. Clothes. Computers. Sports equipment. Emergency room visits. College. It does pile up.

To be precise, it piles up to $233,610.

That is the estimate of the U.S. Department of Agriculture, which has produced regular reports on the cost of raising children since 1960. And that very precise number is what the Agriculture folks came up with in their 2017 report, based on the estimated expenses for a middle-income family (that's making between $59,200 and $107,400 a year before taxes) with two kids, from birth to the age of 17.[1]

It breaks down to nearly $13,000 a year, which makes the matter of the graphing calculator look kind of picayune. The estimates, based on statistics from 2015, varied based on family income (parents making more than $107,000 spent about twice as much as those making less than $59,200) and also from place to place. Married couples in the urban Northeast (that's us!) have the highest estimated costs, while those in the urban and rural Midwest had the lowest.

Bear with me for just a little more statistical fun: how the money is distributed. The kid's share of housing costs comes in at 29 percent of the total; food makes up 18 percent. For couples with kids who have to spend money on child care and education, that comes to 16 percent. And as you would expect, the cost varies greatly depending on household income and the number of family members. Families with one kid spend, on average, 27 percent more; families with more than two kids spend 24 percent less per child. Raising a child will only get more expensive: the report states that a child born in 2015 to a middle-income family will cost an average of $284,570. The children in the highest-income group will cost an estimated $454,770. The USDA even has an online calculator for figuring out the cost of raising your own child— ostensibly so that you can plan your expenses, but I've gotta believe it's also because you can hold the sum over your kids' heads in arguments about their allowances and whether they should have their own cars.[2]

Because the USDA report stops counting parental expenditures at the age of 17, it doesn't cover the scariest cost of all: college. For that one, you go to the College Board, which tells us that in the 2016–17 academic year, going to a four-year public college and paying in-state tuition and fees will cost $9,650; total cost of enrollment is $20,090. At private colleges, the tuition and fees run an average of $33,480, and the total cost of attendance hits $45,370. These are averages. While the median cost of private school education is $35,020, 10 percent of those students go to schools that cost less than $12,000, and 7 percent go to schools that charge $51,000 or more. Many students get a discounted rate. In the 2015–16 academic year, 401 private colleges in a survey reduced nearly half of the tuition for freshmen with grants-based financial aid.[3] But even with discounts, these sums are jaw-dropping.[4]

And did I mention that a lot of us help our kids out with extra cash after college?

Even before then, though, there are plenty of other costs outside the federal estimate. Don't forget those supposedly optional expenses that can be so important, like summer camp for the kids. The USDA report doesn't mention camp. Jeanne and I became big believers in the great things that the right camps do for kids in terms of self-reliance, confidence building, and just plain fun. But . . . spendy!

And that's why summer is a looming horror for many of us parents: we don't know how we will possibly pay for it. A 2014 survey for American Express estimated that nearly nine out of ten parents expect to pay an average of $958 on each of their kids during the summer. The survey found that 77 percent of them were taking day trips costing nearly $300 in 2014, compared with a cost of just over $200 in 2012. A quarter of parents would be sending kids to sleepaway camp with an average cost of $234 per kid in 2014.[5]

I have no idea what planet these summer camps could be found on, but they sure didn't reflect what we were paying for our kids' sleepaway camps. Campexperts.com, a clearinghouse for information on camps, estimates that traditional sleepaway camps cost from $450 to more than $1,000 per week.[6] The American Camp Association says the average cost is more than $630 per week, and notes that it can be $2,000 or more.[7] I used to talk with a boss of mine about French Woods, the incredible theater camp in upstate New York that did so much for our youngest, Joseph, and which was his daughters' camp as well. The boss, Adam, said, "I guess you did what I did: counted the bunks, multiplied that by the camp costs, and then counted up the number of cabins." Well, no, I didn't, because (as this book has made painfully clear) I'm not great with numbers. But the vastness of the amount of money sloshing around was clear even to a financial illiterate like me. The place has five theaters and a 12,000-square-foot circus pavilion with trapezes, for Pete's sake.

And camps are getting even more expensive. In a 2013 article in *Slate*, Matthew Yglesias noted that a $690-per-week figure often cited from the American Camp Association was a 74 percent jump from 2005's $397 per week. Gross domestic product rose just 24 percent in that time. "In other words, if these alarming spending trends continue, summer camp is going to end up swallowing the entire American economy in the long run."[8] He was kidding! But his serious point was that parents will spend ridiculous amounts of money on their kids, and don't necessarily look for discounts.

So there we were, squeezed for cash but wanting to give our kids the benefits of camp.

Other people make family vacations a top priority, and I have no argument with their approach; it's just not the way we did it. Wendell Jamieson, the Metro editor of the *Times*, splurged on a big family vacation every April during their kids' teen years. Wendell said that for these trips—four to Europe, one to Hawaii, one to the West Coast, he and his wife "went all in," which meant "dipping into the home equity account some years, and letting my American Express travel account grow alarmingly." But he felt that they had a window, he said, in which the kids "would be old enough to get a lot out of these journeys, and be fully mobile, yet young enough that they enjoyed spending time with us."[9]

They sound like great trips.

"WE HAVE ENOUGH MONEY"

When it came to trying to economize, we weren't above lying to the kids occasionally. When we moved to New Jersey, we didn't subscribe to cable television. In Takoma Park we'd watched so much Nickelodeon that we could sing all the words to the *SpongeBob SquarePants* theme. After the move, we simply didn't sign up for cable, saving more than a hundred bucks a month. We told the kids that the neighborhood we'd moved to didn't have cable. Internet? We couldn't do without that. But we could live a SpongeBob-free life.

Kids want to know where their family stands. Are we rich? Are we poor? We always told them, "We have enough money." It wasn't completely true, but it wasn't wrong, either.

Even so, life throws things at us that we aren't prepared for. At one point in our life in New Jersey, a dentist told us that Joseph's canine teeth were not coming in properly. His little mouth was too crowded, and the canines were impacted, trapped above the other teeth. An oral surgeon told us he would have to expose the teeth and bracket them, which is about as horrifying as it sounds. Ultimately, tiny chains and rubber bands are involved, and the teeth are gradually coaxed down into place.

Then came the bad news: my insurance plan said it would not pay for the procedure, which they said was not covered. Apparently, the program considered this method of getting the canines to come down to be an unnecessarily expensive alternative to simply pulling some of Joseph's teeth to make room. If we wanted the more complicated procedure—one that our orthodontist and oral surgeon had convinced us was preferable—we'd have to come up with a few thousand dollars on our own.

We could have put the surgery on a credit card, but the balance on the one credit card we use was already too high for comfort. I scanned all the assets we had and remembered one: my *New York Times* stock.

Like many companies, the *Times* had long offered employees shares of stock at reduced prices—about 15 percent less than the market price. A friend advised me to get into the employee stock plan the moment I could: the discount was helpful, and the stock almost inevitably rose. Colleagues had paid for their kids' college years largely out of the appreciated value of their *Times* stock.

So I bought in early, again with the money flowing directly and relatively painlessly from my paychecks. The shares we bought were in the $40 to $50 range, and we hoped for the best. Then the Internet happened, ad sales plummeted, and newspaper stock prices followed that sickening trajectory.

This is my timing; this is my life. Money decisions that are good for others tend to go badly for us. Now it was March of 2009, and the price of a share, of which I owned several hundred, was $4.01, less than a tenth of what I'd paid for it.

But it was money, and it was there. I told the brokerage that handled transactions to sell it if it rose to a price of five dollars a share. It did, and we were able to pay for the surgery.

At the moment, the stock is trading at better than $14 a share. I appear to have sold, predictably, very close to the bottom. But Joe's teeth look great.

Our children, who, for the most part, are just plain wonderful, understood the notion that there were things we could not buy. We would turn ourselves inside out to make sure they had the things they truly needed, but they had grown accustomed to hearing "we can't afford that."

So how much should we do for our kids? Many financial sages advise parents not to support their children in adulthood, or even to help them pay their college debt unless they've already provided for their own retirement. And it does make sense to advise people not to hollow out their retirement funds to get their adult children out of debt, lending them money for homes they can't afford and to start businesses that have little prospect of success, even if they plead.

Financial journalists and money advisers put it this way, repeatedly: just as the flight attendant tells you to put your own oxygen mask on before putting one on a child, you have to make sure that your retirement is taken care of before dealing with your kids' problems. They tell horror stories of parents who bankrupted themselves helping their kids and forgetting this one basic truth: you can get a loan for college, but you can't get a loan for retirement. Besides, the financial journalists say, wagging their fingers, you don't want to teach your children to be dependent, do you?[10]

That's not the way most people do it, of course. A survey conducted in 2011 for the National Endowment for Financial Education found that 59 percent of parents provide support to adult children between the ages of 18 and 39.[11] About half of those parents provide housing or help with living expenses. These decisions can cause problems for the parents, the survey showed: 26 percent of them took on additional debt to help the kids, while 13 percent said that they delayed life events such as getting married, taking a vacation, or buying a home. Seven percent said they delayed retirement.

We help, too. While we haven't bankrupted ourselves for our kids, and we have kept our contributions steady going into our 401(k), we can't imagine not helping them with their college costs, even after they've graduated. Jeanne frequently pops a payment over to one of the kids' college lenders for the loans taken out in their names, trying to take a little of the burden off them and to let them know we've still got their back.

They remember our lie about not having cable. They were no more convinced of it than they were in earlier years about the tooth fairy, but they have always been good enough to play along. And they knew the deeper truth: there was only so much we could pay for. But no matter what, we were going to help them get through college.

Paying for college can be as big a financial obligation as buying a house. And it's been a national financial mess that burdens families and young people with mountains of debt. We went through the process with three kids, and it put us under a mountain of financial strain. But . . .

We were not alone.

Paying for college, saving for college, and worrying about how any of it can possibly happen loom over anyone raising children. Jeanne and I would joke about putting a toy wrench instead of picture books in Elizabeth's hands when she was a toddler. "No book! Wrench! Plumber!"

But we also knew that a college education is not something that pays off just in terms of increased income over a lifetime, as the Pew Research Center has found.[12] In a 2014 report, the organization said that the median monthly earnings of young adults with a bachelor's degree was $3,836 in 2009 (the most recent year available at the time of the report), a 13 percent increase from 1984. In the same amount of time, the median income of young adults with less than a college degree has declined.

Jeanne and I both feel that we benefited from the mental flexibility that comes with a liberal arts education—supposedly useless, but anything but—and we wanted to be sure our kids had that same opportunity we'd had to become lifelong learners. So we knew that we would be paying large for the kids to get college degrees. And dreaded it, as we have dreaded all financial decisions.

COLLEGE SAVINGS: THE HARD SELL

Back when the kids were little, I attended a seminar on saving for college. The financial adviser presenting the seminar was offering his services, if those of us attending wanted to go deeper.

Jeanne and I decided to meet with the adviser. He talked largely about himself, and about his son who was going to a school that was actually an elite tennis academy. It seemed bizarre to us, but was something along the lines of what we would eventually read about in David Foster Wallace's *Infinite Jest*. The adviser suggested that, rather than simply arranging our college funds through him, we turn our entire 401(k) over to him for investment vehicles that he said consistently outperformed the market. He had slick handouts that showed this was true, though of course past performance is no guarantee of future results, but, you know, these funds are great. He came up with a rather complicated investment fund that acted like an annuity we could use to save for the kids' college, one for each child. We needed to start out with a set amount in these investment funds for the kids and to continue making contributions into them. We could never lose what we put into these funds, but they would grow in value, he insisted. When the kids got to college, he said, we could take out college loans and draw down the loan payments from the annuity, so they wouldn't be a burden on our cash flow. In the meantime—and this, he said, was the beautiful thing—these special instruments would not have to be declared on the main financial aid form used by schools, so our income would appear to be lower and we would qualify for more financial aid.

Or so his spiel went.

Colleges, you see, want proof of your income through a form, the Free Application for Federal Student Aid, which goes by the unappealing acronym FAFSA. Once you fill that out, the government looks at the cost of attending the college you are applying to, and compares that with your income as declared on the FAFSA. The resulting number is your "expected family contribution"—that is, how much the government thinks you can afford to pay for college.[13] The difference between your expected family contribution and the cost of attendance is the amount, ideally, that the school will use to reduce your tuition. (The Department of Education, which administers the FAFSA, can help you roughly predict what mix of government aid will be available to you through a form called the FAFSA4caster.)[14]

Hiding the assets, the logic meant, would mean a smaller expected family contribution and lower payments.

It seemed a little sleazy to us, but what did we know? He seemed to have a grasp of the ins and outs of college financial aid and suggested that this was the way all the smart people did it. We did buy the annuities from him, one for each child. We made regular contributions to the funds through automatic payroll deductions.

The financial genius's advice all turned out to be laughably off-base. When the time came, the supposedly shielded assets did nothing to help us. We had saved some money for college, which is good. We had also paid a percentage of those investments to him as fees, which was also good—at least for him.

Here's what went wrong. For one thing, if we'd gone for a fancy school, it would have required a financial aid form that does require the annuities to be declared. Maybe. My income was pretty good, even though living in New Jersey meant that my expenses were high enough that my take-home pay was meager. For most schools, my income disqualified us for quite a bit of financial aid, though we hoped that our expected family contribution, determined from the FAFSA, should have reduced our tuition by something like $10,000 a year.

But here's the part they don't tell you until you show up for orientation, and the peppy orientation advisers take the kids into one room to talk about how fantastic the school is going to be, and the parents are taken into another room to hear a grim lecture from the financial aid office. And on a lovely day in Ann Arbor, where my daughter had been accepted at the University of Michigan (Go, Blue!), I heard the lecture for the first time, and it hit me like a gut punch:

If you're coming in from out of state, you can kiss all that expected-family-contribution stuff goodbye. In that parent-orientation seminar, what they told us is that they meet the need of in-state students with financial aid. They don't do it for out-of-state students.

Oh.

At the suggestion of a colleague who lived in Michigan and knew everyone at the university, I called a friend of hers who happened to run the university's financial aid office. What could we do? Were there any reductions in tuition available?

She was calm and practiced in her delivery. The school costs what it costs, she said, adding, "Maybe you can't afford to send your daughter to the University of Michigan." She didn't mean it in a cruel way; she was simply stating a fact.

"But she loves Michigan!" I replied.

The official suggested that our children might want a large number of things, but that didn't mean we had to provide them all. I thanked her and told her we would try to find a way—but that I would appreciate anything that she could do. She said she would take a look at Elizabeth's transcript and application.

A few days later, we got a note saying that Elizabeth had qualified for a scholarship that would reduce her tuition by a few thousand dollars a year. It was basically a 10 percent discount. We took a deep breath and enrolled Elizabeth at Michigan, the school of her dreams. We're suckers that way.

We cashed in the annuities to pay for Elizabeth's first semesters at the University of Michigan. Jeanne hated the idea of continuing to pay money into a financial instrument just so we could receive money out of the same financial instrument, especially if it didn't provide any of the promised advantages in lowering the expected contribution from our family to the school. And despite our years of savings, the expected payments from the annuities, as it turned out, were not going to cover the cost of these college loans.

So we decided to eliminate the middleman and pay the money we'd collected directly to the school. I hope that the fees we paid him helped pay for his own son's tuition at tennis school. At least we hadn't given him our 401(k) to manage.

The next year, when we saw the accountant who does our taxes, he pronounced himself annoyed that we had bought into those financial instruments. A plainspoken guy, he pointed out that these annuities are something that are designed for long-term accumulation, like decades, and they were completely inappropriate for a shorter-term payout like a college savings account.

Once again, we had learned a valuable lesson of investing, which is to choose advisers wisely; vet anyone who is trying to sell you something. Ask the right questions about their conflicts of interest. Other lessons: A fool and his money are soon parted. Don't be an idiot. Something like that. We didn't lose a lot of money on the accounts, in any case, and cashing them in didn't incur a big penalty.

Cashing in those accounts, however, still would not be enough to pay for college. The cost of going to Michigan at the time was something like $38,000 a year. We needed more.

Along with our misguided attempt at clever annuity management, we ended up with a nice windfall that helped put our girl through college: oil and gas money. Some years back, Jeanne's dad had given her and her brother the mineral rights to property his family used to own. (Mineral rights can be owned separately from the "surface rights" to the land itself.) Every few months, a royalty check would show up in the mail for Jeanne's share of oil production from the land, or natural gas.

Most of the time it was enough for dinner for the whole family at McDonald's. It was never enough for dinner at a steakhouse. But it was always welcome, and felt very Texan.

Once in a while, a "landman"—the people who buy up mineral rights for oil and gas companies—would send us a letter asking if Jeanne wanted to sell and would name a price. Generally the money offered was in the range of a couple of thousand bucks. Such offers represented years' worth of the payments, but not a lifetime's worth. And we liked holding on to the rights. Because, you know, Texas.

Jeanne's dad told us that he considered the mineral rights to be like an annuity, the kind of thing you never sell. Being crude (har, har), I liked telling her how nice it was to be sleeping with an oil heiress.

She'd joke back, "I've got gas, too."

One day, though, during a long run-up in the price of oil, we got a different kind of letter. These new folks offered $25,000 for Jeanne's oil rights. We saw the offer as the product of a speculative bubble that might not show up again for a long time. We took the deal.

That money paid for a little more than one semester of her college.

Jeanne still had her gas. Those checks have been getting smaller and smaller. The fracking boom has driven the price of oil and natural gas down. But somehow, in an age when sea levels are rising and 196 nations agreed to the Paris climate accord, pledging to do what they could to limit warming and stave off the most catastrophic damage of climate change—well, the romance of having gas had faded. We weren't unhappy to see it dwindle. A climate change reporter profiting off fossil fuels? Awkward. Still, we've held on to it. Because Texas.

There was another windfall for us when it came to the kids. Jeanne's father also, at one point, told us that he was creating funds for the kids' college savings funds, setting aside $10,000 apiece. The idea was that they would grow in value over time. They also went, all three funds, to pay Elizabeth's tuition. We'd figure out what to do for the other kids when they hit college age, we decided; we needed to pay today's bills today.

This is the way it goes for many families—whatever you are able to save for your kids' college educations, it won't be enough. In most cases, you will cash out all the savings to pay for the first child's education and will take care of the rest with loans.

It worked out. Elizabeth got a great education at Michigan. It prepared her for the intellectual rigors of law school. Michigan also introduced her to Matt.

Tell me that wasn't money well spent.

The out-of-state tuition squeeze put us on the hook—for Elizabeth at Michigan, for Sam at Penn State, and for Joe at Iowa. Yes, the kids all chose state schools, out of state. A blessing, because even at inflated out-of-state rates, it was far less expensive than comparable private schools. But still.

PAYING FOR COLLEGE

Let's go a little deeper into how college gets paid for. According to SLM Corporation, the company known as Sallie Mae, which provides student loans, just 40 percent of families have a plan in place to pay for all four years of college before enrollment.[15]

College aid comes in three forms: grants and scholarships (which don't need to be paid back), loans (which do), and work-study jobs.

The biggest federal grant program, the Pell Grant, is generally available to children of families earning $50,000 a year or less; for the 2016–2017 school year, recipients could get a maximum of $5,815. Families with more kids might qualify for Pell Grants even though their annual income is somewhat higher than $50,000, because the financial pressure of the number of children is taken into account. Scholarships come in two basic flavors: merit based and need based. Merit-based scholarships require some qualification or achievement—say, great grades. Need-based scholarships are, as the name suggests, about financial need.

The Sallie Mae report found that 35 percent of college costs are paid from scholarships and grants, 23 percent by parent income and savings, 8 percent by parent borrowing, 19 percent by student borrowing, and 11 percent by student income and savings. Four percent comes from other relatives and friends.

Scholarships are great, but they only defray some costs; few students are going to get a free ride on their athletic skills or math scores. Elizabeth's grant helped us at Michigan, but some friends scoffed when I told them that it amounted to just 10 percent of our costs. I guess their young geniuses did better. Who knows? It was money, and we took it. Joseph, too, qualified for a tuition reduction at Iowa because of his good ACT scores.

Most scholarships don't actually bring in all that much money, and so many students apply for dozens, even hundreds of them. That method is a little like extreme couponing: you can make money at it, but you have to ask whether the game is worth the candle. Many of the available scholarships are very specific in nature—what I like to think of as the left-handed, blue-eyed Norwegian problem. It is worth scanning sites like Fastweb.com and Cappex.com, Scholarships.com and BigFuture, the scholarships site of the College Board? to see what you might qualify for. Absolutely; you never know what you'll find. But, at least for Elizabeth, it didn't seem like something worth turning into a full-time job of essay writing. In her junior and senior year, she made more money babysitting than she would have from minor scholarships.

I called Mark Kantrowitz, the former publisher of Fastweb and current publisher of Cappex. He said that many parents delude themselves about paying for college. "Parents have a tendency to overestimate eligibility for merit-based aid and underestimate their eligibility for need-based aid," he said. Only one in eight students uses scholarships to help pay college costs, he said, and the average is about $4,000. "So scholarships are part of your plan for paying for college, but they aren't your entire plan," he said. Less than 1 percent of students get a full ride, and very few scholarships are generous enough to cover all college costs. Even athletic scholarships aren't as juicy as they seem from the outside, he said: "Less than 2 percent of high school athletes go on to receive college athletic scholarships, and the average amount is $10,000," he said.

He said I was wrong, however, about the efficacy of having kids apply for lots of smaller scholarships. "Every dollar you win is a dollar you don't have to borrow," he said, and "every dollar you borrow will cost two dollars by the time you pay it off." Doing a large number of scholarship applications is not much more trouble than doing a few, he said: the essay questions tend to be fairly repetitive, and the process, after a while, becomes a matter of cut and paste. The most important things, he said, are to never pay a scholarship search service ("probably a scam") and to get an early start so that your child doesn't miss deadlines in applying for scholarships. By the time a student has been accepted at a school, a number of the deadlines for independent scholarships have passed. He acknowledged that students who make As are twice as likely to get those scholarships as B students, because the skills that win those grades also work to their advantage in the application process. But he estimated that a teenager spending 10 hours applying for smaller scholarships—they have fewer applicants than the ones that provide $500 or more—can bring in $500, he said, and "I don't know any high school student who can get $50 an hour doing something legal," he said.

If you plan to save for your children's higher education, there are plenty of ways to do it through a variety of programs at the state and federal level. The best known are called 529 plans because they were created under section 529 of the Internal Revenue Code, and they are administered by states or schools.

This brings up a question all parents wonder about: Do savings plans affect your college aid eligibility? In other words, do we hurt ourselves by saving? The answer is yes, kind of, but not much.

Yes, savings are counted against your estimated family contribution, but in a way that is weighted to minimize the damage to you for having been good. Parental assets are counted at a favorable rate, to encourage savings. So only 5.64 percent of parental assets are counted toward the expected family contribution. So if you saved $10,000 for your student, it will increase your expected family contribution by $564. The higher your expected family contribution, the less money you'll get. But 5.64 percent allows you to save a lot with a fairly low penalty.[16] And money drawn from a 529 plan does not count as income for purposes of the next year's financial aid assessment.

Saving for college, as important as it is, rarely works out as well as we'd hope. According to Fidelity Investments' college savings indicator study, the average family will get less than a third of the way to meeting its college savings goals before their child graduates from high school.[17]

The fact is, unless you have planned things exquisitely well, have a winner of the Regeneron Science Talent Search on your hands ($250,000 scholarship for first place!), or have deep financial resources of your own, you are almost certainly going to be paying for college with loans. Those can come from private lenders or from government programs provided by Uncle Sam and many states.

Some friends told us that they had put all the college loans in their kids' names, putting the burden of repayment on them. Other friends told me that they split the debt with their kids. Considering the cost of a college education, either option helps the parents save for retirement but puts the next generation in a deep, deep hole.

Jeanne and I discussed this and realized that we did not want our kids to start off in life with crushing undergraduate debt. We couldn't afford to pay for college for the kids outright, but we told them that we would take out the lion's share of the loans, applying to the federal government under the federal loan program known as PLUS.[18] Our kids also qualified for smaller amounts of money under the federal Stafford Loan program, which goes directly to them.[19] Elizabeth took on the loans for law school—again, at a public university, UT Austin—in her own name.

Note well, dear reader: we paid for their college educations with loans from the government, not from private lenders. This is another of the rare things we did right. Private lenders will bombard you and your kids with education loan offers, but the risks are high. The private lenders can jack up the interest rates on the loans. Federal direct loans, by comparison, come with a fixed rate.

You don't want that kind of burden, especially since student loan debt is forever. Congress passed a law in 2005 saying that you could not even discharge your student debt in bankruptcy.[20] So it's important to avoid a debt treadmill that is even worse than the one that federal loans put you on.

If you haven't saved at all and college is staring you in the face, there are still options. In addition to loans and those scholarships, there are also ways to stretch those dollars, notes Ron Lieber.[21] A gap year can help you and your student build up cash that can help reduce the amount you have to borrow. Another option is military service, which can lead to education benefits that will help pay for college. Lower-cost options like community college can give your student a start in higher education that can lead to a transfer to a terrific four-year school.

This is just an introduction to the enormously complicated world of college financial aid. If you've read this much, you're ready to dig deeper. For more information, check out the federal Department of Education financial aid information site (studentaid.ed.gov/sa) and savingforcollege.com, which specializes in 529 plans.

OKAY, THAT'S MONEY. BUT WHAT ABOUT VALUES?

How can we make sure that our kids have the right values, especially when it comes to money? The best way is setting an example and discussing money with the kids openly—everything from the tooth fairy to college tuition. That is the lesson of my *NYT* colleague Ron Lieber's book *The Opposite of Spoiled: Raising Kids Who Are Grounded, Generous, and Smart About Money.*[22]

I can't say we're the best example of financial stability, but we had good lessons before us when it comes to energy and drive, at least. My father, A. R. Schwartz, was a scrapper and a striver. He was born dirt poor. When he'd get mad at us kids for complaining about money, he'd say, "We didn't have a pot to piss in and throw away," which quieted us down—at least partly because I'd have to stop to think through why anyone would piss in a pot. Life in the Depression was, I decided, confusing.

In fact, Dad's father and mother divorced when he was a little boy, and his mother had next to nothing to live on. She would send my father into the bars where my grandfather was entertaining women. Dad would have to walk up to him and say, "Hi, Pop," and ask for the child support he owed them. Before long, Dad got good at making his own money, renting beach chairs and umbrellas on Galveston's beaches from the age of 11, and later working as a lifeguard. "I was earning more tips than I was getting in child support," he told me.

In college, Dad worked at the dining halls, and would buy plastic rain ponchos for pennies and sell them in the stadium at football games for 50 cents or a dollar when it started to rain. In the Navy, during aircraft ordnance training in Norman, Oklahoma, he and some buddies would hitchhike south to Dallas during breaks and bring back $3 bottles of whiskey, which they would raffle off for 50 cents a ticket.

"I had entrepreneurship," he told me. He became a lawyer and legislator and provided well for us. He always worked, though over time it was clear that he wasn't working to get rich. He put more faith in his legislative pension than in investments, and while he played with some individual stocks, as a child of the Depression, he put most of his savings into certificates of deposit that were rock solid in terms of safety but paid little interest. To Dad, work was about buying the life you want, but not building a mountain of cash.

By the way, when Dad turned 90, Galveston dedicated a stretch of beach for him: Babe's Beach. It was a great tribute, and it will probably attract plenty of Houston bros hoping to see babes.

Jeanne's father, John Mixon, had also come up through poverty; his own father had died when he was just a boy, and he and his mother kept a small farm going. He came through the experience with the same entrepreneurial spirit as my dad had, driven by poverty to work both as a law professor and as an independent researcher in urban issues, investing cannily. Jeanne said that when she was growing up, he refused to have chicken on his table; he'd had to eat too many of his family's chickens as a boy, and it tasted of poverty.

Our mothers, too, worked; my mom had an insurance company, and Jeanne's mom was a nurse.

From childhood on, we saw and we learned. In elementary school I teamed up with a friend, Brad Schreiber, to form a company. We drew up cards that read, "S&S Enterprises—we'll do anything for money." We planned to do odd jobs but were held back by a lack of odd jobs that needed doing, and our own lack of general competence. In high school and college I had a string of part-time jobs.

I finally found something I wanted to do: journalism. I'd like to think that I work at it as hard as my dad works at the things he loves. But it's not a trade that can make me rich. Like Dad, I haven't focused on trying to amass wealth. I love that line from *Citizen Kane*: "It's no trick to make a lot of money if all you want . . . is to make a lot of money."

Jeanne grew up wanting financial independence and worked her way through college and graduate school: burger joint, legislative clerk, transcriptionist (she's a hellaciously fast typist), and other jobs.

Have we instilled good money sense in our own next generation? As I've mentioned, Elizabeth is a lawyer, like her husband, and is aggressively paying down her law school debt. Sam, who has worked aboard cruise ships and is preparing to teach English overseas, makes me as proud as Elizabeth does; the money he saves goes to further travels. He is happy. I think he will find a way to a good living; he's in his 20s, and there's time to explore. Joseph is working full-time, having taken a break from college after two years. He is money-conscious and careful about spending. But he has also had to deal with clinical depression, and helping him get to a life of satisfaction and happiness means far more to me right now than whether he has chosen the right balance of risk and reward in his 401(k).[23]

All three of our kids are good people. They are well read and generous, and each is touched with a generous measure of sweetness—even acerbic, snarky Joe—that thrills me. I admire friends whose kids are super achievers, get into Ivy League schools, and go on to beat the world. These things are easy to brag on, and I don't blame the parents for doing so.

We've focused on something more fundamental: happiness. And I have to say, the return on that investment has been splendid.

PUNCH LIST

SAVING FOR COLLEGE. IF IT'S TOO LATE FOR YOU, SHOW THIS TO YOUR KIDS

As with all things financial, the earlier you start saving for college, the better. But how much should you save? And how should you do it?

There are just three rules when it comes to saving for college:

1) **Start as early as possible.** Vanguard calculates that if you open an account right after your child is born and contribute $3,000 a year, and if your investments earn 5 percent a year, you'll end up with nearly $90,000 by age 18. Start at 9, and you'll earn $54,000 less. Which is still $35,000, which is great! But it could be so much more.[24]

As with so many things, there is a rule of thumb for college savings. And as with so many rules of thumb, it's partly right and partly wrong. The "2K rule of thumb" for figuring out how much you should have saved already, devised by Fidelity, is disarmingly simple. If your goal is to save enough to pay half of college costs, assuming the rest will come from sources like scholarships and loans, the rule calls for you to multiply your child's age by $2,000. For a seven-year-old, that means you'd better have saved $14,000.

This is, of course, not very helpful when you consider the enormous range of costs in higher education; the economical state college versus stratospheric tabs at private schools like Middlebury or Tulane or the University of Southern California. But, as the folks at Fidelity will tell you, it's a source of incentive to start saving and keep saving. The company offers a college savings calculator on its website, as well.[25] The questions are likely to induce hyperventilation: "Today, what is the approximate one year cost of the school your child may attend?" and "What percent of the cost do you expect to cover from savings?" Try it as an exercise. Get used to the idea that these are questions you'll have to answer.

You can find other college savings calculators at Vanguard,[26] Charles Schwab,[27] and any other investment firm.

2) **Come up with your own savings plan and start contributing to it.** A 2016 Sallie Mae report says that 61 percent of parents

use only savings accounts, and 38 percent use only checking accounts to save for college.[28]

DON'T DO THAT. Use a special college investment account that can help you save and invest at the same time, with tax advantages along the way.

The most common savings accounts are the 529 plans mentioned in this chapter. State sponsored and tax advantaged, the money is generally invested in mutual funds.[29]

You can also save for college using so-called custodial accounts created under the Uniform Gifts to Minors Act (UGMA) or Uniform Transfers to Minors Act (UTMA). Once the child comes of age, whatever has been saved goes to that student and the money can be used for any purpose. Some parents are uncomfortable with that idea, though I'm sure you trust your own children completely.

Both the UGMA and UTMA plans are available through investment companies like Vanguard, Fidelity, Schwab, and the rest. You can save for college with the same people who are helping you save for retirement.

3) **Stick with it.** Be strong! As with other investments, if you possibly can, set it and forget it.

8

MEDICAL DISASTERS

UNLESS YOU ARE truly wealthy, your financial world could be upended with startling suddenness by illness. In 2001, then–Harvard Law professor Elizabeth Warren and her research colleagues found that illness and medical bills were partly to blame for about half of personal bankruptcies in the United States.[1] By 2007, an updated report found that the percentage of illness- and injury-related bankruptcy had grown to 62 percent.[2]

The actual percentage is still a matter of some dispute. A later paper by a lawyer and bankruptcy researcher, Daniel Austin, arguing that bankruptcies are rarely caused by a single factor, said that medical costs were the "predominant causal factor" in 18 to 26 percent of cases. Still, he acknowledged that medical costs are nonetheless the "single largest causal factor" in consumer bankruptcy.[3]

Warren, of course, is now a United States senator from Massachusetts and often makes the point that, as she said in a January 2017 tweet, "Most people in this country are one health crisis away from financial ruin."[4]

There's little doubt that the Affordable Care Act has alleviated some of this financial pressure. A research paper from the National Bureau of

Economic Research suggested that Obamacare reduced medical debt among low-income people by $600 to $1,000 a year.[5] One of the researchers, Robert Kaestner, a professor of health economics at the University of Illinois, told Margot Sanger-Katz of *The New York Times* that medical financial distress has ripple effects. "If people are skipping bills and going into debt, then it can have other repercussions."

As Elizabeth Warren showed, it doesn't take much to go from financial debt to bankruptcy. But Obamacare showed that it's possible to improve things. In 2010, when Barack Obama signed the Affordable Care Act into law, personal bankruptcies in the United States stood at 1,536,799. Six years later the number had dropped by half, to 770,846. Of course, some of these can be attributed to the end of the Great Recession and to a tightening of bankruptcy rules. But the role of Obamacare in reducing the number of financial shipwrecks can't be ignored.[6]

There were problems with the law, of course, especially in states that didn't implement the Medicaid expansion part of it. Though the program is not in what Donald Trump and many Republican members of Congress call a "death spiral,"[7] at this writing, some marketplaces are down to a single insurer, and the premiums in many states have jumped. That has meant that many people whose income is too high for government insurance subsidies have been squeezed, and hard. Like the majority of Americans, I'd rather see the problems with the program fixed than see it repealed. Because we've had our own scrapes with medical disaster, and insurance was the difference between keeping on and going down in flames.

The call you never want to get

Our closest call came in the spring of 2015. Things seemed to be going great for us. Selling our house the previous year had gotten us out from under the college loans and paid off our credit cards. We had more money at the end of the month than ever before. I still couldn't buy dinner at expensive restaurants, but I could indulge in a couple of thick steaks for the grill without fretting too much about it. I could even buy the good stuff over at Whole Foods. The cloud of financial worry had become less threatening than at any time I can remember since our college days.

That is, of course, when life reminds you that there's still plenty of chaos and pain out there waiting for you to drop your guard.

I was driving around the campus neighborhood of Iowa City with our youngest, Joseph. He was 19 and had just finished his first year of college. I had moved him out of his University of Iowa dorm room and had driven over to the apartment he had rented for the coming school year. We were going to check it out before making the drive back home. Jeanne stayed home for this one. No sense in both of us making that 1,000-mile drive if we could help it. And besides, she didn't want to take time off from her job as a crossing guard. When Jeanne doesn't work, she doesn't get paid, and that paycheck is an important part of keeping us afloat.

As I was parking the car, a message popped up on my phone:

Your wife is ok but had an accident Pls call me 862216xxxx

I didn't recognize the handle, but of course I called. A woman whose voice was unfamiliar to me told me that Jeanne had been hit by a car.

The person at the other end of the phone was Gabby Stern. Joseph had gone to high school with her daughter, who was walking with her father by Jeanne's corner. They saw Jeanne lying on the ground, bleeding from a gash at the back of her head. Cops were all around and an ambulance was pulling up. The daughter recognized Jeanne and called her mother, who was at that time an employee of *The Wall Street Journal*. Gabby didn't know how to reach me at first, then remembered laughing at my tweets. She sent me the note through the direct message function on Twitter.

So now you know that Twitter is good for something.

I called Gabby and gave her my phone number; she had her husband, Jeff, call me. He was still on the scene and let me know briefly what was going on before handing the phone to a police officer. The officer explained that an elderly woman in a Volvo had smacked into Jeanne while she was helping kids cross the street during the after-school rush. The impact had knocked Jeanne down, and she hit her head hard enough to be knocked cold. They were sending her to a hospital in Morristown—a surprise to me, since there are closer medical centers. Why there? I asked.

"It's the regional trauma center for head wounds," he said.

Wait. What? How serious was this? I asked. The officer couldn't say, but he did tell me that she was no longer unconscious. "She's been talking," he said, "but there's a lot of blood."

Horrifying. I was, at that moment, 1,000 miles away; the drive home would take at least 15 hours. No one could tell me how badly she was hurt. Joseph and I had planned to take two days to drive home, with a night in a hotel to rest. I was frantic, jumpy, frazzled.

"Joe," I asked, "do you mind if we try to drive straight through?"

We stopped by the local Starbucks for a quad espresso and started the drive. Along the way, I reached friends who agreed to go to the hospital to be with her. When the hospital discharged her later that night, they helped her get home. (Whether she should have been discharged with a serious concussion is another matter, but we don't need to get into that.) Later that evening, she got on the phone with me to tell me to find a hotel and not to push myself too hard.

As if.

Joseph and I pulled up to the house around 7:00 a.m.; he went up to his room to sleep, and I climbed into bed next to Jeanne. She was wearing what looked like a bloody turban that cushioned her head and left an open space to expose the stitches. She was groggy and miserable. It would be days before she could focus her eyes enough to read again, and more than a week before she could follow the plot of a novel. But we were together.

And we felt lucky. She was injured on the job; workers' compensation would pay all her medical costs. It's a cumbersome process, but we did not have to deal with tens of thousands of dollars in bills. Even if it had not been a work-related injury, my health insurance with the *Times* would have covered much of the cost. And, thanks to Obamacare, even if I did not have a job that provided me with insurance, I'd have been able to buy it.

We would not be the medical bankrupts that Elizabeth Warren has written about. But every time we saw a bill, and saw the mounting costs that somebody else was paying, we had to wonder how other people dealt with this. Without adequate insurance, all our financial gains of the previous year would have been wiped out. We'd have been back in the hole. I'd have been back on fries and gravy.

Jeanne returned to work, though the police moved her to a less busy corner. It earned her less money per month—the risks tied to the old corner had come with rewards—but her safety was our first consideration.

Because of a quirk of New Jersey law, we were not eligible to sue the driver who hit her. The Garden State's auto liability laws are no-fault, which basically means that policyholders recover their financial losses from their own insurance company. It simplifies insurance, but the dozen states that have no-fault insurance limit the ability of people to file lawsuits in auto accident cases. Under New Jersey law, Jeanne would have had to have suffered a permanent or disfiguring injury in order to qualify to sue the driver over the accident. Apparently, we could have retained the right to sue for less grievous injury by checking a box on our auto insurance company's policy form, and paying dearly for the right every year. But we never even noticed it.[8]

At the urging of friends, I spoke with two lawyers about whether there was a way to sue anyway. One was aggressive and explained that we could probably establish that there had been a permanent injury if we set up an MRI to look for herniated disks or other soft-tissue damage. "If they do an MRI and find there are disk herniations, that gets you over the threshold," he explained. Other forms of injury might be established. He said he had a friendly neurologist up in Hackensack who worked on a contingency-fee basis and would get part of our settlement or jury award. There would be no hourly fees along the way. "What I say is 'get what you can get,'" he explained.

A second lawyer, a second opinion. This guy was less interested in the battery of tests than how Jeanne was doing and how she was feeling. The restriction on lawsuits, known as the verbal threshold, is hard to overcome, he said. "A scar to the back of the head is not going to be a disfiguring scar," he told me. He also wasn't big on a paying for a lot of tests or the idea of claiming some permanent damage. In any case, he said, "this is all way too premature to be talking about." Once her medical treatment was complete, we could see whether there was evidence of permanent injury or persistent pain. "You won't know until the treating doctor says we can do no more," he said. "Hopefully, the stitches will heal, and she won't have recurrent headache, post-concussion syndrome—whatever—or other aches, pains, and injuries that she might have."

He then asked me the only really important question: "Does it look like she's going to make a full recovery?" It did. That, he said, was the outcome we really wanted. "Have a good life," he said. Even over the phone I could tell that he was smiling.

I don't know for sure, but I'll bet the second lawyer had read Dickens's *Bleak House*, the story of families destroyed by being sucked into the courts in never-ending litigation. *Bleak House* was the first Dickens novel I read, just before starting law school. Its law-related tragedies, the infinite cross-generational tangles of the famous case Jarndyce and Jarndyce through the British chancery system, was one of the things that helped convince me that writing would be a better path for me than litigating. I was haunted by the words spoken by Mr. Gridley, a man destroyed by the legal system, and who says of his friend Miss Flite, "There is a tie of many suffering years between us two, and it is the only tie I ever had on earth that Chancery has not broken!"

Which lawyer's advice do you think we took? By now, you probably know us well enough to have figured out that we went with the option of not pushing things. Jeanne had been through an awful time—a lot of pain, a lot of trauma. She didn't want to relive it with more medical tests and a court fight over some ill-defined injury. And the first lawyer's tactics made us uncomfortable. So we didn't go forward with a lawsuit.

Jeanne, meanwhile, kept getting calls from the driver's insurance company, asking her to sit down with them for an interview. They never explained what they wanted to know, though it appeared that they were bracing for litigation. They didn't know whether we could sue; they hadn't asked about the verbal threshold. Jeanne told them that her medical bills were being paid by workers' comp, and she did not want any representative of the company coming into our home or meeting her in a coffee shop. Finally, she agreed to go to their offices, but soon became agitated by the agent's repeated questions about the accident, where Jeanne had been standing, whether she had run out into the crosswalk as the driver had insisted. (The driver's lies were pathetic.)

"It's all in the police report!" she said, her voice rising.

The representative, flustered, asked her to calm down and reminded her that he had not caused the accident.

"I didn't, either!" Jeanne shouted, shaking with anger. "Your client *hit me!*"

The interview ended. Jeanne went home. The calls stopped.

Well, almost. Sometime later, Jeanne called me at work to say the insurance company had called her one more time and had offered a settlement of $10,000. Jeanne accepted it on the spot. I might have tried to negotiate, but Jeanne wanted it all to be over, over, over. And we knew that people with serious, lasting injuries had received settlements that did not amount to much more than that, especially after the lawyer's cut.

So we were done, and we moved on.

Over the next year and a half, Jeanne would have other medical emergencies, including gallbladder attacks that required two surgical procedures in three days, ending with the doctors taking out the offending organ. I developed an unasked-for familiarity with the offerings at the Saint Barnabas Medical Center cafeteria in Livingston, New Jersey. (Try the fried chicken.) She has come through each of these incidents in good health, and we were grateful not to be financially devastated by adventures that start with a late-night visit to the emergency room.

It all drove home an important message: Life is chaotic. It will mess with you.

Is this news? Of course not. But it all reminds me of *The New Yorker* cartoon by Lee Lorenz from 1989 that shows a businessman swaggering down the street, thinking to himself:

Less cholesterol
Regular checkups
No nicotine
No alcohol
Low sodium
Moderate exercise
No sugar

He is oblivious to the steel safe plummeting toward him from above.[9]

I especially love this cartoon because of where I first encountered it: in the Bethesda, Maryland, bedroom of Jules Lodish, a brilliant hematologist and oncologist who I met during my years at *The Washington Post*. Several years before my visit, Lodish had been struck by amyotrophic lateral sclerosis (ALS), or Lou Gehrig's disease. He had been slow to notice a growing weakness in 1994, until "one day, I couldn't turn the keys in my car," he told me, even using both hands.

When I visited him in 2000, he spent his days unable to move, a machine at his side doing his breathing for him. But he was still able to talk—eloquently, endlessly, with humor and wisdom, his brain unaffected while his body went slack. He called the condition "having a ringside seat at your own demise."[10]

He had insurance and pressured the company to allow him to be treated at home. He had been told he would likely survive just two years after his diagnosis. He believed that he could manage his own care more effectively there, which would be likely to help him survive longer. He wrote up a 35-page instruction manual for nurses that would prevent the infections that cause the death of many ALS patients. It worked; he lived for 15 years with the condition, dying in 2008.[11] In that time, he saw two of his three children marry and counseled many patients and their families about living with crushing medical conditions. As he wrote to a friend—using a computer equipped with a sensor that registered keystrokes through twitches of his cheek—"Quintessentially, I have found that ambulation, movement, swallowing, eating, talking, breathing, and self care are not me. They are substantial physical losses; but they are not me."[12]

I don't bring up Jules Lodish's story because it is depressing—or even because it is inspiring, which it surely is. I bring it up because his illness came out of the blue, like that hurtling safe.

Again, I've leaped from the financial to the metaphysical. But let's circle back. Thanks in part to my experience with Lodish, I keep the health insurance paid up and have insisted that the kids have insurance as well. Without it, problems quickly become crises. And you never know when. We also built up a cushion of several thousand dollars for emergencies. (I set aside the most recent nest egg from the advance payment for this book.) It sits there, waiting for us to need it. But when an unexpected car problem or home repair comes up, it's a comfort not to have to borrow money for the fix.

Jeanne just celebrated her 60th birthday. Her dad called and said, "I'm glad you're still here." Then a friend from our college days called and said exactly the same thing. Which unsettled her a bit—as if there's a betting board up somewhere with her name on it. So I didn't say it to her. But I felt it.

WHEN MEDICAL CRISES TAKE EVERYTHING AWAY

While our medical emergencies haven't shipwrecked us financially, we know people whose own health crises have.

I spent an afternoon recently with Jolie Solomon, a good friend and a successful journalist who is now living in poverty. Illness—hers, and her daughter's—were major factors.

We worked together nearly 30 years ago. We were on similar paths. We made similar salaries, and at her peak she was outearning me by quite a chunk. We both were building savings in a 401(k) with generous contributions.

There are differences, too, of course. She was a single mother, and I had a supportive partner. I stayed well; Jolie got sick. It was the kind of illness that Elizabeth Warren was talking about.

Jolie came up through the trade press and local newspapers and worked up to publications like *The Wall Street Journal* and *Newsweek*, where we worked together in the business section. Funny and creative,

Jolie was a joy to work with and had deep expertise in the business world and personal finance. Within *Newsweek*, she rose to the position of deputy chief of correspondents, and went on to Time Inc., where she served as the deputy managing editor at *Fortune Small Business*. By then, she was making very good money—$125,000 a year. And she was funneling a fair amount of that income into a retirement account that, by 2006, had come up to $350,000. She figured that she had 20 years of work ahead of her and was on track to build a very comfortable retirement.

"Baby boomers grew up with this idea that we were going to have things better, easier than our parents," she said, and it seemed to be working out that way. Her father, a schoolteacher, had gone hungry as a child. Jolie, by the time she was just two years out of graduate school, was earning more than him.

She bought a lovely house in Maplewood, New Jersey, in 1995 for $175,000. It was the town she'd grown up in and where her parents still lived, so it felt comfortable. A year later, direct train service opened from Maplewood into Manhattan, and property values began to soar.

In the mid-2000s, she applied for a $75,000 home equity line of credit. The genial banker urged her to take twice as much as she had asked for, and she found herself questioning him like a skeptical journalist about whether they were doing enough to assess whether she was a good credit risk. "You guys don't ask very many questions on this thing!" she said. "Should I really be taking this much?" But the offer was hard to resist, and she figured that she would never need more than a fraction of the credit that was being made available to her. "I'm ashamed to say I took the whole $150,000 because I was amazed, and felt 'rich' to be able to do such a thing."

And things would have been fine if her earnings and home value had stayed high. But they didn't. In 2001, she took a buyout at Time Inc., which was under financial pressure to downsize, thanks to its spectacularly ill-advised merger with America Online. Jolie found work at another magazine, but the money wasn't as good as it had been at *Time*. A buyout there led her through a succession of jobs, in a changing media environment. Most of the gigs offered lower pay and stingier benefits than she'd gotten in the past, but by 2006 she had landed at *More* magazine and was earning six figures again.

She tried not to show it, but Jolie was also in near-constant pain because of conditions that had been worsening, including a chronic bladder inflammation that had tormented her since childhood. In her 30s, she also got a diagnosis of fibromyalgia, a painful condition that can also be accompanied by sleep problems and other health issues. During these years, her father developed Alzheimer's disease and died; her mother, too, would develop the disease. Worse, her daughter, Lily, was in trouble. She had developed a neurological condition in elementary school that contributed to depression and anxiety; those conditions would worsen in middle school and high school.

Lily's health problems meant a punishingly expensive seven-year search for effective treatments, and the best doctors and most effective treatments often were not covered by insurance. Jolie was struggling to find medical treatments for them both, while also trying to get the schools to provide her daughter with services she was entitled to under the law. That required a lawyer, meaning thousands of dollars more to spend. And all the while, she was trying to hold down her high-powered job.

Something had to give. She asked her employer for unpaid time off, the right to work from home, even a less senior job—all options under the Family and Medical Leave Act. "I would have swept the floors—I just wanted to keep my medical benefits," she said. After more than a year without action on her requests, she hired a lawyer, who wrote to the company with demands for her rights under the act. Two weeks later, the company told her that her job had been eliminated. The lawyer said that the company had broken the law, but that it would be grievously expensive to fight. He negotiated her severance package.

After that, she told me, "There was no way I could take another full-time job—I couldn't show up and immediately demand time off to care for my sick kid." She was back to cobbling together freelance gigs. They didn't provide insurance, and her annual income was dropping: $60,000, $50,000, $30,000. Buying insurance on the open market was costing her $1,500 each month, with medications alone costing an additional $1,500.

She was digging deep into her IRA. "I had to take chunk after chunk out of it." She felt that she was running out of options. Her $2,100 monthly mortgage payment had become impossible. A broker who had become a friend advised Jolie to sell the house, and "it seemed abundantly clear that I should." But it wasn't easy to begin "in the middle of this nightmare."

She brought in brokers who told her that the old-fashioned house, which had been deteriorating for years, would require a lot of work. Could she sell it as is? "Nobody buys fixer-uppers anymore," they said. An "as-is" sale might have gone nowhere. She thought of the effort of supervising a contractor, and spending money she didn't have on fixes that might not help; her brain cycled. "I obsessed and ruminated," she said, and was paralyzed.

Even now she can't stop wondering how she could have saved the house. She said, "It still drives me crazy" that, if Obamacare had arrived even a year earlier than it did, she could have saved $100,000 in medical costs that could have gone to housing.

A bankruptcy lawyer helping her deal with her medical debt suggested that foreclosure might actually help her: for the 18 months that the process would take, she could live without having to make mortgage payment or rent. In the end, the process took four years.

Her focus, she told me, remained on her daughter. "You know, they say you're supposed to put the mask on first"—on an airplane that has a sudden drop in air pressure—"but there's only so much of that you can do when the kid is right in front of you." After all, she asked, "What is the best investment you can make, but your kid?"

Jolie had tried to keep the growing money mess from Lily, "but she's too smart," Jolie said, and Lily was growing up. One day during Lily's senior year, on the way to a doctor's appointment, Lily told her that the high school yearbook would cost more than $75.

"What? No!" Jolie burst out. Both of them were soon in tears.

Jolie found herself pouring out a rapid-fire explanation of the underlying causes of their troubles. "This is *not* your fault," she told Lily. "And I made some mistakes, but it is not *my* fault. This is the fault of the system"—on the government, with its toothless rules on family leave, on insurance companies and school systems and banks.

The memory of that drive is hard; it brought Jolie to tears again. "The safety net is, like, it strangles you; it doesn't support you," she said. "And any tiny bits you get, you have to fight endlessly for."

With good medical treatment, Lily stabilized. She graduated from high school and went off to college, where she won scholarships and received financial aid. Jolie went back to work. But it didn't last; her health was declining. On a trip to Denver in 2012, she got so sick that she had to be hospitalized. During her time in the hospital, however, she missed her insurance payment and the insurer canceled her policy. She had no recourse; it was her second late payment, and the terms of her policy were clear. So she found herself saddled with some $60,000 in bills from that stay alone.

"You know that cliché, you're one catastrophic illness away from financial ruin? We were already close to ruin with one catastrophic illness. With another one, forget it."

In 2013, on a trip to Boston, she collapsed again, nearly paralyzed with pain and weakness. She and Lily got her on a bus back to New Jersey. "I got home, and I really have barely been out of bed since." She now has a diagnosis of chronic fatigue syndrome along with the other medical conditions.

She vacillates between beating herself up and defending herself. "Most of me says, 'you have been doing an incredible job in spite of so much.' But I still spend a lot of time second guessing."

In 2016, through scrambling and her reporter's skills, she was able to work through bureaucratic mazes and paperwork to find and nail down federally subsidized housing: $880 a month for a lovely apartment. Each bit of aid can be a mixed blessing; now that she has to pay rent, she has to dip even further into the last of her IRA to cover it. In 2015, she began getting $2,400 a month in disability payments—another victory over bureaucracy. It is her only income, and doesn't go far—but it is enough to disqualify her for the food stamps and utility subsidy she had been getting before.

On the positive side of the emotional ledger, Lily was thriving in college. And Jolie was emerging from the nightmare of eviction. But "it's terrifying to be this sick and this poor," she said. They even had to give up the family dog; she could no longer afford the food and vet bills. Jolie told me that she feels she has lost the life she'd hoped to have. "I thought it was going to be a life worth living, and it was going to protect Lily."

Sobbing, she added, "Even if I get healthy enough to get a little work, there's still no way to rebuild $350,000 and to buy a house. There's no way to recover the future I built for myself, that I was so careful to build." In the meantime, she said, "I'm working on the Serenity Prayer thing, and I know the only way to do this is to change the way I see it."

She kept coming back to the sorrow. "There are rituals for grief over the loss of a parent, of a child," she said. Grave markers and ceremonies. "But how about grief over a future? There's no marker for how to deal with this."

==

There are so many health care casualties like Jolie. I encountered another person in trouble recently, Joyce Lacovara. Remember that Federal Reserve survey with the startling finding that 46 percent of Americans couldn't come up with $400 in an emergency? When *The Washington Post* wrote about it, many of the comments from readers were dismissive and smug.[13] Their basic point: these people are losers who cause their own problems through imprudent living and bad choices. This angered Lacovara, who lives in Woodbridge, Virginia, and has survived two bouts with cancer and who, she said in a comment on the site, "can barely cover the cost of my food":

> Your denial that anyone who isn't somehow irresponsible couldn't possibly wind up in this situation is based on your own fear that if it could happen to someone else who wasn't somehow asking

for it well, then it could also happen to you. Here's the thing. It can. It might. Stop blaming people to make yourself feel safe and better. It won't help you one bit and prevents you considering helping others by making sure our society takes such things into account. Have you ever tried selling a flat screen TV to cover the cost of cancer? Or a smartphone? Good luck with that.[14]

I hunted around and found Joyce's email address. It turned out she'd been the lead singer in a Washington, D.C., heavy metal band, Murder Ink. They had a good reputation, and I'd heard of them, but had never been to a show. (I'm more of a Nick Lowe kind of guy.) Joyce had been a bartender, among other jobs, but the bouts of cancer and the cost of treatment, and painful fibromyalgia, took everything away. In a lengthy, impassioned email, she told me that she now lives on food stamps in a 30-year-old trailer, and "one good meal a day is the best I can hope for."

She lives in poverty but is confronted daily with the excesses of others. "It's like living an 18th Century pioneer life while 2016 dances, glitzes, and glimmers obscenely around me," she wrote. And so the accusations in the comments on that *Washington Post* article infuriated her, she explained. "Stop condemning me for being ill, or just get on with setting up those euthanasia centers!" And, she added, no one should preen about how they could stay out of financial trouble if problems swarmed.

"Believe me, it can happen to any of us."

It's depressingly common, and nothing new, to blame the poor for being poor. Every once in a while, the issue shows up starkly in a sound bite, as it did when former congressman Jason Chaffetz, a Republican from Utah, suggested as Congress was discussing the repeal of Obamacare that people should "invest in their own health care" instead of "getting that new iPhone that they just love."[15] The ugliness of that comment led many people to note that health care costs much more than an iPhone, that a smartphone is, in fact, an important tool for finding work and more. But the comment really put that old theme on display: the idea that poverty is a choice. Stephen Pimpare, who teaches politics and public policy at the University of New Hampshire, flayed that logic in a powerful essay for *The Washington Post*. "Chaffetz, Ryan and their compatriots offer us tough love without the love," he wrote, "made possible through their willful ignorance of (or utter disregard for) what life is actually like for so many Americans who do their very best against great odds and still, nonetheless, have little to show for it. Sometimes not even an iPhone."[16]

My friend Jolie freely admits having made mistakes and bad decisions that contributed to her problems. But there's clearly more to it than that. There are amazing recent works that deal with the causes and the difficulties of rising out of poverty. The book I've been pushing on people since it came out in 2016 is *Evicted: Poverty and Profit in the American City*, by Matthew Desmond.[17] The deeply reported and compellingly written book combines journalism and sociology, and will tell you more about living with poverty than just about anything I've seen.

Desmond takes a hard look at the idea that people's bad choices lead them into poverty and keep them there. He lays out a nuanced psychological point: the notion that bad decisions are not just the cause of personal financial crises but can also be caused by them. In unflinching prose, he details moments of improvidence that were part of the mix of factors that led to a wandering life of eviction and loss. At one point, Larraine, a woman he interviewed, blew her monthly food stamp allowance on lobster tails, shrimp, and king crab legs, cooking a feast for herself shortly before getting kicked out of her rented trailer home. Even her friends complained about her spendthrift ways, and thought, as Desmond wrote, that "Larraine was poor because she threw money away." Instead, he said, the opposite was true: "Larraine threw away money because she was poor." If she saved $50 a month by cutting out cable and visits to Walmart, she would end up with $600 by the end of the year—just enough for one month's rent. "People like Larraine lived with so many compounded limitations that it was difficult to imagine the amount of good behavior or self-control that would allow them to lift themselves out of poverty," he wrote; they had so little hope of climbing out of poverty that "they tried to survive in color, to season the suffering with pleasure."[18]

Desmond then asked the right question: "Would people behave differently if they were provided with a real opportunity to break out of poverty?"[19]

He cited the work of Sendhil Mullainathan, a Harvard professor of economics, and Eldar Shafir, a Princeton behavioral scientist. In their 2013 book, *Scarcity: Why Having Too Little Means So Much*, they write, "Poverty *itself* taxes the mind." That simple yet evocative sentence is based on research suggesting that poverty dampens intelligence and lowers impulse control—"not because they are less capable, but rather because part of their mind is captured by scarcity."[20]

That makes poverty, so often brought about by illness, sound like an illness. And, in a way, it is.

THE SKYROCKETING COST OF KEEPING AN ANIMAL COMPANION ALIVE

It's not just the humans whose medical costs can be a drain—healing our pets can be stupendously expensive. It's been on my mind because recently Ace, the sweetest cat we've ever had, stopped eating and was clearly ailing. The vet, after charging us $300 for a first look, sent her to an animal hospital, where they charged us a jaw-dropping $5,000 to keep her over the weekend for tests. (The hospital staff estimated the cost range between $2,800 and $5,000 when we dropped her off; when we picked her up, they told us that her treatment had come in at the high end of the estimate, which is an amazing coincidence.) The cat turned out to be suffering from a bone marrow shutdown, and while the weekend in the pet equivalent of the Mayo Clinic extended her life by several weeks, with some additional vet visits and medications to try, we eventually had to face the inevitable.

We grieved, and paid the bills. We did not have pet insurance, so the effort to save Ace wiped out that cash cushion I mentioned a few pages ago, and then some. We were back on our credit cards.

We might have spent far more; the vets at the pet hospital had been recommending a bone marrow aspiration that would have cost $2,000. They had other ideas as well. Pet care is more high-tech and capable than ever before, and that ability to do more carries a price tag: Healthy Paws Pet Insurance issued a "cost of pet care" report in 2016 with sobering figures that were drawn from 215,000 claims over the course of a year. The report, clearly intended to scare people into buying the company's product, cited stunningly expensive claims: $44,296 for a dog with spinal disease and pneumonia. The most expensive cat: $14,582 for liver cancer.[21]

Some people, of course, will pay any amount of money to save an animal companion, even going into debt to do so. They have my respect, but they are in the minority. A survey conducted back in 2010 by the Associated Press and petside.com found that 62 percent of people would be likely to approve medical care for pets if the cost was $500 or less, but just 35 percent would if the cost was $2,000; once the cost hits $5,000, just 22 percent would say yes.[22] In the industry, they call the decision not to pay for expensive care "economic euthanasia."

I haven't written up this little aside on pet medical costs to recommend that you buy pet health insurance. Even after what we've been through, I don't think I would take on that monthly expense, though 1.6 million pets in North America have some form of coverage, according to the North American Pet Health Insurance Association.[23] A 2016 review of the field by *Consumer Reports* did not come down to a strong recommendation either way, but said it's important to read the policies from several providers and compare the premiums, copays, and deductibles, which undercut the savings provided by the plans they reviewed pretty extensively. (Unless you've got that $44,296 dog.) The report concluded, somewhat wishy-washily, "If you'd like help with unexpected, large vet bills, a plan may be worth considering."[24]

PUNCH LIST

———●———

MEDICAL DISASTER

Get a health insurance checkup. Do you have enough? Are you overpaying?

1) **If you don't have health insurance, get it.** Let's say you don't have insurance—maybe you just lost a job or quit, or maybe you didn't want the government ordering you to get health insurance under Obamacare and so you paid the penalty instead and are working without a net.

   If so, get health insurance. Whether you are buying it through an employer or going out in the world of Obamacare plans, or you just turned 26 and have aged out of your parents' insurance plan, or you are the parent helping that new 26-year-old, you need to learn the ropes and get that coverage.

2) **Study up.** If you're an absolute beginner, here are some basic terms you need to know. While there are a number of different types of plans, here are the two main ones:

   Health Maintenance Organization (HMO): These tend to be relatively inexpensive, as insurance plans go, because the plans limit your coverage to the doctors and hospitals in or linked to their networks. In most plans, out-of-network care is covered only in emergencies.

   Preferred Provider Organization (PPO): More choice, relatively higher prices. You get a broader choice of doctors, with better prices for getting your treatment from doctors in the PPO network. Go outside the network, and your deductible and copay costs are likely to rise. Most PPO plans don't require you to get a referral before seeing doctors.

   There are also Point of Service (POS) and Exclusive Provider Organization (EPO) plans. POS plans let you find doctors inside or outside of the plan, but only after getting a referral from your primary care physician. EPO plans limit you to certain health care providers.

   Within the two main categories, the various plans come in tiers: platinum, gold, silver, and bronze. The platinum plans offer the broadest coverage and lowest deductibles and copays, but the premiums cost more; bronze plans cost less in premiums and more when you need medical treatment. People with low taxable income or high family expenses can qualify for subsidies, and low-cost "catastrophic plans" are available, mainly for people under 30.[25]

Obamacare enrollment comes once a year, in November and December, but you can always enroll after a major life change, which includes losing your coverage, getting married, or having a baby. You can also enroll year-round in the Medicaid or the Children's Health Insurance Program (CHIP) if you are eligible.[26]

You can find out more about what you need to know about health insurance from HealthCare.gov, the national site for administering the Obamacare plan.

3) **If you already are insured, figure out whether you're paying too much.** Healthy people might be able to get away with plans that trade somewhat lower premiums for a higher deductible, especially young folks. But recognize that if you do opt for the higher deductible and need a lot of medical care, that higher deductible will sting. You have to be able to pay that higher cost if you get into trouble. And if you have to borrow to pay off the deductible, your costs will grow with the interest added to those loans.

Consider the network as well. If you love your current doctors, make sure that they are covered under your new plan—if not, and you want to stick with them, you could spend way too much on out-of-network costs. As you narrow down your choices, compare the benefits. If things like maternity, physical therapy, and mental health care are important to your family, make sure they have got decent coverage under the plan you select. If you take expensive prescription drugs, check on how they are treated under the various plans.

4) **Consider seeking professional assistance.** HealthCare.gov has a guide to local helpers, known in the bureaucratese of the program as navigators.[27] You can also rely on licensed insurance agents or brokers who work with the Obamacare program—the same people who helped sell you health insurance before Obamacare entered the world. They generally get paid by the

insurance companies; if you do decide to go that route, make sure that they can get you the full range of plans available under Obamacare. You can also work online with providers like eHealth insurance.com.

5) **Look beyond retirement.** What about insurance in retirement? At 65, fingers crossed, Medicare kicks in. It doesn't cover everything, though—at that point, you'll want to look into the world of supplemental plans, including Medigap. You can find out more about the range of options at medicare.gov.[28]

9

DEBT

Our interest rate just went to 29 percent
  Even though we've never failed to pay
  It's always Christmastime for Visa
  An American Expression of good cheer
  The payments that we're making are the gift that keeps on taking
  And leaves us buried deeper, leaves us buried deeper every year
    "XMAS TIME FOR VISA," AUSTIN LOUNGE LIZARDS[1]

WE ARE A nation swimming in debt. Mortgage, college loans, home equity, credit cards—it all piles up.

How much debt does the average American family lug around? A lot. Nerdwallet.com, a financial tools and advice company, reports that the average household that has any kind of debt owed $134,642.86 in 2016. (Since some families have no debt, the overall average is somewhat lower, $99,835.73.) Credit card debt alone hit $16,747.98 in the average indebted household. The interest on those credit cards costs Americans an average of $1,292 a year.[2]

Oddly enough, though, 29 percent of American consumers with a credit record actually have no debt—they borrow nothing. Another 22 percent have only credit card debt. That's the startling conclusion of the Urban Institute, which sifted the data on more than five million credit reports. Many of those people are just starting out: some 55 percent of 10- to 22-year-olds are debt-free, as are just under 40 percent of those between ages 23 and 27. Older Americans also ease out of debt, the Urban Institute study showed: past the age of 77, about 36 percent of consumers carry no debt.

The rest of us, those in the middle? Slammed.[3] As always.

Much of the debt that Americans have is overdue. About 35 percent of adults with a credit file have in their credit report some kind of debt that's in collections—that is, more than 180 days past due and handed off to a collection agency. That's about 77 million Americans, owing an average of $5,178, according to another Urban Institute study.[4]

Debt is a personal story, but it has enormous implications beyond individual families. There's medical debt, of course: remember Elizabeth Warren's research showing illness and medical bills were partly to blame for about half of personal bankruptcies in the United States.[5] Those bankruptcies have been a factor in the nation's economic troubles, and led to the years-long fight over Obamacare and replacing it, tying up the nation's politics in an endless war.

The housing crisis, too, was essentially a crisis of debt, with millions of people losing their homes after the real estate bubble burst. It was also, of course, a crisis of too-loose regulation of the financial sector and rampant conflicts of interest. But things started to go south when larger and larger numbers of homeowners couldn't pay their mortgages, and default rates grew high enough to tip the burgeoning market in mortgage-backed securities into failure. But to an enormous extent, the financial bust that almost brought down the global economy came down to whether people could make that monthly payment.

So the nation's addiction to debt has led to many crises. What's more, household debt has been rising. In the first three months of 2017, total household debt reached $12.7 trillion, with a *t*. That's more money than people owed in 2008 during the credit bubble that came just before the crash. The figure, which comes from the Federal Reserve Bank of New York, showed the effects of ballooning student loan debt—it now makes up 11 percent of total household debt, and was just 5 percent in the third quarter of 2008. Auto lending and credit card debt have grown, too. A story about the new peak in *The New York Times* pointed out that in some ways, the growth in debt is good news, since it shows that banks are more willing to lend, and because it means that consumers who were squeezed during the recession may have repaired their credit enough to qualify for loans. But of course, the trend also "could put many Americans back into a hole, prompting a new wave of defaults, much like the ones that accompanied the mortgage meltdown a decade ago."[6]

GETTING MIRED IN DEBT: THE LITERARY VERSION

Plenty of people don't come out on the right side of those moments. What happens to them? They tend to drown in debt.

And, if they are journalists, they then write about it. Take Edmund L. Andrews, a former economics reporter for *The New York Times* who wrote *Busted: Life Inside the Great Mortgage Meltdown*, which appeared in 2009.[7] Or check out the journalist, film critic, and historian Neal Gabler's cover story in *The Atlantic*, "The Secret Shame of Middle-Class Americans," in 2016.[8] Even my friend Joe Nocera, a terrific financial journalist, has admitted in print that after tapping his 401(k) for divorce and home repair, and big losses from heavy investment in tech stocks, his "faith-based" retirement fund was "in tatters."[9]

I am obsessed with these stories, in no small part because, since I am a journalist, they contain a kind of there-but-for-the-grace-of-God comfort. And since these are professional wordsmiths, their stuff tends to be well written. Still, what they write tends to be more about misery than money, and their works resemble addiction memoirs—those books that grip us by showing how low their authors will go. They generally don't give you a sense of how you might live a better financial life. (In this same way, the wisdom of scientist and author Jared Diamond's *Collapse: How Societies Choose to Fail or Succeed* can be boiled down to "don't cut down all your trees." Good advice, but not helpful on a personal level.)

Andrews wrote about his descent into disastrous mortgage and credit card debt, even though he was one of the nation's most knowledgeable economics writers. He fell months behind on his mortgage and risked losing his home. The book ends without resolution on that point: "My wife Patty and I may or may not hold on to our house."

It's compelling stuff, but Andrews has a deeper goal: pointing a finger at a broken system of corrupt banks and asleep-at-the-switch regulators who helped bring about the 2008 mortgage crisis. "No matter how egregious my judgment may have been, it pales in comparison with the self-enriching recklessness of those at the top of the financial ladder," he wrote. And so, "I wish I could send one message to the millions of home buyers who made bad choices: don't beat yourself up over your mistakes."

Gabler's story involves a writer seemingly on top of the world who found himself sliding into a financial mess. He cited those figures from the Federal Reserve stating that nearly half of Americans couldn't come up with $400 right away, though instead of the 46 percent in the survey, he said it was 47 percent. He wrote:

Four hundred dollars! Who knew?
Well, *I* knew. I knew because I am in that 47 percent.

Gabler directly confronts the stigma of loss and people's reluctance to talk about their financial woes. (Unless, as I said, they are journalists.) "To struggle financially is a source of shame, a daily humiliation—even a form of social suicide. Silence is the only protection."

Reaction to these works can be scornful. Gabler came in for criticism from the personal finance writer Helaine Olen in *Slate* magazine, who called it part of "the long-standing genre that I like to call all the sad, broke, literary men." Gabler, she noted, drained a retirement account to pay for his daughter's wedding, and had a home in one of the nation's fancier precincts, East Hampton, New York—a home that could, she said, be rented during the summer for thousands of dollars a week.[10]

The writer Gene Lyons took a shot at Gabler's piece on Facebook: "It's proverbial: a fool and his money are soon parted. Except this guy thinks his profligacy represents a failure of the American Dream."[11]

Easy targets, these money memoirs. But they do strike at something more universal than just saying "poor, pitiful me." Many people feel left behind by an economy that can seem designed to make the rich richer and leave the rest of us to valet-park their Teslas. The anger that comes with that feeling—of being economically at risk, of being ignored— helps explain, in part, why so many voters were drawn to the critique of income inequality from Bernie Sanders. Stoking that anger with fire-brand rhetoric also helped the candidacy of Donald Trump.

If you've read this far, you already know that Jeanne and I have struggled with debt. At the peak, we were carrying nearly $400,000 in mortgage, college loans, and car payments. Mortgage and property taxes were costing us about $2,400 each month, and college loans more than $1,300 a month on top of that. Even with a combined income of more than $10,000 a month before taxes, that didn't leave a lot to spare. Over the years, even as we held ourselves to a single credit card, we still had a stubborn balance of thousands of dollars, with a monthly pay-ment of more than a hundred bucks.

How did we pay it? Jeanne's fretful accounting kept us in line, for the most part. We had occasional late payments, but she was adamant about not letting things go to collection. Jeanne carefully watched grace periods on demands like the mortgage, though, to leave her the wiggle room to put paying one bill before another and waiting, if necessary, for the next paycheck to send in a particularly troublesome one. Some-times, if my health insurance refused a claim, the fight over it would last so long that a hospital would threaten to send the bill to a collection agency. But it was always possible to get them to agree to hold on while the claim was still being disputed.

We were squeezed, but we had never been extravagant. No fancy vacations, and in fact few vacations at all. Our kitchen does not have $1,000 sets of pots and pans. In fact, I don't remember buying them at all, so we probably got most of them as castoffs from my mom's kitchen. Similarly, our dishes are mismatched, some dating from our college days. Our cars are functional, and we drive them into the ground.

So we make choices. I walk an extra third of a mile to my train so that I can park for free, but we saw *Hamilton* on Broadway. Not at

$3,000 a ticket; we paid the original ticket price of less than $200 by buying when the first Broadway tickets went on sale. That's still pricey, sure; but well short of financial disaster.

We haven't been cheating spendthrifts like Dickens's Mr. Micawber; instead, we are more like Trollope's Graystock family in *The Eustace Diamonds*, who are "a race who could not pay their way with moderate incomes." One character, Lizzie Graystock, becomes quite wealthy but still falls into debt. Frank Graystock, the hero of the tale, is honorable and hardworking, but heedless about money: "Small economies in reference to cab-hire, gloves, umbrellas, and railway fares were unknown to him. Sixpences and shillings were things with which, in his mind, it was grievous to have to burden the thoughts."[12]

As a member of Parliament living in fashionable London, his lifestyle and profession required him to live among those born to wealth, "And, indeed, he had so cleverly learned the ways of the wealthy, that he hardly knew any longer how to live at his ease among the poor."

He reminds me of myself in those early days in New York, when money could slip out of your pockets for so many small things: Overpriced lunch. Taxis. Drinks. Many financial guides will wag a finger at people like us and point out that we should be reducing out debt through frugality. And that sounds great. You can get that message, for example, from the guru of getting out of debt, Dave Ramsey—on the radio and in his many books and on his website, where you can be badgered into strict household budgeting, cutting up your credit cards, and eating rice and beans until you pay off that mortgage.[13] You can read David Bach, who has sold millions of books on building a solid financial future by eliminating "the daily extravagances that drain your resources," cigarettes, bottled water, and that latte at Starbucks. He calls this finding your "Latte Factor," and has registered the trademark.[14] In his book *Smart Women Finish Rich*, he estimated that cutting out that daily Starbucks run and investing it would add $2 million in a retirement account.[15] "Are you latte-ing away your financial future?"

I'm all for quitting cigarettes. Those things will kill you, and they are getting more expensive all the time. And I love a good plate of rice and beans.

Still, I disagree. Buy the damned coffee if it makes you happy. When I used to drop Sammy off at school in the morning before going to work, I would often stop by Starbucks and pick up a latte for Jeanne on the way home. When I would present it to her, she would exclaim, "My hero!" After more than 40 years together, this was about the only time I got called that. She's cut out a lot of dairy since then, so no more lattes—but the memory is precious to me. And I still get a double espresso most mornings on my way to the office. I like saying hi to Kerwin and Shaquan and the rest of the gang at the Starbucks in Penn Station, and I pick up a second cup from Nathan, the Bukharan guy in the cart in front of the Times building who charges $1.25, even though there's free coffee once I get to work, because it means saying hi to the sunniest guy in Manhattan. "It's a beautiful day!" he tells me, even when it's sleeting.

My point, however, is that there are many reasons that I spend that money. Even without strict budgeting, I am pretty frugal in other aspects of my life. I'm a fan of street hot dogs, dollar-a-slice pizza, and food truck fare, and am deeply familiar with the Dollar Menu at McDonald's. I get lunch most days in the subsidized cafeteria at my office. While some items there can be pricey—there is a sushi chef, and the food-by-the-ounce line can deliver real sticker shock—I can order two vegetable sides and get past the cash register for less than five bucks. My little rattletrap of a Smart car gets about 40 miles per gallon, and I'm still driving it after nine years. So I do get tired of that latte cliché and its hectoring tone. If I really need to save my pennies, I'll set up a cuss jar in the kitchen and put a quarter in every time I say a bad word. Now that's a road to riches—at least as good an idea as fancy apps like Acorns, which automatically invests your spare change by rounding up your purchases to the nearest dollar and putting the saved pennies in an investment account.[16]

There are things that everyone can do, and should, every year to make sure money isn't leaking out of your house like heat through poor insulation. Keeping a zero balance on those credit cards is important, but so is making sure that your interest rate isn't higher than it needs to be. Check those bills, and look for a better deal. Examine your phone bill for mysterious charges and call the help line to see if you can get a better rate. The cable company, too, might have a new deal they didn't tell you about. Ask. Other subscriptions are creeping into our lives: Are you really listening to Spotify? If not, why are you still paying for it? Netflix, Hulu, Apple Music—make sure you're getting the most out of what you pay for, or don't pay for it.

For Jeanne and me, the most effective technique for economizing is arguing ourselves out of new purchases. That's how I ended up using Sam's woodshop-built Adirondack chair for a few years instead of buying a new recliner. It's why I haven't bought an Apple watch, even though all the cool kids at work have them. When I last mentioned it to Jeanne, she raised an eyebrow. "Do you really need that?" The question irked me; I yearn to be like my other Apple fanboy friends who tell the company at each new product announcement, "Shut up and take my money!"

But that eyebrow. It's just enough to make me think about whether the watch will, in fact, do that much for me when I already listen to my music and track my exercise with my iPhone 6. (No, I haven't bought the 8 yet, either; do I really need that?)

There's a decent analogy to that exercise tracking software. I became a runner in midlife. It was 2006, and spending a week out of every month or so in New Orleans, writing about the rebuilding of the city and eating in its restaurants, was adding pounds. The *Times* was renting a big house on Audubon Park, near the zoo, and there was a running track there that people used all day long. One day I went out in my tennis shoes and ran the 1.8 miles of that track—slowly, and miserably, but I made it around. A couple of days later, after the initial soreness receded, I did it again. And I got stronger, if not faster, and over time it became part of my routine. My weight came back into line.

Once I was working up a sweat every day, dessert became less of a treat and more of a threat. How many miles would I have to run to make up for this serving of bread pudding with white chocolate bourbon sauce? The fitness tracker will tell me, and I pause. Gradually, I came to order dessert less often and to eat less of it when I did. One bite of bread pudding brings ecstasy; downing a portion of New Orleanian generosity will fill me with regret to go with the calories.

But yes, buy the damned latte. There's a little bit of Frank Graystock in all of us, but we can accommodate him and still get by, enjoying a taste of luxury without making pigs of ourselves. We can find other ways to economize, striking a balance between thrift and misery.

You might think that any reasonable financial advice guru would tell you to buckle down and work up that family budget, maybe as Dave Ramsey suggests: with envelopes for each monthly expense, like this much for gas and this much for groceries, and down the line. Well, I'm not a reasonable financial advice guru, and thank heaven for that.

I'm not being some kind of libertine here. A Gallup poll in 2013 found that just one in three Americans has a detailed household budget.[17] And that's not necessarily dumb: strict budgeting does not prepare you for unexpected costs that strike us all. More important, other really smart financial advice people have questioned these systems and their gurus. Helaine Olen has written, "Budgets assume a level of consistency in our finances that doesn't exist." Track spending carefully, she advises, but actual budgets "offer the illusion, not the reality, of financial control."[18] Along with *The Index Card*, her book about personal finance with Harold Pollack that I mentioned earlier, Olen has written a fabulous skewering of the money guru game, *Pound Foolish: Exposing the Dark Side of the Personal Finance Industry*, in which she questions the Ramsey envelopes and the true value of those lattes.[19] Nor, as she says in the 2016 Slate Academy podcast series "The United States of Debt," is it helpful to blame people for being spendthrifts over small indulgences when the real causes of debt are often related to deeper sources of our financial woes: "You see people buying a latte, you don't see them buying their Lipitor."[20]

That's my kind of financial adviser! She's not saying that we should just throw up our hands and forget about managing our finances, but she's not wagging a finger at us and telling us to obsess uselessly. Yes, you shouldn't be too prodigal. But it's also a mistake to be too parsimonious with yourself.

Jeanne agrees that keeping a strict budget is impossible. "You have to know your priorities," she says. "I'm always looking at the accounts—

what's something we're spending money on that we can cut back?" But she was also willing to spend thousands of dollars a year on summer camps, because that was important. She calls it "knowing your priorities," which you balance against "know when you're sinking." Remember: it was her decision to sell the house in Millburn and wipe our slate clean.

Some debt, by the way, is useful. The people with no debt in that Urban Institute study had lower credit scores than those people with some debt but no blots on their record. The authors of the study suggested that if you don't build a credit record, it becomes harder to get credit—a kind of cycle that can keep people who might benefit from having a loan from getting it.[21]

Debt that you take on with the goal of making money is called productive debt; a mortgage gets us shelter, but it's also an investment that we hope will rise in value. A college loan is a kind of productive debt as well, with the expectation of a higher salary and faster advancement thanks to the degree. Nonproductive debt, sometimes called consumptive debt, is the stupid shit: borrowing money for a vacation or meals that you should be able to pay for with your ATM card.

If you can't pay for it out of your checking account, it's worth taking a moment to wonder whether you need it at all. Think about Professor Jack Gladney in *White Noise*, making his way through the mall and buying things to feel better about himself. Buying stuff generates something like a sugar high; it doesn't last, and is generally followed with a crash. The psychologists Leaf Van Boven and Thomas Gilovich have found that buying goods is not as satisfying as buying experiences like tickets to concerts or vacations.[22] In later research, Gilovich and Emily Rosenzweig found that the reason for dissatisfaction with material goods comes down, largely, to buyer's remorse.[23]

Does that mean I'm suggesting that you stop buying stuff? Or course not; I'm no anti-consumerist nag. I have bought things that still please me every time I look at them. (Hello there, beloved Krups coffeemaker.) But it's good to think before buying. And to try to buy things and experiences that will count.

MORE ON CREDIT CARDS

My cousin Nancy was shocked when I told her I don't have a credit card that gives me miles. "I just got a trip to Africa for free!" she told me, a little exasperated. It looked like a fabulous vacation; you should see the pictures! Actually, you can. They're on Facebook.

Smart financial guides teem with information about how to make the most of your credit cards. Clickbait websites offer to tell you about the best credit cards to have RIGHT NOW. Some people clearly benefit from playing the credit card game. My friends go on lovely trips and stay in hotels for free.

But Jeanne and I had made our decision during our worst days to have only one credit card, and it had to be one that would not penalize us. We had been badly burned by previous cards. One day in the 1990s I noticed that my AT&T Universal card, which I got in my first year of employment at *Newsweek*, all of a sudden soared to nearly 30 percent interest. I called the card company and was coldly told that we had been late on a payment, and they had jumped the rate. It was their legal right to do so, and there was nothing I could do about it. The people on the phone from these companies have the judgy sensibility of old deacons, even though they sound like they are 22 years old. What's more, whenever we neared the credit limit, the company would suddenly expand the limit—I would call to complain, and the company reps would tell me it was done as a "service" to us. I didn't want more rope to hang myself with, and more fees for these helpful people. I would demand the limit be brought back down again, and the helpful people would eventually do it. But it was a hassle.

We also tried points, the road to freebies for many of my friends. But an early experiment with enrolling in a program that would reward me with points for using my company-issued American Express card back in my *Washington Post* days also left me feeling burned. I paid to enroll in the program, and the points began to stack up as I traveled for work. But the moment we were late on a payment—and slips of a week were sometimes inevitable for us—the points went into some kind of point jail. To be able to get them back, we would have to pay a penalty. It became clear that we were losing money on the deal, and not able to take advantage of a system that made us spend so much to get so little. And if you keep a balance on your credit card, unless you spend a tremendous amount of money, then you're likely to end up spending more on interest payments than the points are worth. As I mentioned at the beginning of this chapter, the average credit card debt held by people with any debt is about $17,000. We are not alone.

These days, as I've mentioned, we maintain just one credit card. I got it from my credit union; it is not black or platinum or some other prestige color. But the credit union promised a reasonable rate with no nasty surprises. It will never get me a free trip to Africa, but it eliminates a big source of worry, and feels like we are not being abused. That's worth a lot.

Even after we were finally able to pay down that card—thank you, house sale!—we still did not get a rewards card. Old habits die hard; old fear grips our bones.

"Things don't work out for us when we try to be smart," Jeanne says. She's not wrong.

It's not just us; when Jeanne worked as a checker at Target, she saw people pulling out wallets stuffed with cards: ten, a dozen, or more. They would pull one out and give it a try at the terminal. Over the limit. Another. No dice. And another.

It's wasted money, that interest, and very expensive. Remember Professor Pollack, the index-card financial advice guru? Along with recommendations like picking low-fee index funds, he stressed paying off credit cards. And he's right.

HOME EQUITY LOANS

We've been similarly conservative about our mortgages and home equity loans. After our first adjustable-rate mortgage, we always got fixed-rate mortgages. No surprises. And while mortgage brokers have pressured us to consider 15-year fixed mortgages, which build up equity faster in your home, our preference has been to take on the lower monthly payment that comes with a 30-year mortgage. There's only so much we can spend, after all.

Home equity is certainly an attractive option, and they can be useful. You can tap the value of your home for a home equity loan for a certain amount, or get a home equity line of credit that you can draw on when needed. The loans are great for one-off projects like redoing a kitchen, while the lines of credit can act more like a credit card. The interest on home equity loans and lines of credit can often be deducted. Home equity loans tend to charge a fixed rate of interest, but the lines of credit tend to have interest rates that can rise over time.

Americans binged on home equity loans, especially in the run-up to the financial crisis and Great Recession. Housing prices were rising, people thought, so why not use your home's value as a bank and draw out some of that equity?

We were reluctant to follow the crowd, and not just because we'd lost one home when the market took a dive. We had seen the advice in newspaper articles about the beauty of using home equity to pay for the kids' college, since home equity interest rates tend to be so charmingly low. But Jeanne was fierce on this point: she wanted no part of anything that might give somebody the right to take away our house. (Lenders don't generally foreclose because of home equity loans, but it can happen.) Maybe that was the daughter of a professor of property wills and estates talking. Maybe she was just being risk averse. When our bank, trying to make lending even more attractive, offered to send us checkbooks that would draw on the home equity line of credit, she would not budge. All I know is that when things got seriously pitched for us, we only had to repay creditors; our home was not at risk.

In crunch times, such as our daughter's wedding, we took a loan from our 401(k), something that Vanguard makes as easy as filling out an online form. The interest rate on the loan was not high, and we were paying ourselves back; the only downside was the loss of potential investment income while the money was missing from our account. But that was a good incentive to pay the fund back, and we did.

PUNCH LIST

─────────●─────────

GETTING OUT OF DEBT

1) **Get a handle on your spending.** Does money seem to just fall out of your pockets? Paying more attention to what you spend your money on, and how much you spend, can help you impose some discipline on your wallet. Apps like You Need a Budget and Homebudget with Sync, available for iPhones and Android devices, can make it easy.[24]

2) **Pay your credit card bills on time.** Late payments show up on your credit report and can hurt your chance of getting good rates on your next mortgage or car loan, which can prove extremely costly. Besides, late fees are exorbitant, and you could be using that money to pay down your cards. Speaking of which . . .

3) **Pay down your cards.** The interest rate is crazy high, anyway. See if you can't find a credit card with a lower interest rate and fees—and then pay that one off as soon as you can.

4) **Don't use the cards for everyday purchases.** If you don't have the money and it's not essential, it can wait until next month. A debit card pulls the money directly from your bank account; that's the way to pay for meals and incidentals.

5) **Check your bills, part 1:** Have you looked at your phone bill lately? See if any odd charges have crept in. Call customer service to find out if there are lower rates available or if you can switch to a less expensive plan.

6) **Check your bills, part 2:** Once you've done that, check your cable bill. Customer service might help you find a less expensive package without losing much in the way of selection.

7) **Check your bills, part 3:** Do you suffer from subscription creek? Look at what you've signed up for with a regular deduction from your bank account or credit cards: take a hard look at recurring monthly charges for services like Netflix, Hulu, Spotify, and Apple Music. Are you really watching Hulu? If not, why are you paying for it? Cut out what you don't use.

10

LIFE INSURANCE

"Maybe it's time we started being sensible. All we've ever thought about is getting out of this house. The more I think about it, the more I think that's crazy. This house is plenty comfortable enough. With nine thousand a year, we could afford some life insurance. Did you ever stop and think what would happen to you if I dropped dead some morning?"

"Don't think about it!" Betsy said. "I'd drop dead right alongside you."

"Then what would happen to the children?"

"What's gotten into you, Tommy? I've never heard you talk like this before."

—SLOAN WILSON, *THE MAN IN THE GRAY FLANNEL SUIT*

LIFE INSURANCE HAS always been especially intimidating to me; it's a black box. A black box about death. Fun! I hated thinking about it. But the need for it creeps up on you, as it did on Tommy, the man in the gray flannel suit. It is the Future.

The longer I put off taking a hard look at insurance, the more expensive the policies would be. But by not getting a big policy yet, I was saving money. It was gambling, with interesting odds. But the stakes had climbed too high to keep putting it off.

So in this year of getting our financial life together, I decided to finally take a look at my insurance situation.

I knew a few things: I wanted to keep it simple. And I didn't want to get hustled.

When the investment adviser who set up the kids' college funds was through getting his fees for creating unnecessary savings instruments for us, he also offered to help me look for life insurance. "You need to be insured for $2 million, minimum," he said—a figure that might have been necessary if we sent the kids to Ivy League schools and needed to pay off their college debt in one swoop, and had a mortgage several times larger than the one we had. I felt, in other words, hustled. I told him I would keep his recommendation in mind. It seemed to me that the family could get by with something less than millions, especially if I'd be impoverishing us in the meantime by signing huge checks over to the insurance company every month. And I was reluctant to deal with somebody who was like the annoying insurance salesman Ned Ryerson from *Groundhog Day*. (Played, in case you've forgotten, by the wonderful Stephen Tobolowski.) An extreme parody, I know. But it was part of what put me off. Along with that bigger part, the part about thinking about death.

What I was hoping for was that fairly straightforward kind of policy known as term life. You get evaluated for the policy, you are told a rate to pay, you make your monthly payments. The downside is that the policy only lasts for a set term, say 10 or 15 years, and then you have to go through the process again.

The other main kinds of policies fall under the broad heading of "permanent life" insurance, with higher premiums and that build up savings as you go. You can borrow money from the savings you accumulate, and often at favorable tax rates; the savings can also be invested. The two main kinds of permanent life insurance are known as whole life and universal life.

A lot of insurance brokers love permanent life policies, and not just because those policies earn them fatter commissions than plain-vanilla term life. But knowing about their incentives was enough reason for me to be wary, along with the fact that I barely manage to keep track of the actual investments in our 401(k) plan. I didn't want to pay more to manage another set of investments. And people who don't make their money off selling you these policies will generally tell you that there's no reason to try to turn an insurance policy into an investment; get an insurance policy and make investments, but don't expect a chimera of the two to perform all that well.

I also already had experience with permanent life: a policy with AIG that my mother set up for me when I was just hitting my 30s. Mom had worked for several years as an insurance agent when I was a kid and knew the business pretty well. She must have figured I was too feckless to arrange life insurance for myself. The death benefit—the amount Jeanne would get when I died—was $100,000, enough to pay funeral expenses and to give Jeanne a financial boost, but not enough to make up for the loss of the family's main breadwinner. Mom hadn't said much about the policy at the time, and she made the payments herself. (Have I mentioned that my mother is great?) Years later, she sent the paperwork to me and told me I could borrow against the savings amount if I needed to. It was around $10,000. She eventually asked me to take over the payments. It wasn't a policy I'd wanted, but I decided not to cancel it—partly because of my usual financial sloth, along with the fact that borrowing against the $10,000 occasionally helped us through financial pinches. The annual premiums of $678 were not horrifying, but the term life I had at work offered a bigger payout for less in premiums.

Yes, Mom, I did have my own life insurance at work, but not very much of it. I'd always just signed up for whatever policies my employers offered. They were simple, requiring no physical exam, at least into my 50s. I figured the policies were reasonably priced—something coworkers generally confirmed, though the most determinedly fiscal of them did say they found somewhat better rates by scouring insurance websites and comparison shopping like mad. As you know by now, that is not me.

At the time I decided to start our financial makeover project, I had life insurance that would pay $275,000 if I died. But what would happen if I left the paper—whether because of another opportunity or because I got laid off? I decided it was time to take my life insurance into my own hands.

I started the way millions of people do: with a web search. I checked out SelectQuote.com, NerdWallet.com and PolicyGenius.com.

On one of the sites, the form confused me. It started out with the questions I expected about my health and things like whether I smoked. Then it asked for my email address, saying that it would hold on to the data that way so I could come back to it later. It then asked questions like when did I expect to pay off my mortgage? I picked the option "30 years," the term of the mortgage. But was that how long I expected to be in the house? We hadn't spent 30 years anywhere yet, but I didn't know when we might sell the house and pay off the mortgage. It seemed to me that the questions were designed to score my answers in ways I didn't understand.

After filling out the form, the site ended up telling me that just $100,000 in life insurance would be enough—much less than I expected. Thus the amount I needed to change my current coverage, the site said, was zero.

Which seemed weird. Hadn't that financial adviser told me I'd need at least $2 million in life insurance? He was probably trying to up the price to get a better commission, so a number somewhere between $2 million and $100,000 made sense.

A day or so later, I got an email from a "Senior Client Service Manager" that invited me to call.

The Client Service Team I lead can help vet your choices, answer questions about coverage, and will help see your insurance applications through from start to finish. We aren't on commission, so you can trust our advice is unbiased.

My confusion, I realized, might be part of the business plan. Simple tests are never as simple as they claim to be. Some people could zip through the site and come up with the answers, but most of us would need a helping hand. To figure out whether my current coverage was adequate, I would need to talk to a human being. Which is, of course, the point of these self-administered tests: to get you talking with an agent. And while they might not get a commission, they aren't working for a charity, either. And who were these people?

I remembered that a former boss of mine, Adam Bryant, had done a thorough job of checking out life insurance the year before. He had worked with an insurance broker who was energetic and smart, and had come up with a life insurance policy that he liked. Then he hit a complication. The agent told him that he could qualify for a special, lower rate if he could get his weight down by a few pounds. He is a high-achieving kind of guy who tries to hit the top of every category; I always figured if he hadn't gone into journalism, he might have been an astronaut. So he started driving his weight down by doing fanatical amounts of exercise. The effort backfired: one day during the period of frantic exertion, he saw blood in his urine. The condition is called hematuria—you can look it up, though I recommend skipping the pictures. Like so many medical mysteries, hematuria is usually nothing, but it can in some cases be Very Bad. It was pretty clear that in his case, the problem was brought on by the exercise, which can have that effect. But no one—especially no insurance company—would assume the best-case scenario, so my boss's sudden complication put off the evaluation and put him through weeks of testing.

By the way, after he was finally ready for the evaluation, he had gotten his weight just under the threshold for that wondrous rate. But, he told me, the nurse who showed up to do his medical exam pulled what he called a "crappy analog scale" out of her bag and had him stand on it. It added a few pounds, and he didn't qualify. Adam told me this with a wide-eyed, "what are ya gonna do?" expression. And yes, he gave me permission to tell this story.

He liked the insurance broker he worked with, however, and gave me the broker's email address. The guy worked for SelectQuote.com. This was not a recommendation on an algorithm. It was the right kind of referral: one from a person I know and respect. Adam is smarter than I am and good with money, and he vouched for the broker, whose name was Lucas.

So I sent an email to Lucas, and we set up an appointment to talk on the phone. On the morning our conversation was scheduled, as I was taking my morning run in West Orange, a guy backed out of his driveway coming straight for me. If I hadn't seen the movement out of the corner of my eye, I'd have been in the middle of his driveway when he slammed out into the street. Instead, I was able to stop at the edge of his driveway and wait, my hands up in warning as he passed. He saw me and slammed on his brakes, going white; he lowered his window and apologized. "One of us needed to be watching, and this time it was me," I said. "No problem." But if I'd been looking at my phone—changing songs, checking an alert—I might have been a casualty of the health-conscious lifestyle, another runner down. I don't believe that the universe sends us messages, but I do believe that coincidences can be instructive. My reminder of mortality made me look forward to the conversation a little more.

When Lucas called, I ducked into one of the newsroom's private work offices to be able to have this personal conversation. He conveyed a sense of competence; he knew his stuff and wasn't just reading from a script. He was nothing like Ned Ryerson. Lucas told me he would interview me about my medical history and then would be able to offer a set of possible life insurance plans that might suit my needs and budget. If I wanted a policy, a nurse would come to my house to take my blood and vital stats.

That first call took three-quarters of an hour. He said that, at my age, my preference for a term life policy was smart, since building up the investment value takes years. He ran me through questions about my income, how much was left on the mortgage, and whether we still had young kids at home. When it comes to knowing how much life insurance is necessary, he said, "if there are kids in the house, the answer usually is, 'a lot more.'"

Still, he said, the $275,000 might not be enough. If I died and Jeanne wanted to stay in our house, the insurance would pay off the mortgage, but her income as a crossing guard might not cover the taxes and living expenses. So what we had "sounds a little bit light," he said, and initially suggested $500,000, "at least until you retire." Once we were drawing down the 401(k), there wouldn't be as great a need for insurance to fill in the gaps. "If something does happen in the next 10 years, your wife is going to need an extra cushion," he explained.

He asked questions, a million questions. Height, weight, blood pressure, medications. Did I smoke? If so, I'd have to pay the "smoker price," a big hike over the price that nonsmokers pay. Not anymore, I said, and started to launch into a description of my past social smoking, maybe three cigarettes a week. But the agent said that as long as I'd been smoke-free for a year, that was all the insurance company cared about. And I had. If I'd lied about smoking, the evidence would show up on the blood test.

How was my blood pressure? It tended to be a little high, I told him, adding that I exercise to keep it in line.

Lucas told me that if I took blood pressure medications to stay at a healthy range, the insurer would look at the number and not care whether I got there with meds. "The insurance company doesn't care about exercise" when it comes to blood pressure, he said. "They care about numbers." (They do care about whether you exercise in general, though.) In any case, he said, if we thought my numbers might be high, he could steer me toward insurers that were more comfortable with higher blood pressure.

More questions. Cholesterol? Diabetes? Cancer? Sleep apnea? Anxiety or depression? How much alcohol did I drink?

How about my parents' health? Strokes or cancer before turning 65?

My answers seemed to satisfy him, though he sounded a bit concerned about my father's two strokes. The first one had definitely hit him before 65. But, I told him, Dad was also still going strong at 95. He liked that.

Then he asked whether I'd ever had a stroke or blood clot.

Well, I explained, "I have a G20210A prothrombin anomaly."

A what?

This, as it turns out, is a long story, one I've had to tell many times. Fifteen years before, I'd been on the commuter train when I realized I couldn't read the sign announcing the next stop with my right eye. I called my little brother, an ophthalmologist, and he told me I was seeing a retina specialist that morning. A forceful guy, my little brother, but he was right: when I saw the doc, he examined me carefully and said that I had developed a blood clot in my retina. It had formed, he explained, at the site of an arteriovenous malformation, a relatively rare tangle of blood vessels that can be found anywhere in the body. They are also known as AVMs and this one happened to be in my eye. If it had been in my brain, I would have had a stroke. In my eye, it meant I'd gone partially blind.

Further testing showed the reason for the incident: a genetic mutation that made me a little likelier than other people to form blood clots. Most doctors know about one of these, Factor V Leiden. Mine was less known; the mouthful of a name meant that I had one amino acid, adenine, where a guanine was supposed to be, or maybe the other way around, at position 20210 in the gene for prothrombin, a clotting factor.

Basically, I was struck half blind by a typographical error, which seems fitting for a writer, doesn't it?

As you can imagine, I learned all this new vocabulary very carefully. And, with watchful waiting, the clot slowly broke up and my distorted vision largely cleared, though I still can't see much in the upper-right corner of my right eye. And we had the kids tested for it, and I told my family about it—my father has had two strokes at the site of an arteriovenous malformation in his brain, and one brother had developed blood clots in his legs after surgery. So it seemed important to let everyone know that we might be at some increased risk.

And that's what I explained to poor Lucas. "I will need to check and see about the AVM," he said.

I told Jeanne about the interview, and how the guy seemed a little shaken when I talked about Dad's heart attacks and strokes and about my own high blood pressure and AVM.

"We might not be able to afford life insurance for you," she said.

That irked me; she seemed to be saying I was old and sick and past my sell-by date—a car with a minor problem that she thinks should be junked. That old fight. But she agreed to wait and see what the broker had to say.

She asked why the guy thought we needed a $500,000 policy in the first place, when we already had $275,000 coming to her if I died tomorrow. I explained his point: that she would want to be able to pay off the house and continue living there.

"I wouldn't want to keep living in New Jersey," she said. "I'd sell the house and move to Texas, which is cheaper. I could live with my mother for free and help take care of her. Her house is paid off." If her mother was no longer with us, Jeanne said, "I could get an apartment in Austin or Pflugerville." So she'd be living near Elizabeth, Matt, and Robin. In other words, the main reason for a big insurance payout was gone.

If she was going to sell the house, though, she'd still need rent money in Austin, right? She said she figured that by then she'd have access to the pension and Social Security—not enough to live high, but enough to get by. So the amount of money that the broker and I were talking about might not be as important to her. She figured she could do with something like the $275,000.

And, she reminded me, there was still that AIG policy.

So get insurance, she said. I could still get hit by a guy backing out of his driveway. We have friends startled by accidents, cancer. But don't go wild.

She said, "I don't think it's worth all the mishegas, as your people say."

About a week later, Lucas called back, apologizing because it took him a little longer to get rates back because of the complications in my history. Did I depress you? I asked. "It's okay," he said, not exactly denying it. "It gets more complicated, but they're not all going to be quick and easy."

He had a range of policies before him, and recommended that I look closely at a policy from Prudential. He had an estimate that I could be insured for $250,000 for $131 a month, or $1,455 a year if I paid a lump sum. Pretty close to what I was already paying, and with a rate that would be guaranteed for 10 years; my work insurance had been bumping up every 5 years. And if I wanted to stretch it to 15 years, it wouldn't cost much more.

It all made sense. I told him I wanted the Prudential plan and set up an appointment for the nurse's visit.

The nurse, whose name was Robin, came by at 7:00 a.m. on a

summer morning. The early hour made the fact that I couldn't eat for eight hours before the appointment easy to handle. She walked into our messy house; I cleared off a space on the kitchen table for her to work and for me to set up my laptop so that I could answer her questions.

One of the cats greeted her by jumping on the table. She asked if I could put the cats somewhere else. "Are you allergic?" No, she said; she was just going to be taking blood and doing things that cat hair would interfere with. These are not the kinds of problems that one has to deal with in doctor's offices, but she handled it all calmly.

She asked the same questions that Lucas had and entered the information on a Samsung pad. I had to dig around and look for the name of the doctor who had treated me for my eye problem in 2001. Like the broker, she stumbled a little over the G20210A prothrombin thingie. And over the fact that my dad had a heart attack and a stroke before the age of 70. But she took it down, had me give her the names of all the doctors.

She took my blood pressure: 120 over 80. She took it two more times. Even better. At a recent checkup, my doctor had advised me to drink less coffee and reduce my salt intake to bring my numbers down, and it was working. I missed french fries, but liked putting off having to take medications for a while longer.

The nurse was pleasant and funny and took my blood painlessly. She asked for, and got, a urine sample. She was in and out the door in a half hour.

"Is she done?" Jeanne poked her head out of the bedroom, having not wanted to take part in my fun. And we went on with our day.

In the end, the AV malformation was not a factor; the rate came in at Lucas's estimate. I signed up for $300,000—a little bump, to be safe—for 15 years, and paid the first year up front.

We had passed through another gantlet.

WHAT ABOUT LONG-TERM DISABILITY INSURANCE?

One topic that Lucas and I didn't discuss was disability insurance—the kind of policy that helps pay your bills if you are injured in a way that leaves you unable to work. You get a portion of your salary during your period of recovery.

Like a lot of people, I get disability insurance through my employer. But with the rise of the gig economy, fewer people get that kind of support. That means more people are exposed to disability risk without resources to deal with it.

Here's what you need to know.

It could happen to you. The Social Security Administration estimates that a 20-year-old has a one in four chance of experiencing disability before reaching retirement age.[1] That frighteningly high figure has been disputed, but the potential for a waylaying injury is there for anyone.[2] Still, 70 percent of Americans don't have disability insurance, according to Northwestern Mutual, a major provider of such policies.[3]

When people become disabled, whether for a while or for a lifetime, they might depend on family to get them through. Not every family has the resources, however. Social Security provides disability payments, but they aren't generous: the average monthly disability benefit in 2015 was $1,165.[4]

So getting insurance to cover some of the costs is a good idea, right? Disability insurance comes in two flavors: short term and long term. The short-term variety gets you covered for injuries or illnesses that put you out of commission for months or, depending on the policy, maybe a year. It tends to be cheaper than long-term disability insurance, which can keep you covered for the length of your expected working life. Depending on the terms of the policy, long-term disability insurance can bridge the gap to retirement age. It also has a longer period before coverage kicks in, commonly three to six months. Neither kind of policy will provide the full income that you've lost—again, how much depends on the terms of the policy you choose—but the policies can provide half or more. Long-term disability insurance can pay as much as three-quarters of your lost income, which can be a crucial source of support in a tough world.

If your employer does not provide the policies, insurance companies will. You can check with an insurance agent or work through an online insurance broker like PolicyGenius. And, of course, if you have your own policy, you take it with you if you change jobs.

Once you start looking, you'll notice that the younger you are, the less you'll pay. You'll see ways to save money, too, by choosing a longer waiting period before coverage can begin or a shorter amount of time that the policy pays out.

PUNCH LIST

———————●———————

GETTING LIFE INSURANCE

1) **Ask yourself:** Do you need life insurance? If you're young and you have kids, you probably need plenty. If you're older, near retirement, and have retirement funds built up, you might not need it at all—or, at least, you'll need less.

2) **Figure out how much you need.** Deciding how much life insurance you need involves, at some level, predicting the unknowable. But life insurance calculators let you fill in some estimates and come up with reasonable answers. You can find good life insurance calculators online. USAA has one.[5] So does Bankrate.com.[6] Others are as easy to find as firing up a Google search. The calculators have you estimate how many years of your potential income will need to be replaced: how much you can expect to have to pay for your kids' upkeep and education; how long your spouse will need support before retiring or dying. They also fold in costs you might not have considered, including the cost of your burial—$7,000 or more!—or of the kids' weddings.

   Play with the calculators. Try a range of answers and see how the results tumble out. You can think of it as a video game, but without extra lives.

3) **Find a broker.** This is another one of those cases where getting expert advice can be a big help. If you have an insurance broker or company you or your family or friends knows and trusts, of course, go with them. But if you don't, sites like Selectquote.com, Policy Genius.com, and Insure.com will compare policies from a range of companies. You can also look for deals from groups like the AARP, which leverages its buying power across its enormous membership.[7] And while you're at it, look into disability insurance, as well.

4) **Vet that policy.** Before signing any policy, make sure that the insurance company you're dealing with is in good financial shape. Your broker should tell you, and help you interpret the ratings from services like Moody's and Standard & Poor's. You can also look into whether the company provides good customer service by

checking the complaints at the National Association of Insurance Commissioners.[8]

5) **Prepare to be probed.** If you are getting a life insurance policy, your insurer will want to know your risk of stroke, heart attack, and other illnesses. You'll go through a lengthy questionnaire, but you're also likely to need a medical exam. There are no-exam policies, but they tend to come with caps on coverage and relatively high prices. But if you're pretty healthy—you don't smoke, you exercise regularly, and keep your weight in a decent range—you'll save a lot by submitting to the medical exam.

11

WRITING A WILL

In case I die in this mess I leave all to the wife.
                    CECIL GEO. HARRIS

OLY GUACAMOLE, GUYS. Prince died without a will.

All that money, and one of the greatest performers I ever saw onstage didn't spend a little of it on sorting out his estate? It amazes me.

Maybe he figured he had time to work all that out. Or maybe he thought he didn't need to work it out at all. I remember a colleague telling me about trying to arrange a video interview with fitness icon Jack LaLanne. He was explaining to LaLanne's assistant that the video would eventually be part of an obituary package; the well regarded "Last Word" videos with the *NYT.* The assistant said that Mr. LaLanne would never participate in such a project. My friend responded that it was not unusual for people to be uncomfortable with talking about death, but that many people had agreed to these interviews.

"You don't understand," the assistant said. "Mr. LaLanne doesn't think he's going to die."

On January 23, 2011, Mr. LaLanne was proven wrong.[1]

So, yes, death is inevitable. Yet we continue to make long-term bets:

we shop at Costco. Jeanne and I might have enough economy-size jugs of Tide and gigantic packages of toilet paper rolls to survive into the next century. Still, preparing for an eventual demise—at least by drawing up a will—is a good idea.

Which is not to say that I had a will, either, at Prince's age. (He died at 57.) Writing a will was another one of the things on the endless to-do list that kept not getting to done. We don't have a Warren Buffett–sized fortune to bestow on the kids, but a house and 401(k) accounts add up to something. Jeanne and I both knew that a will smooths the way for your heirs to inherit whatever you're going to give them, saving time and money. Wills can also help you avoid tax pitfalls and feuding heirs. Remember: the conflict at the heart of Dickens's *Bleak House* is a generations-long lawsuit over an inheritance. No spoilers, but the case did not end well for anyone involved, over several generations. Wills provide control over more than money: for people whose children are still minors, the will names the guardians.

If you haven't written these decisions down, the government will make the decisions itself, based on a legal formula. You'll be beyond caring by then, but why not do what you can ahead of time to see that the assets get distributed as you'd like?

Those are all good arguments, but they hadn't gotten me to spring into action. We had put it off, like everything else that involved thinking about money and death. We were in good company: fewer than half of Americans have written a will, according to Gallup. In a May 2016 poll, just 44 respondents said that they had a will, down from 51 percent in 2005. But 75 percent of people aged 55 and over who earned more than $75,000 said they had a will. For our age, we were in the minority.[2]

So! A will.

Besides, I didn't want to leave it to the very last minute, like poor Cecil George Harris. Mr. Harris, a farmer in Saskatchewan, died in 1948 in a gruesome way: he got pinned under the wheel of his tractor and lay there for nearly 10 hours until his wife found him. He died the next day of his injuries, but during his painful time under his red tractor, he'd used his penknife to scratch a brief attempt at a will into its fender. It read, in full, "In case I die in this mess I leave all to the wife.

Cecil Geo. Harris." A quick-thinking local lawyer had the fender removed and brought into court as proof that Mr. Harris had left a true last will and testament, and a judge ruled it was valid. The fender is on display at the law library of the University of Saskatchewan, in Saskatoon, and the law nerd in me hopes to see it someday.[3]

With our project to get our financial lives in order, we knew it was time to move forward before getting pinned under the tractor of fate. Jeanne and I believe that simpler is better: We want to die peacefully, with family gathered around us, listening one last time to the Ramones. And to leave our estate issues tied up neatly.

Which also meant that any will we wrote should be as straightforward as it could be. I'd seen what could happen when things got complicated. I had a friend from my college days, Bob Solomon, a professor of philosophy and a corporate ethics consultant who wrote wonderful books, and even appeared in Richard Linklater's trippy film *Waking Life*. Bob, who had a congenital heart condition, died with shocking suddenness in 2007 after collapsing in the Zurich airport.

Some months later, his widow, Kathy Higgins, got in touch to tell me that he had written a will intended to give his good friends some money. Not enough to buy a car, but enough to be a nice surprise, and to make a fond final memory. The problem, she said, was that while the original will had been written by a lawyer, Bob had decided to revise it on his own. Now there was something of a mess that could be resolved only if I and the other would-be recipients signed a waiver of some kind that would be sent by the lawyer. She just wanted me to know that it was on its way.

So much for nice surprises. I thought about Kathy having to deal with this complication—and having to pay the lawyer to sort it all out—in the middle of her grief. I told her that I didn't want the money if it was going to cause her trouble, but that I would sign whatever got sent to me. It came; I signed it and forgot about it.

Nearly two years after Bob died, I got an envelope in the mail. It contained a check and a handwritten note from Bob. When had he written it? It was overwhelming. And so sweet.

I wrote to thank Kathy, and she replied, "Actually, it was enjoyable to do, since it was something I could do with/for Bob. The whole point of the exercise of the lawyer and the letters was to undercut Bob's intention of just surprising people—though of course the lawyer thinks that this was necessary. I'm glad you were surprised anyway."

It was a wonderful gesture, odd and warm, like Bob. But the experience showed me that maybe I wanted to keep things a little less surprising. Our wills, Jeanne's and mine, would just be about family. And while we were at it, we figured, we should take a look at other end-of-life decisions such as how far we wanted doctors to go with our medical treatment.

First, I tried going online for a do-it-yourself approach. Several products can help you write your own will and other estate documents, including financial guru Suze Orman's "Will and Trust Kit" and an assortment of products from LegacyWriter.com, LegalZoom.com, BuildaWill.com, and Nolo.com.

Tara Siegel Bernard of *The New York Times* tried out four will-writing programs a while back and showed the resulting documents to an attorney. She found that the programs varied in quality, thoroughness, and ease of use—and that for all but the simplest situations, legal help was worth getting.[4] *Consumer Reports* has also argued in favor of lawyers over software in most cases: "Your needs are too complex for a do-it-yourself estate plan if you must provide for a disabled child, you owe estate taxes, or you own a business."[5]

I went to the websites of several of the online options, started reading the descriptions, and quickly realized that I had no idea what I was doing. This comes back to my earliest point in this book: I am, in fact, an idiot.

Yes, I am a lawyer. But I'm not a practicing lawyer. I didn't even take will and estates in law school. (Hey, I didn't take oil and gas law, either, and that topic is also on the bar exam. I made up for the holes in my legal education for both topics in the cram review course before the test. And I passed the bar exam. By two points.)

While some of the products, like LegalZoom's "comprehensive" "Last Will and Testament" package (but not the basic version) offer consultation with an attorney who will vet the resulting document,

Jeanne and I decided to go through the process with an attorney from the get-go. Our wills were going to have a few complications; we wanted to explore the question of whether we might want some kind of a trust for Joseph, who might need some help on money matters because of his depression.

This is one more of those situations when consulting with an expert makes a lot of sense. When it came to the potential complications of a will, and the downsides of doing it wrong, I wanted to sit across from a human being.

While we were at it, we figured on also getting a living will—one of those documents that tells doctors how far to go in saving your life. These days, you almost can't walk by a hospital or get a medical procedure without someone asking you, "Do you have an advance medical directive? A living will?" Then they offer you materials. It's gotten to be so commonplace that I'd come to ignore it.

But giving instructions about how you want to be treated in case of dire illness is important. As a reporter, I have covered the Death with Dignity movement and talked with terminally ill patients who wanted a say over how they left this world. When I was reporting in Oregon, which pioneered physician-assisted suicide laws, I met a hospice nurse who told me she had gotten a big purple tattoo reading "DNR"—do not resuscitate—on her left breast, over her heart. It was the sort of thing an emergency responder wouldn't miss, she explained.

She offered to show the tattoo to me. I thanked her, and said I trusted her on that point.

I also covered the legal and political mess around the death of Terri Schiavo, the Florida woman who suffered extensive brain damage in 1990 and was kept alive in a persistent vegetative state. Her husband, Michael, and parents squared off over whether to follow what Mr. Schiavo argued were her wishes: not to be kept alive artificially under such circumstances. That case became a circus, and made its way to Congress and the Supreme Court before her husband won the right to have her feeding tube removed in 2005.

Who needs that? Aren't illness and death painful enough for the whole family?

So, yes, I knew the importance of getting those instructions out there, and Jeanne and I had talked about not wanting extraordinary measures that would keep us suspended hellishly between life and death after hope of recovery is gone. Dementia, irreversible brain damage, end-stage terminal illness: we agreed that we didn't want doctors to take heroic measures that would torment everyone involved while zeroing out family assets.

I'd tried to let the kids know my wishes in an informal way. When our daughter Elizabeth was 13, I accompanied her on a volunteer trip to spend an afternoon with people living at the Hebrew Home for the Aged near Washington, D.C. She did art projects and played games with the residents and talked with many of them. But we both noticed the other residents, the ones who couldn't play cards, who were tied into their wheelchairs and looking blank and empty. And drooling.

On the way back to our car, I said, "Now, sweetie, listen to me. If I ever get to the state some of those people were in, I want you to buy a gun . . ."

"Daddy!" she shouted with the kind of disgusted exasperation that is a hallmark of so many of our conversations. But she was smiling, too.

"Laugh now," I said. "Remember later."

As striking as the moment may have been—and she recently told me that she remembers it well—it was not an advance directive. Not in writing, not specific, not available for strangers to find in an emergency. And that's what Jeanne and I realized we needed to have. On the other hand, getting such things down on paper is One. More. Damn. Thing. And we hadn't gotten around to it.

I joked to Jeanne that I hadn't written up a directive yet because she would be managing my care; she is *such* a pessimist. Jeanne is the one who, when the boiler went out, predicted that we would have to replace the whole thing. Then the repairman showed up, put in a new thermocouple, and we were back in business for about 200 bucks.

I've got the opposite problem: I try to hold on to things long after they are beyond hope, spending good money on hopeless cases like automotive lemons.

I joked to Jeanne that I had visions of her telling doctors, "Pull the plug—he's a goner," and hearing myself shouting, *"but it's only a broken arm!"*

That grim fantasy made her laugh. She opened her arms wide, saying, "But I loooove you!"

She told me that the reason to worry about the medical directive is the opposite of the scenario I'd laid out. "I'm going to keep you alive *forever*," she told me. "The doctors will say, he's brain-dead. I'll still—"

I cut in, "You'll say, 'nothing new there!'"

"I'll still say," she said, pushing my shtick aside, "no, keep him going. I'll move into your room and just sit next to you."

"Like a plush toy," I said.

"I'll never let you go," she said.

So it was time for the living will, too. When I got my colonoscopy shortly after turning 59—it was just fine, thanks for asking, let's not talk about "bowel prep"—I asked the nurse for the information that had been offered to me on living wills instead of waving it off.

He handed me a poorly photocopied printout from the American Hospital Association with the title "Put It in Writing: Questions and Answers on Advance Directives." That phrase, "advance directives," is the umbrella term for living wills and the "durable power of attorney for health care," which set out your medical wishes. To be specific, the living will is a set of guidelines you choose for your treatment; the durable power of attorney for health care sets up another person as the decision maker for health crises. These days the two categories tend to be blurred and can be combined.

The brochure the nurse handed me was not a workbook or tool kit; laws and forms for advance directives vary from state to state, and so it dealt in generalities. But these were helpful, with a discussion about people "stating their health care preferences in writing, while they are still healthy and able to make such decisions." It pointed out that in 1990 in the case of Nancy Cruzan, the Supreme Court said that a state could require "clear and convincing evidence" of a patient's wishes before withdrawing life support, and that Congress passed the Patient Self-Determination Act of 1990 that requires hospitals to bring up advance directives with patients. Which helps explain why I'm always getting brochures offered to me on hospital visits.

Between the brochure and other information I started to gather online, I learned that while state laws do differ, most of the differences concern what's required to validate the document—in some jurisdictions, two witnesses. In others, a notary public or an attorney. The name of your health care decision maker also changes from state to state: you might appoint a proxy or a representative. Because of these differences, if you plan to do this form yourself, then it's important to know what your state requires.

The basic information and the forms can be found in bookstores and on the internet at sites like the National Hospice and Palliative Care Organization, which offers customized forms for each state that combine elements of living wills and proxy assignment, and the American Bar Association, which provides a comprehensive directive form that it developed with AARP and the American Medical Association; the site provides extensive background information as well. And yes, there's an app for that.[6]

These are the kind of papers you want everybody to have: your family, friends, clergy, lawyer. It should be on file at your doctor's office, as part of your medical record. You don't want to go to all of this trouble contemplating horrors and then not have people know about your wishes when you're lying unconscious in a hospital bed. Some of the terminally ill people I met on my Oregon reporting trip had a brightly colored advance directive folder on their refrigerator door with the forms inside so that paramedics wouldn't have trouble finding it. And the more I thought of it, the more that nurse's purple DNR tattoo sounded like a good idea. If I got one, I wouldn't be alone. A Google image search for "DNR tattoo" brings up plenty of examples. Though purple is not my color.

Not so fast, though. A formal DNR order instructs ambulance and hospital emergency department workers not to revive you in an emergency, when they are legally obligated to try to revive you unless there are explicit orders to the contrary. DNR orders are favored by some people in poor health who are unlikely to benefit from CPR. The nurse had seen too many people suffer after resuscitation; the rest of us might want to let the emergency responders take their initial shot.

The problems with a simple DNR tattoo are easy to grasp. Two doctors wrote them up in a 2012 article in the *Journal of General Internal Medicine.*[7] The tattoo, they said, is "intuitively appealing, but flawed as policy." As an instruction, it is both stark and broad, and might confuse emergency workers. "Errors in interpretation may have life and death consequences." And while DNR forms can be revoked, the tattoo will be there even if you change your mind, unless you want to go through the trouble and pain of removal.

So I won't make a statement with my flesh. Forms will do.

I started looking for a lawyer, spending time with my chief legal adviser, Google. It showed me a number of lawyers specializing in wills and estates in our area. There was the firm in a rich town whose big partner graduated from Harvard before I was born. Its website was so tastefully designed that it seemed to say that they wanted a certain class of clients, say, country club members who also hired wealth advisers. There was also a woman who practiced out of her home just a couple of miles from us. I also saw a small firm in a more down-market town. After this quick scan of the legal landscape, I was about to call the solo practitioner when Jeanne told me she'd rather have a recommendation from a friend than simply trust my gut.

Dang.

So I sent notes out to friends who, it has always seemed to me, are grown-ups. One of them offered a name and this ringing endorsement:

I use a guy in town called Nate Arnell. I have zero standard of comparison and have no idea if his fee was high, low or average, but he's a nice guy and seemed fine.

I'm not so big on extreme vetting. He's the one I called.

"How can I help you?" he asked.

I told him we needed a will. "That's a good thing, because that's what I do," he said.

We got an appointment. He said he would provide the will and our advance directives as part of a package, though he could not say ahead of time how much everything would cost.

The day we met him at his office in Millburn, New Jersey, we played the game of Jewish Geography. He was born and raised in Kansas City. He didn't know my friends the Firestones, but his big sister grew up with Calvin Trillin. He'd see Trillin—"Everybody called him Buddy"— at family events. Growing up around my literary heroes is the kind of qualification I look for in a lawyer. He was a vigorous guy with a neatly trimmed beard.

The will didn't have to be a final, huge deal, he explained. He could make the document flexible enough to serve for some time but easy to change if need be. "You can make a new one every single day." That, however, would be expensive. "Good for me, not so good for you." The process could cost as much as $3,000 if we had a lot of changes or complications, but would be less if things were straightforward.

We talked for a bit about the tax implications of our deaths—that the federal estate tax affects only people with millions of dollars' worth of assets. Currently, he said, it's $5.42 million for each of us. We assured him that we did not have $11 million in assets. Only 4 percent of people end up triggering the tax. New Jersey's estate taxes start at a lower level: $647,000 apiece. With the two of us, that means the potential for our heirs to pay no inheritance tax unless we top $1.35 million. There could be income taxes tied to, say, my pension, and further implications depending on the amount that gets paid out from the estate in a short time. "If you take it out all in one year, you take it out in a very high rate; if you did it in bits, it might hit lower brackets," he said.

He also laid out the scenarios that cause wills to become complex and fractious—multiple marriages, blended families with stepchildren from those various marriages, families in conflict, and more.

"We've only been married to each other," Jeanne told him. "All of our children are our children. And we all get along."

You could see Nathan's shoulders relax. He then asked what our assets might be: house, 401(k), life insurance. He would include clauses giving the surviving spouse lots of flexibility in planning how to get the money and to do tax planning around the inheritance.

We told him about Joseph's depression and the possible need for some kind of continuing support. He described wills he had written in the past, including provisions for a child who was unable to manage his affairs. Jeanne explained that she wasn't trying to keep him from getting money, but she would like the money to be administered by his big sister, who is a lawyer. She asked, "Could it be his sister?"

"It could be," he said. "That's why I was asking whether they get along." He discussed taking that son's share and setting up a system that would allow him to get 5 percent of his share every year, like a salary. He told us to make sure that Elizabeth was up for the responsibility. (She later told us that she was willing to take it on—if nothing else, she said, it would mean they would have an excuse to hear from each other on a regular basis.)

He then moved on to the advance directive and also power of attorney—the ability of a person designated by us to make decisions for us if we were incapacitated. And, he said, we should think hard about giving medical power of attorney to one of the kids. "If you don't think she could pull the plug, then she's not the right person," he said. I asked, again, what all this would cost; he said it depended on how much time it would take to draft everything.

He told us that he would work up the documents and send them our way. Jeanne and I thanked him and walked over to a nearby Starbucks for a break.

"That was really depressing," Jeanne said.

"Contemplating mortality?" I asked.

She looked at me. "Death! Death! Death!"

=

A few days later, I was going over what we needed to do before our next meeting. Nate had ended the first visit with a homework assignment: track down our pensions, insurance policies, retirement accounts, and anything else that will pass to heirs when we die. We would need to make sure that the beneficiaries named in all those documents line up with what we're putting into the will. In most cases, the contract terms of the beneficiary statements will control what happens.

"This is why people don't make their wills," Jeanne said. "It's too much fucking trouble."

A few weeks later, Nate sent a stack of digital documents—a will for me and for Jeanne, a durable power of attorney for each of us, and his and her living will/health care directives. The wills were 41 pages apiece; the other documents came to a dozen pages more for each of us. Dry stuff, though he included a very readable summary. I was on a reporting trip when they showed up in my email; I read them on the plane on the way home. I sent Jeanne an email telling her she needed to read them, too, and she wrote back, "I leave it in your hands. You are da man."

I wrote back, "No no no no no we are partners you are woman an equal this is important oh what the fuck all right."

We went back to his office, briefly discussed the provisions of the wills, and signed them. A short time after that, we got the final bill: a little less than $2,000.

Now we have wills. One more worry is gone, or maybe it was a source of guilt. Or maybe it was just a nagging thought. I won't be happy to die, but I won't be tormented over leaving that particular loose end undone.

And there's something to be said for that.

PUNCH LIST

———— • ————

GETTING A WILL

1) **Get a will. Really.** Dying without a will—intestate—is a drag for everyone. Things can get tied up in court, and many of the decisions will be decided under rules of law that might not reflect your wishes.

2) **Get a lawyer.** Yes, there are websites and services that can help you do it yourself. You might be one of those people who will do a perfect job of writing a will, and your family and assets might be uncomplicated enough to take a stab at it. If so, Godspeed—but then get a lawyer to check your work.

    For most of us, using a lawyer for this important document is a good idea. If your family situation is complicated—if you have family members who might benefit from a trust or other arrangement for continuing care—have a lawyer do it. A lawyer can help explain the benefits of having things like a "dynasty trust," which sounds like it would only be for rich people but which can help protect an inheritance from being lost in a divorce.[8]

3) **Decide on your beneficiaries.** These are not usually complicated decisions. People leave their property to their spouses and kids. But you should plan it out. And don't use your will to settle old scores; what's the point? This is also the moment to think about any charitable bequests you'd like to create. This is especially important for dual-income couples with no kids who might have substantial assets to spread around when they no longer need them. Whether it's gifts to charities, hospitals, political parties, religious organizations, your alma mater, or other organizations, the choices you make with a portion of your assets now can make a difference in the world when the time comes.

4) **Decide on your executor.** Who will make sure the provisions of the will are carried out? Your executor. Choose wisely; it's a lot of work and requires good judgment. If your estate will be complicated, you might want to have a lawyer or other professional do it instead of leaving the mess to one of your kids. Make sure the

guardian knows of your decision and agrees to it. The executor can be paid.

5) **Got young kids?** Set up a guardian. Someone has to be there for them; in a will, you get to decide who that is. Without a will, a court will appoint one. Again, this is a role that you don't spring on somebody after you're gone; talk it over with your prospective guardian, and sign up an alternate to be safe.

6) **Put it somewhere safe, but easy to find.** We left a copy of ours at our lawyers' office. You can keep it in a safety deposit box or a good fireproof safe, or with a trusted relative. Make sure family members know where to find it—it would be a shame to go to all that trouble for nothing.

7) **Once it's written, revisit the will at least every five years.** Things change. Marriages end; children grow to independence; executors and beneficiaries die. Don't let your will get out of date, or you could cause much of the confusion you tried to avoid by paying for the thing in the first place.

12

OLDER AGE

Someday, if you are lucky, the nightmare of paying for your kids' college will all be over. The kids will be out of school, and the loans will be paid off. (More than one friend called life after finishing the college debt payments "the biggest raise I ever got.")

But for many of us, as the kids are getting older, a big truth drives up: our parents are getting older, too. Things start to get complicated. And that can mean money, too.

And we are all aging. There's nothing new in discovering that you are part of the sandwich generation. With that comes the worry about our parents, if we're lucky enough to still have them in our lives, and the fretting over how the financial side of things will work out.

WHAT ABOUT THE FOLKS?

Some 70 percent of people turning age 65 will probably need long-term care at some point, according to the U.S. Department of Health and Human Services.[1] And it's expensive. A 2010 HHS report estimates that costs in a nursing home can be more than $90,000. Which is, you know, even more expensive than college. How in the world does that get paid for?

Jeanne and I are the tail end of the baby boom. Our parents are from what has been called the Silent Generation, born between the 1920s and 1940s. The Silent Generation accumulated wealth. As they have aged, an industry has grown up, with federal assistance, to make sure much of that wealth got transferred to the eldercare system.

This is how Medicare works: you pay your assets down until you are broke, whether living independently or in an assisted-living facility or a nursing home, and then Medicaid takes over. That is the way it is supposed to work, at least.

We have known people who handled the transition poorly. Some try to make sure that the aged parent will be eligible for Medicaid coverage—and not let the assets go directly to health care providers, draining away any possible inheritance—by drawing down the parent's assets. But Medicaid has what is known as a "five-year look-back" period; the feds check to see if someone applying for long-term care support has dumped assets to qualify for the coverage. If there's evidence of that kind of transfer, the government can impose a period of ineligibility. The result can be very expensive for the Sandwich Generation kids.

It's complicated! And scary. Money worries and old age—two great fears that go great together. Overhanging all of it is the worry that our folks won't get the care they need and deserve.

We got our wakeup call about these issues when Jeanne's mom, Doris, needed a hip replaced. Having to figure out her care, and what would happen if the recovery didn't go well, sent us into fits of apprehension and research.

We're lucky in some ways; Doris's sister was able to stay with her for the surgery and for a couple of weeks after. Jeanne and I were able to fly in to provide some help at that point, but we live 2,000 miles away and couldn't stay long. So we hired a home health aide to come in three days a week. We were told it wasn't covered by Medicare, but we knew it was important. And, in fact, the home health aide saved Doris's life, spotting a skin infection, cellulitis, three weeks after the surgery that was growing and could have been life-threatening. She got her to the hospital, and treatment began to clear the condition.

Worth it? Absolutely. But still, expensive. Jeanne started signing up to work every festival and parade that the cops needed crossing guards for in order to help pay the home aide company.

And as her mother's recovery dragged on, we asked ourselves whether her mother might need to be in an assisted-living facility.

My folks had looked into the same issues and initially decided on a very nice assisted-living complex in Austin, where they live. They put down a substantial deposit. But they thought better of it after my younger brother reviewed the charges and told them they were exorbitant compared with what he could help them find nearer to him, in Florida. The decision was put on hold until 2017, when Dad had a few hospitalizations and it was time to make a decision. Working with my older brothers in Houston, my parents decided to move into a senior living complex in Houston, where they had ready access to medical care. With the money they hope to make from selling their condominium in Austin, they expect to be able to afford the new place for years to come. Jeanne's father has also been thinking about these issues; he and his wife have been planning to move into a smaller home without stairs that would be easy to maintain.

Jeanne's mom, however, had no such plan, except to occasionally tell Jeanne, "I'm going to die at home." And we didn't want to have to make a decision quickly if the surgical recovery didn't proceed well, or if other health problems came up.

So we started doing some research. The federal government offers an online tool for comparing nursing homes at medicare.gov/nursinghome-compare/search.html, and has a great deal of other information besides at sites listed at this endnote.[2] There are also referral companies like A Place for Mom, a free service that helps people explore the options for caring for elderly parents.[3] However, A Place for Mom gets its fees from the institutions it helps place people in; to writers like Paula Span of *The New York Times*, this raises questions of potential conflict of interest.[4] Span has noted that local agencies on aging can provide the same information, without the financial incentives.[5]

Jeanne and I began to study up on assisted-living places. We looked up complexes in Houston but had another thought as well; if need be, could we move her closer to us? Our house is three floors, and not suited to an older person with mobility problems. But, we thought, maybe she'd be willing to live near us in an assisted-living place in New Jersey.

We took a tour. A facility wasn't far from our home; it was part of a chain, Care One, a New Jersey–based company that has about 70 centers across the mid-Atlantic and New England states.

After making an appointment, we walked into a place that looked like a Homewood Suites or Hampton Inn: pleasant and generic, if not luxurious. The explosion of inexpensive architecture that put decent hotels at every interstate exit seemed to be helping to build this booming industry, as well. This building had nice floors and a soaring entryway, with a dining hall directly across a lobby from the front door. The building was just 11 years old and still looked new.

A boom box sitting on top of a piano played oldies rock and roll—annoyingly loud for us, but probably okay for anyone hard of hearing. You could smell the food—it was 2:00 p.m., and lunch hadn't been over for long—and the smells weren't institutional. They made me hungry, which was a good sign.

Charles, a friendly guy from Kansas, was the executive director of the place, and he sat us down to go over the basics. There's a lot of confusion about terms, he said, and people think of nursing homes when there's actually a range of living arrangements depending on how much help people need. It's not just putting people in nursing homes anymore, he explained, adding that "'nursing homes' is an outmoded term." He was using a lot of terms whose precise definitions I didn't know, and I was getting confused.

"We don't know what we're talking about," I said.

He explained that assisted living is for people who need some help getting by from day to day but don't have the kinds of health problems that require extensive medical care and a nursing home. I was familiar with the latter; my father's mother lived out her final years in a nursing home after an incapacitating stroke in her 50s.

He told us that, with the aging of baby boomers, his industry was expected to triple in size in the next 15 to 20 years. People stay healthier longer now, and by the time they are ready to move into a place like CareOne, they need a degree of help. To qualify for Medicaid, they must need help with at least three areas of life, like taking medications, getting around and getting food, and having motivation to take part in activities.

He handed us a glossy folder with information about the facilities and a couple of pages of the charges, which were a little startling. Besides a "community fee" on moving in of $3,500, the basic room and board for what they called a studio apartment—essentially, a hotel room—was $5,680 a month. Share a room, and it could cost $3,853 a month. Then additional charges were tacked on, depending on what level of service you need. They were called "activities for daily living" and could run from $30 to more than $100 a day. On top of that, medication assistance cost from $19 to $25 a day, depending on whether you take up to 15 medications a day or 16 or more. Yes, that's 16 or more.

Beyond that were the ancillary services and charges, including about $12 for room service if you didn't want to go to the dining hall—a charge, he said with a smile, that's meant to encourage people to be social. A "call system pendant" would cost $175 a month, as would "wander care."

Chris said he understood that we were at the beginning of a confusing process and that we might not end up bringing Doris to New Jersey after all. Still, "I'm happy to be a resource for you guys," he said.

He walked us around and showed us the studio and the larger suites, which run $6,800 a month. Jeanne had told him that, with her mom's house and other assets, she estimated that she might have about $300,000 to deal with. Chris did the numbers in his head. A one-bedroom mid-size room would cost $6,300 a month, or about $76,000 a year. Doris's savings would pay, then, for about four years on her own dime; if she had continued income of $1,000 a month from Social Security or other sources, that would bring it down to about $64,000 a year, stretching out the assets to five years.

The showrooms were nicely appointed—you bring in your own furniture—and on a dresser sat the book *A Bittersweet Season*, by Jane

Gross, which is about her care for her aging mother.[6] (Another terrific book on dealing with aging parents is *When the Time Comes: Families with Aging Parents Share Their Struggles and Solutions*, by Paula Span.)[7]

As our tour was ending, a piping alarm went off. A "memory care" patient was standing too close to the door of the locked wing she was in; she had to be persuaded to move.

We walked by residents who seemed happy—a tall older man who, in his youth, had played basketball for Rutgers. A woman with a walker. A cluster of people sharing a couch, looking like the grown kids visiting Mom.

That night, Jeanne called her mom and asked the most important question: What do you want?

The two of them had arranged her powers of attorney and medical directive in case Doris had a medical crisis, but Jeanne wanted to know her wishes explicitly, and now. If she could no longer live alone, would she want to move in with her sister, Mary? Stay with her son, Steve, who lived near Dallas? Come up to New Jersey and live near us in an assisted-living facility?

"First Mary," she replied, "then you."

Jeanne then called her brother and her aunt to tell them the score. Everyone seemed relieved to have answers.

The next night I was reading a little more about assisted living, and came across this advice in *The New York Times* from an elder-care counselor who said that many older people "will never agree to have 'the conversation' until a major medical catastrophe occurs."[8]

I turned to Jeanne, sitting across the living room with a book. "This is what you just did!" It took a medical problem to broach the subject effectively, but she had at least made a start.

AND THEN, WHAT ABOUT OUR OWN RETIREMENT?

We've done our planning for retirement as far as the money goes, but what will we actually do with ourselves when we are ready to quit working?

Staying in the Northeast would not suit us; once out of the daily working world, I'd sooner never pick up a snow shovel again. And please don't mention snowblowers; after a friend lost three fingers on his right hand to one, I lost my enthusiasm for them. While we can avoid snow duty by living in an apartment or condo, we would like to live in a place with a lower cost of living.

Two-thirds of retirees are likely to move at least once, according to a 2014 retirement study by Merrill Lynch and Age Wave, a company that studies aging issues. The survey found that only half of those retirees downsize; some move into bigger places.[9] By the age of 61, the majority of those surveyed said that they were free to choose where they wanted to live.

How about traveling? Jeanne and I have talked about it, off and on. We like the idea of travel, but in our way. Her dad bought a camper customized from the big Mercedes-made Sprinter van. It's a popular option for people who want something more manageable than the behemoth Winnebagos and King Aires. He and his wife have driven Moby, their Sprinter, from Texas all over the continental United States and into Canada.

All the RVs, however, were awfully expensive. And what suited her father didn't sound like something that would be a good fit for us. We're comfortable in smaller cars and can see ourselves traveling the country and staying in cheap hotels. It would take a lot of nights at Hampton Inns to make a fancy motor home look more affordable by comparison. This is the sort of question that travel buffs debate endlessly: RV fans argue that buying smaller, used vehicles can change the cost comparison and can be cheaper than driving and staying in hotels.[10]

Other folks find even more unusual ways to live in retirement. In 2015, when I traveled across the Atlantic on the *Queen Mary 2* as part of a *New York Times* "Times Travels" voyage, I met a couple who are always on the move. Robert and Beverly Johnson are, in retirement, living without a home. "We've now been traveling, basically with a rolling suitcase and a backpack apiece, for nearly five years," Bob told me in a note after the crossing. "We typically spend about half a year in the states and half a year elsewhere, but this varies." Without housing expenses, he said, they have enough money to see the world. He referred to the two of them as "geriatric hippies" who aren't rich but who are lucky enough to have held on to the disappearing three-legged stool of pensions, Social Security, and invested savings. They make it work by traveling cheaply: on cruise ships, they take interior cabins; "no Ritz-Carlton hotels," he wrote. They rent a room in Bob's sister's house, which serves as their legal address for credit card bills, taxes, and the like.

It's a fascinating idea. It suggests that there are possibilities out there that most people have never thought about. Another weird-but-interesting notion: living aboard a cruise ship as an alternative to a retirement home. If you look into the idea, you might see stories about the late Beatrice Muller, a widow who lived for many years aboard the *Queen Elizabeth II*.[11] She was spending about $100,000 a year to live full-time on the luxury liner. "Why should I go home to my vacuum cleaner?" she said to the writer Mimi Swartz in 2006. "If I run out of money, my sons will keep me here to keep me out of their hair. They're delighted I'm safe and happy." A 2004 paper in the *Journal of the American Geriatrics Society* even suggested that the cost of cruise ship living could be comparable to the cost of assisted living.[12] Assisted-living companies, of course, dispute the math, and also make the point that while the meals and entertainment might be better aboard a cruise ship, geriatric medical care and other specialized treatment for older folks are not generally available on board ships, where such services are more general.[13]

Still other retirees find ways to travel from place to place without constantly being on the move. Some senior living chains offer residents the option of moving from one facility to another, whether for brief visits or for a substantial part of the year.[14]

For more independent seniors, there is house swapping, sort of a mutual Airbnb. The movement that has been around for decades, with dozens of services like HomeExchange.com, Home Link International (homelink-usa.org), and LoveHomeSwap.com creating networks of people all over the world who vacation in one another's homes. It's not a vacation for last-minute dashers, but for those who can plan, the system seems to work; some of the sites, including Intervac.com, offer long-term exchanges that can provide housing for months at a time.

House-sitting sites include Trustedhousesitters.com and MindMy House.com.

There are networks that cater to over-50 travelers, whose schedules tend to be more flexible than families looking to head somewhere on school spring break, including Home Exchange 50 Plus (homeexchange-50plus.com), Senior Home Exchange at IVHE.com, and Homebase Holidays (homebase-hols.com/page/Seniorshomeexchange), which offers stays of up to six months.

None of that sounds like Jeanne and me, though. We don't see ourselves roving the seas forever, or even the interstates, or crashing at a stranger's house. We really like the morning oatmeal at Hampton Inn. What can I say? Besides, at some point, we'd want to settle again.

In the last year or so, the conversation has grown more serious. We've seen the articles, like the regular pieces in *Forbes* touting the "best places to retire."[15] They focus on factors like the local economy, home prices, and air quality, as well as whether the town is walkable. The latest list has places like Blacksburg, Virginia (I've been there—it's terrific) and Fargo, North Dakota ("CONS: Cold winters." You don't say!). The Milken Institute has produced its own data-driven report ranking 352 metropolitan areas to find the "best cities for successful aging."[16] They really like Madison, Wisconsin. But who doesn't?

All these reports are fine, as far as they go. More than anything, they help you figure out how other people figure out where they want to live in their retirement years, and the criteria that people sift through, and which you could sift through in your own way. How is the cost of living, relative to the rest of the country? You can find cost-of-living calculators to do your own comparisons at sites like Bankrate.com, and extensive city comparisons on the basis of factors like income, crime, and climate at sites like City-Data.com.

Whatever the lists and reports might say about uprooting yourself and moving to a place you've never lived before, Jeanne and I feel the tug of our home state, Texas. We want to be near family. We want to spend time with that granddaughter, and whoever else might come along.

But where? Austin, the city we love most, has become crowded and expensive. If we lived in Pflugerville, the same town as the kids, though, there's always the possibility of being too much in their business. Jeanne had no interest in her own hometown, Houston, which she thinks of as unmanageably large.

Then she surprised me by talking about my hometown, Galveston, with enthusiasm. "I've never lived in a beach town," she said. It would be just a few hours' drive to get to Pflugerville and the kids, and an hour to see our Houston family members and to see theater productions there. Houston also has some of the best hospitals in the world, and that's no small consideration. More important, I love the salt air and the feel of sand between my toes. (Please don't sing Jimmy Webb's song "Galveston." Growing up there, I've heard it enough for a lifetime.) The Wall Street of the South before the devastating 1900 storm, the island town retains some of that old grandeur.

Jeanne's dad, who lives in Houston, owns a trailer home in Galveston right off the beach that he and his wife love. When we came to visit, he pointed out toward the water. "This is the million-dollar view," he said proudly. He then pointed just a few hundred feet to the right, where actual million-dollar houses, the vacation houses of rich Houston folks, stood. We checked and found that we could buy a small condo or house there for around $100,000—the kind of place we might be able to buy with cash when we sold our home in New Jersey. Not one of the glorious old Victorian homes on the East End, or the expensive places down the island to the west, but something nice. And because the island is only two miles wide, you're never far from the beach.

Galveston is not at the top of anyone's "best places to retire" list. It is not even listed in the Milken report. Its beaches are not pristine, and the parts that are not spruced up are run-down; the poverty rate, according to the U.S. Census, is about 25 percent.[17] City-Data.com says its crime rate is higher than the national average.[18] (The FBI, however, which collects those statistics, regularly warns people not to read too much into them, for a number of reasons: for example, some cities have a comparable amount of crime, but the police department in the supposedly higher-crime city does a better job of recording offenses.)[19]

But the Texas Gulf Coast is getting more attention as a place to retire as an alternative to more expensive beach towns in Florida. As a writer for the *Huffington Post* put it, "when you combine affordability with natural beauty, it's surprising it's not up there with Florida as a top retirement destination."[20] This was sounding better and better!

The only problem with this idea, of course, is that it is absolutely nuts. Galveston gets smacked by hurricanes on a pretty regular basis. The house I grew up in, a solid brick structure that had survived a number of fierce storms, was destroyed by Hurricane Ike in 2008. What's more, climate change promises rising sea levels in the coming decades, and the potential for even more violent storms hitting Gulf Coast towns. As a reporter on the climate change beat, that possibility hit me hard. Jeanne's dad can lose that trailer; for him, it's a vacation home, not a primary residence. We would have to be prepared to lose everything if we bought there.

We're not so attached to our possessions, though. The move from the big house in Millburn to the little place in West Orange meant getting rid of enormous amounts of stuff. Downsizing again, to an even smaller place, whether a condo or a tiny house, would impose that discipline again, and underscore the message. We would evacuate before any storm; no hurricane parties for us. FEMA has a good guide online about storm preparation and what to take when you evacuate.[21] The list includes valuables, important papers on a thumb drive, and a "go bag" with food, medications, phone chargers, and other essentials. Buying an inexpensive place, or renting, at least until assisted living beckons, could lessen the financial sting if we lost in a storm. Flood insurance could mitigate losses. As long as we survive, the rest is just stuff.

We could live with less risk in a place like Boise, Idaho. I like Boise. The state capitol building is a gem, and the river is lovely. You can get Basque food downtown! But I don't want to live in Boise. And it gets more than 20 inches of snow a year.

The purpose of this exercise is not to convince you to live in Galveston—though, you know, check it out. Our level of risk acceptance could well be very different from yours (I still eat Gulf oysters and shrimp, remember?), and you might find sand between your toes annoying. But you can go to the same sites we did, think about what's important to you in finding a place to live. And make your own decision.

By the way—between my writing the first draft of this manuscript and the second, Hurricane Harvey hit the Texas coast with a wet fury that left Houston struggling with about 50 inches of rain. I flew to the Gulf Coast to report on the disaster. Galveston took a less dire hit, but things could have been much worse. While I was driving to dinner after flying with a cowboy who saved cattle by helicopter near Bay City, southwest of Houston, I got a call from Jeanne.

"I'm going to betray you," she said. "I don't want to live in Galveston anymore." I told her I understood. A couple of days later, though, she was rethinking her rethinking. We're like that. We're still discussing our options.

We're considering the very last steps, too. When we do pass away, we're leaving behind one very important thing: a book for the kids. Not Bogle, or Trollope. Its title: *What if . . . Workbook.*[22] It's basically a death organizer: a place to put bank accounts, retirement fund information, online accounts and passwords, life insurance information, credit cards, and suchlike. Jeanne ordered a copy after reading about it in a newspaper article; there are plenty of other books like it out there. She made filling it out a project, and it's ready when it's needed. We hope it saves the kids a lot of trouble.

And as far as that final piece of real estate goes, we're not sure we want a burial plot. We don't want to be that much trouble. And no urn, please. We'll be all right in the ash heap of history.

More important, we'll take a pass on those heavily marketed prepaid burial plans. They don't seem like a good deal and can cost more than going over our preferences with the kids, who will take care of business at the right time, paid for out of a bank account they have access to so it won't cost them anything. Your banker can even set up a separate account, payable after death. Prepaid plans, I have read, often go undiscovered and only show up in the family papers after you've been buried.[23] Haven't I wasted enough money during my life? I don't want wasting money to be the very last thing I do.

13

THE END

"Yet, sir, married men with families have lived on my income."

"And on less than a quarter of it. The very respectable man who brushes my clothes no doubt does so. But then you see he has been brought up in that way. I suppose that you as a bachelor put by every year at least half your income?"

"I never put by a shilling, sir. Indeed, I owe a few hundred pounds."

"And yet you expect to keep a house over your head, and an expensive wife and family, with lady's maid, nurses, cook, footman, and grooms, on a sum which has been hitherto insufficient for your own wants! I didn't think you were such an idiot, my boy."

"Thank you, sir."

—ANTHONY TROLLOPE, *PHINEAS REDUX*

I AM *STILL* an idiot.

Okay, that's not fair. I've absorbed a lot, which must have raised my money IQ by a few points, and maybe I've even improved my money sanity. There's no better way to learn about something than writing a book, at least so long as you take the work part seriously.

I am still basically scared of money. I've just gotten used to paying more attention to it: Zero out credit card balances. Invest in index funds. And, I've learned, it's never too late to start building a retirement fund, though earlier is better.

And—let's face it—I didn't actually make myself a financial expert. I picked up some information, but it's not as if I went back to college for an MBA. The lucky thing is that you don't have to be an MBA to fix your financial life. Even those supposed financial geniuses, as we found out, don't consistently beat the market. A few simple rules did the trick, and when it came to everything else—insurance, a will, and the rest—I found good people and listened to them. That doesn't make me an accredited financial maven, but it did get the job done. When Kinky Friedman, the singer and comic novelist, was running for governor of Texas, he argued that his lack of experience was not a problem. "I tell people, 'Trust me, I'm a Jew, I'll hire good people.'"[1]

And I am, like Kinky, a Jew. I am, in fact, a Jew who is not particularly good with money, even now. (So much for that stereotype.) But after some false starts, I have learned enough make some good decisions. And how to hire good people. If I've done my job right, then you've learned those things, too.

That would be so great. If you meet me somewhere—say, at a book talk—please come up to tell me that you learned something. Lie if you have to. I'm insecure.

And while I'm confessing here, let me admit that this project took a little more than a year, despite the title of the book. Sue me.

But you don't need to take more than a year to do what we did. Here's one last punch list: a task a month for a year. The list won't fit on an index card, but it's pretty concise. And now that you've seen us do these things, you have a better sense of the terrain. Give it a year: make this the year that *you* get your financial life in order. Whether or not you think you can make it, take the steps. As Hamlet told his mother, "Assume a virtue if you have it not." Or, as people in Alcoholics Anonymous say to those trying to put themselves on the path to sobriety and wonder whether they are up to the challenge, "Fake it till you make it."

January—Are you on track for retirement? If you have a 401(k) fund, check it to see if you're on track. Check the composition. Are you in low-fee funds—preferably, index funds? If you have a pension, what will it pay you? Check your expected Social Security payment for whatever year you think you might retire. Will the combination give you a substantial portion of your current income? (Remember: the rule of thumb is about 75 percent, but you should think of what you'll really need.)

February—What do you need to do to catch up? If you're not going to get to the 75 percent, or whatever you're hoping for, you need to find a way to get there. That means paying the maximum into a 401(k), and if you are 50 or older, taking advantage of the senior bump-up to put in more. If you haven't got a fund yet at all and you're in your 50s, you've got a tough climb ahead. Skip vacations if you have to—yes, even skip those lattes. This is emergency mode, and you can still build up a cushion with effort and discipline. Remember, Carrie Schwab-Pomerantz says that if you are starting in your 50s, you need to put away 40 percent of your income. And maybe more. It might call for a lifestyle change, and this is the month to see if you can put these processes in place.

March—Read a book that will make you think about money. It could be any of the books from my financial bookshelf. But why not *David Copperfield*, so you can meet Mr. Micawber? Or, if you're feeling ambitious, start Anthony Trollope's Barsetshire novels or Palliser series. Those books say more about getting and spending than any financial guide.

April—Write a will and take care of the medical directive and power of attorney documents. We got a lawyer to do it; you probably will, too.

May—Check your life insurance. Have you got any? Have you got enough? Do you understand what it will do or won't do for your family?

June—Clean up your credit cards and other debts: renegotiate interest rates, examine your phone bills for mysterious charges, and see whether a call to the phone company's help line won't get you a lower monthly rate. Do it again with your cable company. And then look at other subscriptions—are you really listening to Spotify? If not, why are you paying for it? Subscriptions creep up all around us: Netflix, Hulu, Apple Music. Make sure you're getting the most out of what you pay for, or don't pay for it.

July—If any of the previous tasks took more than a month, you've got this one to take up the slack.

August—It's August. You don't want to work in August.

September—Begin the conversation with your kids about how much support they can expect from you; their needs and yours. And, looking further forward, be sure to talk with them about your own choices for end-of-life decisions, with copies of your own financial assets workbook, will, and medical directive documents.

November—If your parents are still around, make sure you know what they want and study up on their care options as their health declines. You don't want to be taken by surprise.

December—It's been a nearly a year. Check back over the list and see if you've handled these things to your satisfaction. Double-check that retirement fund and look at whether you're making the progress you need to be. It's not a onetime set of decisions, it's a process. And then congratulate yourself on a year well spent.

Here we are at the end of our story—though, I hope, nowhere near the end of our lives.

Indulge me for a moment: I want to talk about another book, one that begins, "In the beginning . . ."

For many years now, I have attended a Bible-study class. Since we're Jewish, our focus is on what Christians call the Old Testament, which

Jews call the Torah, or the Pentateuch: the five books of Moses. I'm not actually religious, but the Torah is just about the most fascinating book I know, and understanding its stories underlies so much of our literature and of Western culture that it's an essential work to know. Besides, the funny, friendly members of Congregation Emanu-El of West Essex have made the classes the best book club ever.

It's a strange project, this book club, because when we started, some 15 years ago, it was decided to go through every word of the Torah, from Genesis to Deuteronomy, from start to finish. In a world that skims, we linger; in a society that has lost its attention span and even "too long, didn't read" is abbreviated on Twitter as "tl;dr," we take the Torah pokily, deliberately. Even so, we recently completed Deuteronomy.

Then we started the book all over again.

Why? Because there's always something new in it. And not everyone was there for the first "In the beginning." I came in a year or so after the class started, when they were already in mid-Genesis, so it was nice to go restart the cycle.

But I digress, yet again. Here's the point. Among the repeated themes in Deuteronomy, this last of the five books, is one of the most searing messages delivered to the gathered Hebrews. They are about to enter the promised land after wandering 40 years in the desert. God tells them, through Moses, that he has set before them a blessing and a curse. Make the right choice—do good, follow the commandments and laws—and you will live, and even prosper. Choose wrongly and, well, things get very bad. The curses are enumerated at length. At great length. Death. Being scattered across the earth with nothing. Hemorrhoids. (Really, it's in the book. I'm telling you, you've got to read this thing. The movies don't do it justice.)

We can argue about deeper meanings, but the fact is that we all have the blessing and the curse before us, however you want to think of it, and whatever the nature of the reward or the punishment. Most of us choose wrongly—punishment for those failings are a major theme of the Book, from the flood to the destruction of Sodom and Gomorrah to the slaughter after the golden calf. It's why there is so very much smiting. (I really enjoy the smiting.) It's why, despite all the wrongness and the smiting, we still get the message to go out there and choose to do the right things.

Is it hard to do these things? Yes. Are they impossible? No. I'll let Deuteronomy 30:11-14 say it better than I ever could:

> Surely, this Instruction which I enjoin upon you this day is not too baffling for you, nor is it beyond reach. It is not in the heavens, that you should say, "Who among us can go up to the heavens and get it for us and impart it to us, that we may observe it?" Neither is it beyond the sea, that you should say, "Who among us can cross to the other side of the sea and get it for us and impart it to us, that we may observe it?" No, the thing is very close to you; in your mouth and in your heart, to observe it.[2]

We can choose to do good—and now I'm back talking about our little book here, not the Book. Because while, yes, we should make the right moral choices on the grand level of life or death, we must also at least try to make the right financial ones. One good act leads to another, and another. Thus are habits built. And if we do make those right choices, and have a little luck, we will enjoy good fortune.

No guarantees! But you could do worse.

ACKNOWLEDGMENTS

A FELLOW JOURNALIST RECENTLY asked me whether I liked writing books. I told him that I *love* writing books, because putting together something at this length, word by word, uses different muscles than quick-hit newspaper stories. Books have that feeling of permanence. People don't use books to line their birdcages. And in an instant-everything digital world, it's important to try to make things that take time. To adapt John Kennedy's inspiring speech about going to the moon, we do these things "not because they are easy, but because they are hard."

But we don't do them alone. My editor at Penguin Random House, Megan Newman, is a source of support, wisdom, and inspiration—the kind of sure-handed editor and friend every writer dreams of. The Penguin folks did amazing things with the book, including Hannah Steigmeyer, and the astonishingly thorough Maureen Klier, Lindsay Gordon, Casey Maloney, and Erica Rose. My agent, Rafe Sagalyn, has spurred me on and guided me, and has put up with me for more than two decades, which is no small thing in this fickle world.

I would also like to thank *The New York Times*, my employer for the past 17 years. The *Times* has been a wonderful place to work and to learn. My editors have helped shape story after story on my wildly pin-balling beats. Passages in this book are drawn from work I have written for those editors, and it is their guidance that made the pieces as good as they are. As for colleagues, there's no beating the men and women of the lunch table in the company cafeteria, which is a little like the

Algonquin Round Table, but with knuckleheads. Ron Lieber read portions of this book, for which I'm deeply grateful, to make sure I didn't
screw things up too badly.

Thanks, too, to my commuter train buddy John Straus, who mentioned the connection between Engels and Dickens that helped me
understand why I was quoting so many novels in my draft and then to
explain it. And thanks to Jolie Solomon and Joyce Lacovara, who let me
tell their stories, and to my friend and colleague Jean Rutter, who suggested the punch lists. The Torah study class at Temple Emanu-El gave
me more than 15 years of perspective on that amazing book. And thanks
also to John Bogle, who, as I said, saved my financial life.

Thanks, as well, to our folks, who have been supportive and generous, and to our children, Elizabeth and Matthew, Sam and Courtney,
and Joseph, and to baby Robin. Without them, none of this would be
necessary.

Among all my debts, of course, ultimately and always, I owe the
biggest, and the best, to Jeanne.

NOTES

Introduction

1 Paul Burka, "A Test of Character," *Texas Monthly* 16, no. 2 (February 1988), 185.

2 Financial Industry Regulatory Authority (FINRA) Investor Education Foundation, *Financial Capability in the United States 2016*, July 2016, www.usfinancialcapability.org/downloads /NFCS_2015_Report_Natl_Findings.pdf.

3 Nari Rhee and Ilana Boivie, *The Continuing Retirement Savings Crisis*, National Institute on Retirement Security, March 2015, http://www.nirsonline.org/storage/nirs/documents/RSC%202015 /final_rsc_2015.pdf.

4 Federal Reserve, *Report on the Economic Well-Being of U.S. Households in 2015*, May 2016, https://www.federalreserve.gov /2015-report-economic-well-being-us-households-201605.pdf.

5 John Schwartz, "Retirement Reality Is Catching Up With Me," *The New York Times*, March 11, 2015, www.nytimes.com/2015/03 /12/business/retirement-reality-is-catching-up-with-me.html.

Chapter 1: The Project

1 Financial Industry Regulatory Authority, http://apps.finra.org /calcs/1/retirement; Fidelity, https://www.fidelity.com/calculators -tools/retirement-calculator/overview; Vanguard, https:// retirementplans.vanguard.com/VGApp/pe/pubeducation /calculators/RetirementIncomeCalc.jsf; Schwab, http://www

.schwab.com/public/schwab/investing/retirement_and_planning
/saving_for_retirement/retirement_calculator; Bankrate, http://
www.bankrate.com/calculators/retirement/retirement-plan
-calculator.aspx; and AARP, http://www.aarp.org/work
/retirement-planning/retirement_calculator.html.

2   "U.S. Survey Data at a Glance," FINRA Investor Education
Foundation, July 2016, http://www.usfinancialcapability.org
/results.php?region=US#.V8x8fao-vNg.twitter.

3   FINRA Investor Education Foundation, *Financial Capability in
the United States 2016*, July 2016, www.usfinancialcapability.org
/downloads/NFCS_2015_Report_Natl_Findings.pdf.

4   Federal Reserve, *Report on the Economic Well-Being of U.S.
Households in 2015*, May 2016, https://www.federalreserve.gov
/2015-report-economic-well-being-us-households-201605.pdf.

5   William Alden, "How a Lopsided Recovery Fueled the Dollar-
Store Wars," September 23, 2014, https://www.nytimes.com/2014
/09/28/magazine/how-a-lopsided-recovery-fueled-the-dollar-store
-wars.html.

6   Ian M. Lyons and Sian L. Beilock, "When Math Hurts: Math
Anxiety Predicts Pain Network Activation in Anticipation of
Doing Math," *PLOS One*, October 31, 2012, http://dx.doi.org
/10.1371/journal.pone.0048076.

7   William Harms, "When People Worry About Math, the Brain
Feels the Pain," UChicagoNews, October 31, 2012, https://news
.uchicago.edu/article/2012/10/31/when-people-worry
-about-math-brain-feels-pain.

8   "Stress in America: Paying with Our Health," American
Psychological Association, February 2015, https://www.apa.org
/news/press/releases/stress/2014/stress-report.pdf.

9   SPENT with Lindsay Goldwert, http://www.spentpodcast.com
/bio.

10 Joan D. Atwood, "Couples and Money: The Last Taboo,"
American Journal of Family Therapy 40, no. 1 (2012): 1–19,
published online January 9, 2012, http://dx.doi.org/10.1080
/01926187.2011.600674.

11 Financial Therapy Association, www.financialtherapyassociation
    .org.

12 Norm Forman, *Mind Over Money: How to Banish Your Financial
    Headaches and Achieve Moneysanity* (Toronto: Doubleday
    Canada, 1987).

13 Don DeLillo, *White Noise* (New York: Penguin, 1986), 83–84.

14 Donald W. Black, "A Review of Compulsive Buying Disorder,"
    World Psychiatry 6, no. 1 (February 2007): 14–18, PMCID:
    PMC1805733, www.ncbi.nlm.nih.gov/pmc/articles/PMC
    1805733/.

15 Piquet-Pessôa, Marcelo, M. Ferreira, Gabriela, A. Melca, Isabela,
    Fontenelle, Leonardo, "T1 - DSM-5 and the Decision Not to
    Include Sex, Shopping or Stealing as Addictions," Current
    Addiction Reports, no. 1 (2014): 172–176, 10.1007/s40429-014-
    0027-6 https://www.researchgate.net/publication/264051559_
    DSM-5_and_the
    _Decision_Not_to_Include_Sex_Shopping_or_Stealing_as
    _Addictions

16 Ibid.

17 Adrian Furnham, *The New Psychology of Money* (New York:
    Routledge, 2014).

18 David Foster Wallace, "This Is Water," http://bulletin-archive
    .kenyon.edu/x4280.html.

19 Adrian Furnham, Sophie von Stumm, and Mark Fenton-
    O'Creevy, "Sex Differences in Money Pathology in the General
    Population," *Social Indicators Research* 123, no. 3 (2015): 701–711,
    published online September 11, 2014, DOI: 10.1007
    /s11205-014-0756-x, https://www.ncbi.nlm.nih.gov/pmc/articles
    /PMC4543416.

Chapter 2: Starting Out

1 Elizabeth Warren and Amelia Warren Tyagi, "What's Hurting
   the Middle Class," *Boston Review*, September 1, 2005, http://
   bostonreview.net/forum/what%E2%80%99s-hurting
   -middle-class.

2   Robert Earl Keen, "Dreadful Selfish Crime," https://www
    .youtube.com/watch?v=GfqYnPjPrOQ.

3   John C. Bogle, *Enough: True Measures of Money, Business, and
    Life* (Hoboken: Wiley, 2010).

4   Daniel Kahneman and Angus Deaton, "High Income Improves
    Evaluation of Life but Not Emotional Well-Being," *Proceedings of
    the National Academy of Sciences* 107 no. 38, DOI: 10.1073/
    pnas.1011492107, http://www.pnas.org/content/107/38/16489
    .full#ref-10.

5   Lara B. Aknin, Michael I. Norton, and Elizabeth W. Dunn,
    "From Wealth to Well-Being? Money Matters, but Less
    Than People Think," *Journal of Positive Psychology* 4, no. 6
    (2009): 523–527, http://dx.doi.org/10.1080/17439760903271421,
    described in Elizabeth W. Dunn and Michael Norton, "Don't
    Indulge. Be Happy," *New York Times*, July 7, 2012, http://nyti
    .ms/PtFC7T.

6   Jennifer Robison, "Happiness Is Love—and $75,000," *Gallup
    Business Journal*, November 17, 2011, http://www.gallup.com
    /businessjournal/150671/happiness-is-love-and-75k.aspx.

7   The Equality of Opportunity Project, "How Can We Improve
    Economic Opportunities for Our Children?" http://www
    .equality-of-opportunity.org.

8   David Leonhardt, "The American Dream, Quantified at Last,"
    New York Times, December 8, 2016, http://www.nytimes.com
    /2016/12/08/opinion/the-american-dream-quantified-at-last.html.

9   Adam Davidson, "It's Official: The Boomerang Kids Won't
    Leave," *New York Times*, June 20, 2014, https://www.nytimes
    .com/2014/06/22/magazine/its-official-the-boomerang-kids-wont
    -leave.html.

10 Richard Fry, "For First Time in Modern Era, Living with Parents
    Edges Out Other Living Arrangements for 18- to 34-Year-Olds,"
    May 24, 2016, http://www.pewsocialtrends.org/2016/05/24
    /for-first-time-in-modern-era-living-with-parents-edges-out
    -other-living-arrangements-for-18-to-34-year-olds.

11 Kate Taylor, "'Psychologically scarred' millennials are killing countless industries from napkins to Applebee's—here are the businesses they like the least," *Business Insider*, Oct. 31, 2017, http://www.businessinsider.com/millennials-are-killing-list-2017-8.

12 Joel Stein, "Millennials: The Me Me Me Generation," *Time*, May 20, 2013, http://time.com/247/millennials-the-me-me-me-generation.

13 Tom Wolfe, "The 'Me' Decade and the Third Great Awakening," *New York* magazine, August 23, 1976, http://nymag.com/news/features/45938.

14 Chris Han, "The Best TIME 'Millennials' Cover Parodies," College Humor, May 14, 2013, http://www.collegehumor.com/post/6890116/the-best-time-millennials-cover-parodies.

15 Doree Shafrir tweet, https://twitter.com/doree/status/576076420322971648.

16 Doree Shafrir, "I Was Sure Freezing My Eggs Would Solve Everything," *BuzzFeed News*, June 22, 2014, http://www.buzzfeed.com/doree/i-was-sure-freezing-my-eggs-would-solve-everything%20.

17 Doree Shafrir tweet, https://twitter.com/doree.

18 Doree Shafrir tweet, https://twitter.com/doree/status/576079955840249856.

19 John Schwartz, "Notes on an 'Idiot's' Guide to Retirement,'" *New York Times*, March 13, 2015, http://www.nytimes.com/times-insider/2015/03/13/notes-on-an-idiots-guide-to-retirement.

20 Bourree Lam, "Why Aren't Millennials Saving Money?" *The Atlantic*, November 12, 2014, http://www.theatlantic.com/business/archive/2014/11/why-arent-millennials-saving-money/382634/?utm_source=atltw%201/4.

21 Josh Zumbrun, "Younger Generation Faces a Savings Deficit: Postrecession Thrifty Ways Fade Amid Weak Jobs Market, Hefty Student Debt," *Wall Street Journal*, November 9, 2014, http://www.wsj.com/articles/savings-turn-negative-for-younger-generation-1415572405.

22 Lam, "Why Aren't Millennials Saving Money?"

23 Transamerica Center for Retirement Studies, *Millennial Workers: An Emerging Generation of Super Savers*, http://www .transamericacenter.org/docs/default-source/resources/center -research/tcrs2014_sr_millennials.pdf.

24 Catherine Rampell, "The Coming-of-Age Ritual of Spend Now, Save Later," *Washington Post*, November 13, 2014, https://www .washingtonpost.com/opinions/catherine-rampell-the-coming-of -age-ritual-of-spend-now-save-later/2014/11/13/5fd9314e-6b73-11e4 -a31c-77759fc1eacc_story.html?utm_term=.20d6f1746c9b.

25 "The Labor Market for Recent College Graduates," Federal Reserve Bank of New York, https://www.newyorkfed.org /research/college-labor-market/college-labor-market_wages.html.

26 Scott Fulford and Scott Schuh, "Consumer Revolving Credit and Debt Over the Life Cycle and Business Cycle," Federal Reserve Bank of Boston, 2015, https://www.bostonfed.org/publications /research-department-working-paper/2015/consumer-revolving -credit-and-debt-over-the-life-cycle-and-business-cycle.aspx.

Chapter 3: Your Investing Primer

1 Nari Rhee and Ilana Boivie, "The Continuing Retirement Savings Crisis," National Institute on Retirement Security, March 2015, http://www.nirsonline.org/storage/nirs/documents /RSC%202015/final_rsc_2015.pdf.

2 Monique Morrissey, "The State of American Retirement: How 401(k)s Have Failed Most American Workers," Economic Policy Institute, March 3, 2016, http://www.epi.org/publication /retirement-in-america/#charts.

3 Ibid.

4 Alicia H. Munnell, Wenliang Hou, and Anthony Webb, "NRRI Update Shows Half Still Falling Short," Center for Retirement Research, December 14, 2014, http://crr.bc.edu/wp-content /uploads/2014/12/IB_14-20-508.pdf.

5 "Personal Responsibility. Public Trust," 2016 Natixis Global

Retirement Index, https://ngam.natixis.com/docs/271/829/2016
%20Natixis%20Global%20Retirement%20Index%20Report
_Final,1.pdf.

6 "Report: Nazi Treasure Hunters Following More Realistic
Retirement Plan Than 86% of Country," *The Onion*, March 4,
2015, http://www.theonion.com/article/report-nazi-treasure
-hunters-following-more-realis-38147?utm_content=Main&utm
_campaign=SF&utm_source=Twitter&utm_medium=
SocialMarketing.

7 David A. Pratt, "Some Implications of the Changing Structure of
Work for Worker Retirement Security, Pensions and Healthcare,"
December 10, 2015, https://www.dol.gov/asp/evaluation
/completed-studies/Future_of_work_worker_retirement
_security_pensions_and_healthcare.pdf.

8 Federal Reserve, *Report on the Economic Well-Being of U.S.
Households in 2015*, May 2016, https://www.federalreserve.gov
/2015-report-economic-well-being-us-households-201605.pdf.

9 FINRA, "Can You Ace This Quiz? Test Your Financial Literacy,"
http://www.finra.org/investors/highlights/can-you-ace-quiz
-test-your-financial-literacy.

10 Erica Goode, "Among the Inept, Researchers Discover, Ignorance
Is Bliss," *New York Times*, January 18, 2000, http://www.nytimes
.com/2000/01/18/health/among-the-inept-researchers-discover
-ignorance-is-bliss.html.

11 "Unskilled and unaware of it: how difficulties in recognizing
one's own incompetence lead to inflated self-assessments,"
Kruger J, Dunning D. *J Pers Soc Psychol* 77, no. 6 (December
1999):1121-34, https://www.ncbi.nlm.nih.gov/pubmed/10626367

12 FINRA, "Traditional and Roth 401(k)s," http://www.finra.org
/investors/traditional-and-roth-401ks.

13 Pew Charitable Trusts, *Who's In, Who's Out: A Look at Access to
Employer-Based Retirement Plans and Participation in the States*,
January 2016, http://www.pewtrusts.org/~/media/assets/2016/01
/retirement_savings_report_jan16.pdf.

14 IRS, "Retirement Topics—IRA Contribution Limits," https://
www.irs.gov/retirement-plans/plan-participant-employee
/retirement-topics-ira-contribution-limits.

15 Center for Retirement Initiatives, Georgetown University
McCourt School of Public Policy, http://cri.georgetown.edu.

16 "Secure Choice," Illinois State Treasurer website, http://
illinoistreasurer.gov/Individuals/Secure_Choice.

17 Ryan Alfred, "The One Chart That Explains 401(k) Fees,"
BrightScope, https://www.brightscope.com/financial-planning
/advice/article/15556/The-One-Chart-That-Explains-401K-Fees.

18 Landon Thomas Jr., "Explaining E.T.F.s and How They Gained
Their Allure," *New York Times*, February 22, 2016, https://www
.nytimes.com/2016/02/23/business/dealbook/good-times-for
-exchange-traded-funds.html.

19 Mark Miller, "How to Make Your Money Last as Long as You
Do," *New York Times*, February 18, 2017, https://www.nytimes
.com/2017/02/18/your-money/retiring-longevity-planning-social
-security.html.

20 John Schwartz and Judith H. Dobrzynski, "3 Men Are Charged
with Fraud in 1,100 Art Auctions on eBay," *New York Times*,
March 9, 2001, http://www.nytimes.com/2001/03/09/business
/3-men-are-charged-with-fraud-in-1100-art-auctions-on-ebay.html.

21 Ron Lieber, "As Stocks Gyrate, It's Time to Measure Your Risk
Tolerance," *New York Times*, February 12, 2016, https://www
.nytimes.com/2016/02/13/your-money/as-stocks-fall-its-time-to
-measure-your-risk-tolerance.html?_r=0.

22 "Investment Risk Tolerance Assessment," Personal Finance
Planning, University of Missouri, http://pfp.missouri.edu
/research_IRTA.html.

23 Investment Risk and Return Characteristics, Rutgers New Jersey
Agricultural Experiment Station, http://njaes.rutgers.edu/money
/investmentrisk.asp.

24 Carl Richards, "No Shortcuts in Evaluating Your Investment
Risk," *New York Times*, February 22, 2016, http://www.nytimes

.com/2016/02/23/business/no-shortcuts-in-evaluating-your-risk
.html.

25 John Schwartz, "A Flying Cowboy Rides to Rescue Cattle
    Stranded in Harvey's Floods," *New York Times*, September 3,
    2017, https://www.nytimes.com/2017/09/03/us/harvey-cattle-
    helicopter.html.

26 John Schwartz, "How I Was Struck by Lightning (and Lived to
    Crack Wise About It)," *New York Times*, May 13, 2008, http://
    www.nytimes.com/2008/05/13/science/13shock.html?ref=science.

27 Jennifer C. Black, Jennifer N. Welday, Brian Buckley, Alesia
    Ferguson, Patrick L. Gurian, Kristina D. Mena, Ill Yang,
    Elizabeth McCandlish, and Helena M. Solo-Gabriele, "Risk
    Assessment for Children Exposed to Beach Sands Impacted by
    Oil Spill Chemicals," *International Journal of Environmental
    Research and Public Health* 13, no. 9 (September): 853. Published
    online August 27, 2016, DOI: 10.3390/ijerph13090853, https://
    www.ncbi.nlm.nih.gov/pmc/articles/PMC5036686/.

28 "Occupational Health Guideline for Turpentine," Centers for
    Disease Control and Prevention, https://www.cdc.gov/niosh
    /docs/81-123/pdfs/0648.pdf.

29 "Chemicals in Meat Cooked at High Temperatures and Cancer
    Risk," National Cancer Institute, https://www.cancer.gov
    /about-cancer/causes-prevention/risk/diet/cooked-meats-fact-sheet.

30 Jeff Donn, "Medical benefits of dental floss unproven,"
    Associated Press, August 12, 2016, http://bigstory.ap.org/article
    /f7e66079d9ba4b4985d7af350619a9e3/medical-benefits
    -dental-floss-unproven.

31 Jamie Holmes, "Flossing and the Art of Scientific Investigation,"
    New York Times, November 24, 2016, http://www.nytimes.com
    /2016/11/25/opinion/sunday/flossing-and-the-art-of-scientific
    -investigation.html?smid=tw-nytopinion&smtyp=cur.

32 Jason Zweig, *Your Money and Your Brain: How the New Science of
    Neuroeconomics Can Help Make You Rich* (New York: Simon &
    Schuster, 2008), 4.

33 Carrie Schwab-Pomerantz and Joanne Cuthbertson, *The Charles Schwab Guide to Finances After Fifty: Answers to Your Most Important Money Questions* (New York: Crown Business, 2014).

34 "The Society of Actuaries Publishes Annual Update to Mortality Improvement Scale," Society of Actuaries, October 20, 2016, https://www.soa.org/press-releases/2016/soa-publishes-mortality -improvement-scale-update/.

35 "2015 Risks and Process of Retirement Survey: Living Longer and Impact on Planning," Society of Actuaries, https://www.soa.org /Files/Research/Projects/research-2016-living-longer-impact.pdf.

36 Josh Barro, "We're Living Longer. That's Great, Except for Social Security," *New York Times*, November 17, 2015, https://www .nytimes.com/2015/11/17/upshot/were-living-longer-thats-great -except-for-social-security.html.

37 Stephen C. Goss, "The Future Financial Status of the Social Security Program," *Social Security Bulletin* 70, no. 3 (2010), https://www.ssa.gov/policy/docs/ssb/v70n3/v70n3p111.html.

38 "Participants Need Better Information When Offered Lump Sums That Replace Their Lifetime Benefits," Government Accountability Office, January 2015, http://www.gao.gov/assets /670/668106.pdf.

39 Engels to Margaret Harkness in London, Marx-Engels Correspondence, 1888, https://www.marxists.org/archive/marx /works/1888/letters/88_04_15.htm.

40 Jane Austen, *Persuasion*, chapter 1.

41 "I Have Arrived!" *David Copperfield* (1935), Turner Movie Classics http://www.tcm.com/mediaroom/video/342914/David -Copperfield-Movie-Clip-I-Have-Arrived-.html.

42 Andrew Tobias, *The Only Investment Guide You'll Ever Need* (Boston: Mariner Books, 2016).

43 Adam Smith [George J. W. Goodman], *The Money Game* (New York: Vintage, 1976).

44 Dave Ramsey, *The Total Money Makeover: A Proven Plan for Financial Fitness* (New York: Thomas Nelson Books, 2013).

45 "Dave Ramsey Doubles Down on His Bad Investment Advice," White Coat Investor, October 16, 2015, http://whitecoatinvestor .com/dave-ramsey-doubles-down-on-his-bad-investment-advice.

46 John C. Bogle, *The Little Book of Common Sense Investing: The Only Way to Guarantee Your Fair Share of Stock Market Returns* (Hoboken: John Wiley & Sons, 2007).

47 Helaine Olen and Harold Pollack, *The Index Card: Why Personal Finance Doesn't Have to Be Complicated* (New York: Portfolio, 2016).

48 Image of the original index card: http://www.samefacts.com /wp-content/uploads/2013/04/advice_to_alexM.jpg.

49 Penelope Wang, "Everything You Need to Know About Money on One Index Card," *Money*, January 5, 2016, http://time.com /money/4161238/index-card-harold-pollack.

50 "Berkshire Hathaway Annual Shareholder Letter," Berkshire Hathaway, Inc., 2014: http://www.berkshirehathaway.com /letters/2014ltr.pdf.

51 Louis Navellier, "(Back to) Earth-Day—the Tech-Stock Crash of 1970," NASDAQ, April 23, 2010, http://www.nasdaq.com/article /back-to-earthday-the-techstock-crash-of-1970-cm19586.

52 "Tesla: Inside the Lab—the Tesla Coil," New Voyage Communications, 2000, https://www.pbs.org/tesla/ins/lab _tescoil.html.

53 "Ancient Jewish History: The Urim & Thummim," http:// www.jewishvirtuallibrary.org/jsource/Judaism/urimthummim .html.

54 John Schwartz, "There's No Future in Being an Oracle," *New York Times*, July 11, 2009, http://www.nytimes.com/2009/07/12 /business/mutfund/12essay.html.

55 Aye M. Soe, "Does Past Performance Matter? The Persistence Scorecard," S&P Dow Jones Indices, https://us.spindices.com /documents/spiva/persistence-scorecard-august-2016.pdf.

56 James B. Stewart, "An Index-Fund Evangelist Is Straying from His Gospel," *New York Times*, June 22, 2017, https://www

.nytimes.com/2017/06/22/business/burton-malkiel-investment
-stock-index-funds.html?mcubz=2.

57   "Frequently Asked Questions," Small Business Administration,
September 2012, www.sba.gov/sites/default/files/FAQ_Sept
_2012.pdf.

58   John C. Bogle, "Lightning Strikes: The Creation of Vanguard,
the First Index Mutual Fund, and the Revolution It Spawned,"
http://www.bfjlaward.com/pdf/25975/42-59_bogle_jpm_0918.pdf.

59   John C. Bogle, "The Index Mutual Fund: 40 Years of Growth,
Change, and Challenge," *Financial Analysts Journal* 72, no. 1
(January–February 2016), DOI: http://dx.doi.org/10.2469/faj.v72
.n1.5, http://www.cfapubs.org/doi/full/10.2469/faj.v72.n1.5.

60   Luke Kawa Bernstein, "Passive Investing Is Worse for Society
Than Marxism," Bloomberg Markets, August 23, 2016, https://
www.bloomberg.com/news/articles/2016-08-23/bernstein
-passive-investing-is-worse-for-society-than-marxism.

61   James B. Stewart, "Endowment Sweepstakes: How Tiny
Houghton College Beat Harvard," Common Sense, *New York
Times*, February 9, 2017, https://www.nytimes.com/2017/02/09
/business/college-endowment-investment-returns.html.

62   Berkshire Hathaway Inc., Chairman's Letter, 1996, http://www
.berkshirehathaway.com/letters/1996.html.

63   Berkshire Hathaway Inc., 2016 annual letter to shareholders,
http://www.berkshirehathaway.com/letters/2016ltr.pdf.

64   Long Bets: "Over a ten-year period commencing on January 1,
2008, and ending on December 31, 2017, the S&P 500 will
outperform a portfolio of funds of hedge funds, when
performance is measured on a basis net of fees, costs and
expenses," http://longbets.org/362.

65   Ted Seides, "Why I Lost My Bet with Warren Buffett," May 3,
2017, https://www.bloomberg.com/view/articles/2017-05-03/why-i
-lost-my-bet-with-warren-buffett.

66   Bogleheads.org: Investing Advice Inspired by Jack Bogle, https://
www.bogleheads.org/forum/index.php.

67 John C. Bogle, "The Arithmetic of 'All-In' Investment Expenses," *Financial Analysts Journal* 70, no. 1 (January–February 2014), http://www.cfapubs.org/doi/pdf/10.2469/faj.v70.n1.1.

68 Penelope Wang, "No Matter What Trump Does, Keep Your Hands Off Your 401(k)," *Money*, November 9, 2016, http://time.com/money/4564295/401k-retirement-inertia-trump-election-aftermath.

69 Matthew J. Belvedere, "Warren Buffett Says the US Will Do Fine Under Trump Because We've Got the 'Secret Sauce'," CNBC, January 20, 2017, http://www.cnbc.com/2017/01/20/warren-buffett-says-the-us-will-do-fine-under-trump-because-weve-got-the-secret-sauce.html.

70 FINRA, "Take the Financial Literacy Quiz," http://www.usfinancialcapability.org/quiz.php. More information on the quiz and scoring can be found at http://www.finra.org/investors/highlights/can-you-ace-quiz-test-your-financial-literacy.

71 Investment Risk Tolerance Quiz, https://njaes.rutgers.edu/money/riskquiz.

Chapter 4: Getting Advice

1 Michael Lewis, *Liar's Poker* (New York: Norton, 2010), 242.

2 Fred Schwed, *Where Are the Customers' Yachts? Or, A Good Hard Look at Wall Street* (Hoboken: John Wiley & Sons, 2005).

3 Tara Siegel Bernard, "Now, Your Financial Advisers Will Have to Put You First (Sometimes)," *New York Times*, June 8, 2017, https://www.nytimes.com/2017/06/08/your-money/now-your-financial-advisers-will-have-to-put-you-first-sometimes.html.

4 Tara Siegel Bernard, "Labor Dept. Seeks Delay of Consumer Protection Rule for Financial Advisers," *New York Times*, August 9, 2017, https://www.nytimes.com/2017/08/09/business/labor-department-fiduciary-rule.html.

5 Tara Siegel Bernard, "'Customers First' to Become the Law in Retirement Investing," *New York Times*, April 6, 2016, http://

www.nytimes.com/2016/04/07/your-money/new-rules-for
-retirement-accounts-financial-advisers.html.

6　FINRA, *2016 FINRA Annual Financial Report*, http://www.finra
.org/sites/default/files/2016_AFR.pdf.

7　"Find a CFP® Professional," Certified Financial Planner Board of
Standards, http://www.letsmakeaplan.org/choose-a-cfp
-professional/find-a-cfp-professional?utm_source=google&utm
_medium=cpc&utm_term=%2Bcertified%20%2Bfinancial%20%
2Bplanning%20%2Bboard&gclid=COqPzoOLvtICFQm
Bswodv1EONw; "Find an Advisor," National Association of
Personal Financial Advisors, https://www.napfa.org; "Find Your
Financial Planner Now," Financial Planning Association, http://
www.plannersearch.org.

8　HighTower Whiteboard Animation: Brokers vs. Fiduciaries,
https://www.youtube.com/watch?v=Dg5RRMAc1GY.

9　"Putting Your Interests First," Committee for the Fiduciary
Standard, http://www.thefiduciarystandard.org/wp-content
/uploads/2015/02/fiduciaryoath_individual.pdf.

10　Ron Lieber, "Your Money: The 21 Questions You're Going to
Need to Ask About Investment Fees," *New York Times*, February
17, 2017, https://www.nytimes.com/2017/02/10/your-money
/the-21-questions-youre-going-to-need-to-ask-about-investment
-fees.html.

11　Ron Lieber, "How a Personal Finance Columnist Got Caught
Up in Fraud," *New York Times*, April 17, 2009, http://www
.nytimes.com/2009/04/18/your-money/financial-planners
/18money.html.

12　Anthony Bourdain, "Don't Eat Before Reading This," *New
Yorker*, April 19, 1999, http://www.newyorker.com/magazine
/1999/04/19/dont-eat-before-reading-this.

13　"Senior Investor Alert: Free Meal Seminars," North American
Securities Administrators Association, http://www.nasaa.org
/1950/senior-investor-alert-free-meal-seminars.

14　Eleanor Laise, "Hybrid Insurance Policies Gaining Steam,"

Kiplinger's Personal Finance, January 2017, http://www.kiplinger
.com/article/insurance/T036-C000-S004-hybrid-policies
-gaining-steam.html.

15 National Association of Personal Financial Advisors, https://
www.napfa.org; "Find a CFP® Professional," Certified Financial
Planner Board of Standards," https://www.cfp.net/utility/find-a
-cfp-professional; XY Planning Network, https://www
.xyplanningnetwork.com; Garrett Planning Network, http://
www.garrettplanningnetwork.com.

16 "Tough Questions to Ask Your Advisor, https://legacy.napfa.org
/UserFiles/File/ToughQuestionsToAskYourAdvisorUpdated
August2011.pdf; Lieber, "The 21 Questions You're Going to Need
to Ask About Investment Fees."

17 "Putting Your Interests First," Committee for the Fiduciary
Standard.

Chapter 5: Houses

1 Michael Neal, "Homeownership Remains a Key Component of
Household Wealth," National Association of Home Builders
Select, September 3, 2013, http://www.nahbclassic.org/generic
.aspx?sectionID=734&genericContentID=215073&channelID
=311&print=true.

2 Karen Weise, "Housing's 30-Percent-of-Income Rule Is Nearly
Useless: The enduring rule of thumb is arbitrary and almost
meaningless in today's market," Bloomberg News, July 17, 2014,
https://www.bloomberg.com/news/articles/2014-07-17
/housings-30-percent-of-income-rule-is-near-useless.

3 "Selected Housing Characteristics: 2010–2014 American
Community Survey 5-Year Estimates," United States
Census Bureau, http://factfinder.census.gov/faces/tableservices
/jsf/pages/productview.xhtml?pid=ACS_14_5YR_DP0
4&src=pt.

4 Joint Center for Housing Studies of Harvard University Press
Release, http://www.jchs.harvard.edu/housing-recovery

-strengthens-affordability-and-other-challenges-remain-harvard
-research-center Full report: http://www.jchs.harvard.edu
/sites/jchs.harvard.edu/files/jchs_2016_state_of
_the_nations_housing_lowres.pdf.

5   Laura Kusisto, "Home Prices Recover Ground Lost During
Bust," *Wall Street Journal*, November 29, 2016, http://www.wsj
.com/articles/u-s-home-prices-set-a-record-in-september
-case-shiller-says-1480428083.

6   "Report on the Economic Well-Being of U.S. Households in
2014," Board of Governors of the Federal Reserve System, May
2015, https://www.federalreserve.gov/econresdata/2014-report
-economic-well-being-us-households-201505.pdf.

7   Mordecai Richler, *The Apprenticeship of Duddy Kravitz* (Toronto:
New Canadian Library, 1989), 65.

8   *Texas Monthly*, March 1981, http://www.texasmonthly.com/issue
/march-1981.

9   "Owning a Co-op: 10 questions to ask before you buy," HSBC,
2015, https://us.hsbc.com/content/dam/hsbc/us/docs/pdf/Coop
%20Guide.pdf.

10 James Dao, "Angered by Police Killing, a Neighborhood Erupts,"
New York Times, July 7, 1992, http://www.nytimes.com/1992/07
/07/nyregion/angered-by-police-killing-a-neighborhood-erupts
.html?pagewanted=all.

11 Michael T. Osterholm and John Schwartz, *Living Terrors:
What America Needs to Know to Survive the Coming
Bioterrorist Catastrophe* (New York: Delacorte Press,
2000).

12 Center for Retirement Research, "Using Your House for Income
in Retirement," Boston College, http://crr.bc.edu/wp-content
/uploads/2014/09/c1_your-house_final_med-res.pdf.

13 Sam Levin, "Millionaire Tells Millennials: If You Want a House,
Stop Buying Avocado Toast," *Guardian*, May 15, 2017, https://
www.theguardian.com/lifeandstyle/2017/may/15
/australian-millionaire-millennials-avocado-toast-house.

14 "SoFi Is Offering Avocado Toast for Buying a Home—Yes, Really," SoFi, June 29, 2017, https://blog.sofi.com /avocado-toast-sofi-mortgage.

15 McKinsey & Company McKinsey Global Institute: "Independent Work: Choice, Necessity and the Gig Economy," October 2016, https://www.mckinsey.com/~/media/McKinsey /Global%20Themes/Employment%20and%20Growth/ Independent%20work%20Choice%20necessity%20and%20the% 20gig%20economy/Independent-Work-Choice-necessity-and-the-gig-economy-Full-report.ashx.

16 Ben Luthi, "30% Credit Utilization Rule: Truth or Myth?," NerdWallet, June 28, 2016, https://www.nerdwallet.com/blog /finance/30-percent-credit-utilization-ratio-rule.

17 "What's Your FICO Score?" Experian, http://www.experian .com/credit-report-partner/index-g.html.

18 "Identifying Your Credit Fingerprint" Equifax, https://www .equifax.com/personal.

19 "Be in the know with TransUnion—see your credit score NOW," TransUnion https://membership.tui.transunion.com.

20 "Know Your FICO° Scores And Stop Overpaying For Credit!" myFICO, http://www.myfico.com/

21 "What is a Credit Utilization Rate?" Experian, https://www .experian.com/blogs/ask-experian/credit-education/score-basics /credit-utilization-rate/.

22 "Affordability Calculator," Zillow, https://www.zillow.com /mortgage-calculator/house-affordability/.

23 "How Much House Can I Afford?" Bankrate, http://www .bankrate.com/calculators/mortgages/new-house-calculator.aspx.

24 "How much house can I afford?" NerdWallet, https://www .nerdwallet.com/mortgages/how-much-house-can-i-afford.

Chapter 6: Bankruptcy

1 Linda Qiu, "Yep, Donald Trump's companies have declared bankruptcy . . . more than four times," Politifact, June 21st, 2016,

http://www.politifact.com/truth-o-meter/statements/2016/jun/21
/hillary-clinton/yep-donald-trumps-companies-have
-declared-bankrupt/.

2 "June 2016 Bankruptcy Filings Down 6.9 Percent," *Judiciary
News*, United States Courts, July 27, 2016, http://www.uscourts
.gov/news/2016/07/27/june-2016-bankruptcy-filings-down
-69-percent.

3 "Bankruptcy," Nolo Press, https://store.nolo.com/products
/bankruptcy?utm_source=nolo-content&utm_medium=nolo
&utm_campaign=nolo-related-products.

4 "Find an Attorney," National Association of Consumer
Bankruptcy Attorneys, https://www.nacba.org/find-an-attorney.

5 "Chapter 11 for Individuals vs. Chapter 13," American
Bankruptcy Institute, http://www.abi.org/feed-item
/chapter-11-for-individuals-vs-chapter-13.

6 "Bankruptcy Filings Decline Is Smallest in Years," United States
Courts, October 18, 2017, http://www.uscourts.gov/news/2017/10
/18/bankruptcy-filings-decline-smallest-years.

7 "Bankruptcy," United States Courts, http://www.uscourts.gov
/services-forms/bankruptcy.

8 *Bankruptcy Basics*, Administrative Office of the United States
Courts, November 2011, http://www.uscourts.gov/sites/default
/files/bankbasics-post10172005.pdf.

Chapter 7: The Kids

1 Mark Lino, Kevin Kuczynski, Nestor Rodriguez, and TusaRebecca
Schap, "Expenditures on Children by Families, 2015," United
States Department of Agriculture, Center for Nutrition Policy and
Promotion, Miscellaneous Report No. 1528-2015, https://www
.cnpp.usda.gov/sites/default/files/crc2015.pdf.

2 Cost of Raising a Child Calculator, United States Department of
Agriculture, https://www.cnpp.usda.gov/calculatorintro.

3 "Tuition Discounts at Private Colleges Continue to Climb,"
National Association of College and University Business
Officers, May 16, 2016, http://www.nacubo.org/About

_NACUBO/Press_Room/2015_Tuition_Discounting_Study
.html.

4   College Board, *Trends in College Pricing 2016*, https://trends
.collegeboard.org/sites/default/files/2016-trends-college-pricing
-web_0.pdf.

5   "American Express Spending & Saving Tracker: A Summer Well
Spent: No Idle Time for Kids This Season," American Express/
Ebiquity, July 3, 2014, http://about.americanexpress.com/news
/sst/report/2014-07_Spend-and-Save-Tracker.pdf.

6   "Frequently Asked Questions About Overnight Camps," The
Camp Experts & Teen Summers, http://www.campexperts.com
/overnight-camps-faq.

7   "Camp Trends: Tuition," American Camp Association, http://
www.acacamps.org/press-room/camp-trends/tuition.

8   Matthew Yglesias, "Summer Camp Cost Growth Will Bankrupt
America," *Slate*, June 20, 2016, http://www.slate.com/blogs
/moneybox/2013/06/20/summer_camp_tuition_inflation.html.

9   Wendell Jamieson, "A Family Travel Playbook: Make Plans,
Prepare to Let Them Go," *New York Times*, September 12, 2017,
https://www.nytimes.com/2017/09/12/travel/a-family-travel
-playbook-make-plans-prepare-to-let-them-go.html?mcubz=0.

10 Rebekah Barsch, "Which Should You Save For First: Retirement
Or Your Kids' College?" *Forbes*, June 30, 2014, https://www
.forbes.com/sites/northwesternmutual/2014/06/30/which-should
-you-save-for-first-retirement-or-your-kids-college/#52f2f4444179;
Elliott Weir, "Securing Your Financial Safety Mask First," III
Financial, https://iiifinancial.com/2015-securing-your-financial
-safety-mask-first; Jeff Rose, "How Supporting Adult Children
Can Flat Out Ruin Your Retirement," *Forbes*, September 17,
2016, https://www.forbes.com/sites/jrose/2016/09/17/how
-supporting-adult-children-can-flat-out-ruin-your-retirement
/2/#142c93de73b8.

11 "Survey: Parents Financially Supporting Their Adult Children,"
National Endowment for Financial Education, http://www.nefe
.org/Portals/0/WhatWeProvide/PrimaryResearch/

ConsumerPolls/PDF/ParentsSupportingAdultChildren
_ExecSumm.pdf.

12 Richard Fry, "For Millennials, a Bachelor's Degree Continues to Pay Off, but a Master's Earns Even More," Pew Research Center, February 28, 2014, http://www.pewresearch.org/fact-tank/2014 /02/28/for-millennials-a-bachelors-degree-continues-to-pay-off -but-a-masters-earns-even-more.

13 "Wondering how the amount of your federal student aid is determined?" U.S. Department of Education, https://studentaid .ed.gov/sa/fafsa/next-steps/how-calculated.

14 FAFSA4caster page, Federal Student Aid, https://fafsa.ed.gov /FAFSA/app/f4cForm?execution=e1s1.

15 Sallie Mae, *How America Pays for College 2017*, https://www .salliemae.com/assets/Research/HAP/HowAmericaPaysfor College2017.pdf.

16 "Does a 529 Plan Affect Financial Aid?," Savingforcollege.com, http://www.savingforcollege.com/intro_to_529s/does-a-529-plan -affect-financial-aid.php.

17 "Don't Know How Much You Should Be Saving for College?," Fidelity Investments, April 20, 2017, https://www.fidelity.com /about-fidelity/individual-investing/ dont-know-how-much-you-should-be-saving-for-college.

18 "PLUS loans are federal loans that graduate or professional students and parents of dependent undergraduate students can use to help pay for college or career school," U.S. Department of Education, https://studentaid.ed.gov/sa/types/loans/plus.

19 "The U.S. Department of Education offers low-interest loans to eligible students to help cover the cost of college or career school," U.S. Department of Education, https://studentaid.ed.gov /sa/types/loans/subsidized-unsubsidized.

20 Preston Mueller, "The Non-Dischargeability of Private Student Loans: A Looming Financial Crisis?," *Emory Bankruptcy Developments Journal* 32, no. 1 (2015): 229–264, http://law.emory .edu/ebdj/content/volume-32/issue-1/comments/non -dischargeability-private-student-loans-looming-crisis.html.

21 Ron Lieber, "Eight Tips for Parents Who Have Saved Nothing for College," *New York Times*, May 1, 2014, https://parenting .blogs.nytimes.com/2014/05/01/eight-tips-for-parents-who -have-saved-nothing-for-college.

22 Ron Lieber, *The Opposite of Spoiled* (New York: HarperCollins, 2016).

23 John Schwartz, *Oddly Normal: One Family's Struggle to Help Their Teenage Son Come to Terms with His Sexuality* (New York: Gotham, 2012).

24 Charu Chander Gross, "The 3 Types of College Savers You'll Meet," Vanguard Blog, August 22, 2017, https://vanguardblog .com/2017/08/22/the-3-types-of-college-savers-youll-meet/? EXCMPGN=EX:EM:RIG:eITV:092117:EDU :Link:slot1:101:EDU:XX:XX:XX.

25 "Are You on Track?," College Savings Calculator, Fidelity Investments, http://www.fidelity.com/misc/college-savings /college_savings.html.

26 College Savings Planner, https://vanguard.wealthmsi.com/csp .php.

27 College Savings Calculator, http://www.schwab.com/public /schwab/investing/retirement_and_planning/saving_for_college /college_savings_calculator.

28 Sallie Mae, *How America Saves for College*, 2016, http://news .salliemae.com/sites/salliemae.newshq.businesswire.com/files /doc_library/file/HowAmericaSaves2016_FINAL.pdf.

29 Ann Carrns, "How to Manage a 529 Plan for Your Child's Education," *New York Times*, https://www.nytimes.com/2017/02 /10/your-money/529-plans-how-to-invest-college.html.

Chapter 8: Medical Disasters

1 David U. Himmelstein, Elizabeth Warren, Deborah Thorne, and Steffie Woolhandler, "Illness and Injury as Contributors to Bankruptcy," *Health Affairs*, February 2005, http://content .healthaffairs.org/content/suppl/2005/01/28/hlthaff.w5 .63.DC1.

2   David U. Himmelstein, Deborah Thorne, Elizabeth Warren, and Steffie Woolhandler, "Medical Bankruptcy in the United States, 2007: Results of a National Study," *American Journal of Medicine* 122, no. 8 (2009): 741–746, http://www.pnhp.org/new _bankruptcy_study/Bankruptcy-2009.pdf.

3   Daniel A. Austin, "Medical Debt as a Cause of Consumer Bankruptcy," *Maine Law Review* 67, no. 1 (2014): 1–23, Northeastern University School of Law Research Paper No. 204-2014, http://ssrn.com/abstract=2515321.

4   Elizabeth Warren tweet, https://twitter.com/elizabethforma /status/820688308393144321.

5   Luojia Hu, Robert Kaestner, Bhashkar Mazumder, Sarah Miller, and Ashley Wong, "The Effect of the Patient Protection and Affordable Care Act Medicaid Expansions on Financial Well-Being," NBER Working Paper No. 22170, April 2016, http://nber .org/papers/w22170.

6   Allen St. John, "How the Affordable Care Act Drove Down Personal Bankruptcy," *Consumer Reports*, May 02, 2017, http:// www.consumerreports.org/personal-bankruptcy/how-the -aca-drove-down-personal-bankruptcy.

7   Reed Abelson and Margo Sanger-Katz, "No, Obamacare Isn't in a 'Death Spiral,'" *New York Times*, March 15, 2017, https://www .nytimes.com/2017/03/15/upshot/obamacare-isnt-in-a-death-spiral -its-replacement-probably-wont-be-either.html.

8   No-Fault Auto Insurance, Insurance Information Institute, February 2014, http://www.iii.org/issue-update/no-fault -auto-insurance.

9   Lee Lorenz, "Less cholesterol, regular checkups . . . ," *The New Yorker*, February 20, 1989, https://condenaststore.com/featured /less-cholesterol-regular-checkups-lee-lorenz.html.

10 John Schwartz, "Stricken With ALS, A Doctor Perseveres," *The Washington Post*, September 5, 2000, https://www .washingtonpost.com/archive/politics/2000/09/05/stricken-with -als-a-doctor-perseveres/c66e632b-07bc-4b88-a04d-a1ea197dee12.

11 Joe Holley, "Jules R. Lodish; Doctor Showed Will to Live as He Battled With ALS," *The Washington Post*, July 31, 2008, http://www.washingtonpost.com/wp-dyn/content/article/2008/07/30/AR2008073003042.html.

12 John Schwartz and James Estrin, "Living for Today, Locked in a Paralyzed Body," *New York Times*, November 7, 2004, http://www.nytimes.com/2004/11/07/health/07ALS.html.

13 Ylan Q. Mui, "The Shocking Number of Americans Who Can't Cover a $400 Expense," *The Washington Post*, May 25, 2016, https://www.washingtonpost.com/news/wonk/wp/2016/05/25/the-shocking-number-of-americans-who-cant-cover-a-400-expense/#comments.

14 Joyce Lacovara, Comment on *Washington Post* story, "The Shocking Number of Americans Who Can't Cover a $400 Expense," *The Washington Post*, May 29, 2016, http://washingtonpost.com/news/wonk/wp/2016/05/25/the-shocking-number-of-americans-who-cant-cover-a-400-expense/?outputType=comment&commentID=washingtonpost.com/ECHO/item/f2106c13-3dd3-40c0-9559-fc4d152ec4c8.

15 Philip Bump, "Jason Chaffetz's iPhone Comment Revives the 'Poverty Is a Choice' Argument," *Washington Post*, March 7, 2017, https://www.washingtonpost.com/news/politics/wp/2017/03/07/jason-chaffetzs-iphone-comment-revives-the-poverty-is-a-choice-argument/?utm_term=.d5a6e8ecd5e1.

16 Stephen Pimpare, "Laziness Isn't Why People Are Poor. And iPhones Aren't Why They Lack Health Care," *Washington Post*, March 7, 2017, https://www.washingtonpost.com/posteverything/wp/2017/03/08/laziness-isnt-why-people-are-poor-and-iphones-arent-why-they-lack-health-care/?utm_term=.7daf565f2ee0&wpisrc=nl_most-draw5&wpmm=1.

17 Matthew Desmond, *Evicted: Poverty and Profit in the American City* (New York: Crown, 2016).

18 Ibid., 219.

19 Ibid., 378.

20 Sendhil Mullainathan and Eldar Shafir, *Scarcity: Why Having Too Little Means So Much* (New York: Times Books, 2013), 60.

21 "Cost of Pet Care: 2016," Healthy Paws Pet Insurance, https://www.healthypawspetinsurance.com/cost-of-pet-care.

22 "The AP-Petside.com Poll," GfK Custom Research North America, http://surveys.ap.org/data%5CGfK%5CAP-GfK%20Petside%20Topline%20for%20final%20060710_4th%20release.pdf.

23 "The Pet Health Insurance Industry in North America," North American Pet Health Insurance Association, https://naphia.org/industry.

24 Mandy Walker, "Is Pet Insurance Worth the Cost?" *Consumer Reports*, March 30, 2016, https://www.consumerreports.org/pet-products/is-pet-insurance-worth-cost.

25 "The 'Metal' Categories: Bronze, Silver, Gold & Platinum," Healthcare.gov, https://www.healthcare.gov/choose-a-plan/plans-categories.

26 "Medicaid & CHIP coverage," healthcare.gov, https://www.healthcare.gov/Medicaid-chip/getting-medicaid-chip.

27 "Find Someone Nearby to Help You Apply," healthcare.gov, https://localhelp.healthcare.gov.

28 "What's Medicare Supplement Insurance (Medigap)?" Medicare.gov, https://www.medicare.gov/supplement-other-insurance/medigap/whats-medigap.html.

Chapter 9: Debt

1 Permissions granted courtesy of Conrad Deisler, Hot Twang Music/BMI; Hank Card, Highway Cafe Music/BMI; Korey Simeone, Kilimanjaro Publishing/BMI; Tom Pittman, Tom Pittman/BMI; and Boo Resnick, NERTFAF Music/BMI. From the album *The Drugs I Need*, Blue Corn Music, 0603.

2 Erin El Issa, 2016 American Household Credit Card Debt Study, Nerdwallet.com, https://www.nerdwallet.com/blog/average-credit-card-debt-household.

3   Wei Li and Laurie Goodman, "Americans' Debt Styles
    by Age and Over Time," Urban Institute, November 2015,
    http://www.urban.org/sites/default/files/publication/72976
    /2000514-Americans-Debt-Styles-by-Age-and-over-Time.pdf.

4   Caroline Ratcliffe, Signe-Mary McKernan, Brett Theodos,
    Emma Cancian Kalish: *Delinquent Debt in America*, Urban
    Institute, July 28, 2014, https://www.urban.org/research/
    publication/delinquent-debt-america/view/full_report.

5   David U. Himmelstein, Deborah Thorne, Elizabeth Warren, and
    Steffie Woolhandler, "Medical Bankruptcy in the United States,
    2007: Results of a National Study, *American Journal of Medicine*
    122, no. 8 (2009): 741–746, http://www.pnhp.org/new
    _bankruptcy_study/Bankruptcy-2009.pdf.

6   Michael Corkery and Stacy Cowley, "Household Debt Makes a
    Comeback in the U.S.," *New York Times*, May 17, 2017, https://
    www.nytimes.com/2017/05/17/business/dealbook/household-debt
    -united-states.html.

7   Edmund L. Andrews, *Busted: Life Inside the Great Mortgage
    Meltdown* (New York: W. W. Norton, 2009).

8   Neal Gabler, "The Secret Shame of Middle-Class Americans,
    The Atlantic, May 2016, https://www.theatlantic.com/magazine
    /archive/2016/05/my-secret-shame/476415.

9   Joe Nocera, "My Faith-Based Retirement," *New York Times*,
    April 27, 2012, http://www.nytimes.com/2012/04/28/opinion
    /nocera-my-faith-based-retirement.html.

10 Helaine Olen, "All the Sad, Broke, Literary Men," *Slate*, April 21,
    2016, http://www.slate.com/articles/business/the_bills/2016/04
    /neal_gabler_s_atlantic_essay_is_part_of_an_old_aggravating
    _genre_the_sad.html.

11 Gene Lyons, Facebook post, April 27, 2016, https://www.
    facebook.com/gene.lyons.7/posts/10208528290057308.

12 Anthony Trollope, *The Eustace Diamonds* (London: Oxford
    University Press), 98.

13 Dave Ramsey website: http://www.daveramsey.com/.

14 The Latte Factor Calculator, David Bach website, http://
davidbach.com/latte-factor/.

15 David Bach, *Smart Women Finish Rich: 7 Steps to Achieving
Financial Security and Funding Your Dreams*, reissued, with two
additional steps, as *Smart Women Finish Rich: 9 Steps to Achieving
Financial Security and Funding Your Dream* (New York: Crown
Business, 2002).

16 Ann Carrns, "Apps That Make Saving as Effortless as Spending,"
New York Times, March 25, 2016, https://www.nytimes.com/2016
/03/27/your-money/apps-that-make-saving-as-effortless-as
-spending.html?_r=0.

17 "One in Three Americans Prepare a Detailed Household
Budget," Gallup, June 3, 2013, http://www.gallup.com/poll
/162872/one-three-americans-prepare-detailed-household-budget
.aspx?g_source=household+budget&g_medium=search&g
_campaign=tiles.

18 Helaine Olen, "Toss Your Budget, Why a Pillar of Personal
Finance Isn't Nearly as Essential as We Think," *Slate*, June 5,
2015, http://www.slate.com/blogs/moneybox/2017/03/16/donald
_trump_s_pointless_budget_is_a_perfect_symbol_of_his
_administration.html.

19 Helaine Olen, *Pound Foolish: Exposing the Dark Side of the
Personal Finance Industry* (New York: Portfolio Press, 2012).

20 "The United States of Debt," Slate Academy, http://www.slate
.com/articles/slate_plus/debt_academy_2016.html.

21 Wei Li and Laurie Goodman, "Urban Wire: Finance," Urban
Institute, November 16, 2015, http://www.urban.org/urban-wire
/six-new-insights-about-americans-borrowing-habits.

22 Leaf Van Boven and Thomas Gilovich, "To Do or to Have? That
Is the Question," *Journal of Personality and Social Psychology* 85,
no. 6 (2003): 1193–1202, DOI: http://dx.doi.org/10.1037/0022
-3514.85.6.1193, http://psych.colorado.edu/~vanboven/research
/publications/vb_gilo_2003.pdf.

23 Emily Rosenzweig and Thomas Gilovich, "Buyer's Remorse or
Missed Opportunity? Differential Regrets for Material and

Experiential Purchases," *Journal of Personality and Social Psychology* 102, no. 2 (February 2012): 215–223, DOI: http://dx.doi.org/10.1037/a0024999.

24 https://www.youneedabudget.com; http://anishusite.appspot.com.

Chapter 10: Life Insurance

1 "The Faces and Facts of Disability," Social Security Administration, https://www.ssa.gov/disabilityfacts/facts.html.

2 Ron Lieber, "The Odds of a Disability Are Themselves Odd," *New York Times*, February 5, 2010, http://www.nytimes.com/2010/02/06/your-money/life-and-disability-insurance/06money.html.

3 "Planning and Progress Study 2017," Northwestern Mutual, http://news.northwesternmutual.com/planning-and-progress-2017.

4 "The Faces and Facts of Disability," Social Security Administration.

5 "How Much Life Insurance Do I Need?" USAA, https://www.usaa.com/inet/life_insurance_advice/LifeInsuranceAdvice/LifeInsInputPage?flowExecutionKey=e1s2&w:pageMapName=w-0.

6 "HowMuch Life Insurance Do I Need?" Bankrate.com, http://www.bankrate.com/calculators/insurance/life-insurance-calculator.aspx.

7 AARP Life Insurance, http://www.aarp-lifeinsurance.com.

8 https://eapps.naic.org/cis/indexReportCriteria.do.

Chapter 11: Writing a Will

1 Richard Goldstein, "Jack LaLanne, Founder of Modern Fitness Movement, Dies at 96," *New York Times*, January 23, 2011, http://www.nytimes.com/2011/01/24/sports/24lalanne.html?mcubz=0.

2 Gallup, "Majority in U.S. Do Not Have a Will," May 18, 2016, http://www.gallup.com/poll/191651/majority-not.aspx?.

3   Geoff Ellwand, "A Dying Man's Short Will Has a Long History," *Lawyers Weekly*, May 10, 2013, http://law.usask.ca/news /LawyersWeeklyTractorWill10May13.pdf.

4   Tara Siegel Bernard, "In Using Software to Write a Will, a Lawyer Is Still Helpful," *New York Times*, September 10, 2010, http://www.nytimes.com/2010/09/11/your-money/11money.html.

5   "How to Create a Bulletproof Estate Plan," *Consumer Reports*, November 2013, http://www.consumerreports.org/cro/2013/11 /how-to-create-a-bulletproof-estate-plan/index.htm.

6   National Hospice and Palliative Care Organization customized forms, www.caringinfo.org/i4a/pages/index.cfm?pageid=3289; American Bar Association directive form, www.americanbar.org /content/dam/aba/administrative/law_aging/Links_to_State _Advance_Directive_Forms.authcheckdam.pdf; ABA, AARP, and AMA background info on advance directives, www .americanbar.org/groups/public_education/resources/law_issues _for_consumers/directive_whatis.html; ABA:healthcare wishes app, www.americanbar.org/groups/law_aging/MyHealthCare WishesApp.html.

7   Alexander K. Smith and Bernard Lo, "The Problem with Actually Tattooing DNR across Your Chest," *Journal of General Internal Medicine* 27, no. 10 (October 2012): 1238–1239, published online July 19, 2012, DOI: 10.1007/s11606-012-2134-1, www.ncbi .nlm.nih.gov/pmc/articles/PMC3445688.

8   "Dynasty Trusts . . . Not Just for the Wealthy," Investorguide .com, http://www.investorguide.com/article/13617/dynasty -trusts-not-just-for-the-wealthy-0613.

Chapter 12: Older Age

1   "Who Needs Care?" United States Department of Health and Human Services, https://longtermcare.acl.gov/the-basics/who -needs-care.html.

2   You can read much more about alternatives to nursing homes, including assisted-living and community services that help

people stay in their homes, on the federal government's Medicare website, https://www.medicare.gov/nursinghomecompare /Resources/Nursing-Home-Alternatives.html. For additional information on nursing homes, see Medline Plus, a site of the United States National Library of Medicine, https://medlineplus .gov/nursinghomes.html. A guide to residential care communities from the Centers for Disease Control and Prevention is at https:// www.cdc.gov/nchs/fastats/residential-care-communities.htm. See also, Ann Carnes, "Searching for Quality in Assisted Living Care," Your Money, *New York Times*, May 15, 2014, https://www .nytimes.com/2014/05/17/your-money/searching-for-quality-in -assisted-living-care.html.

3 A Place for Mom, http://locate.aplaceformom.com.

4 Paula Span, "A Helping Hand, Paid on Commission" *New York Times*, September 2, 2011, https://newoldage.blogs.nytimes.com /2011/09/02/a-helping-hand-paid-on-commission/

5 National Association of Area Agencies on Aging website: http:// www.n4a.org/

6 Jane Gross, *A Bittersweet Season: Caring for Our Aging Parents— and Ourselves* (New York: Vintage, 2012).

7 Paula Span, *When the Time Comes: Families with Aging Parents Share Their Struggles and Solutions* (New York: Grand Central Life & Style, 2009).

8 "Advice About Assisted Living for Aging Relatives, Part 2," October 23, 2013, http://www.nytimes.com/2013/10/23/booming /advice-about-assisted-living-for-aging-relatives-part-2.html.

9 "Home in Retirement: More Freedom, New Choices," https:// mlaem.fs.ml.com/content/dam/ML/Articles/pdf/ml_Home -Retirement.pdf.

10 Darrow Kirkpatrick, "The Cheapest Way to Roadtrip Might Surprise You," *Money*, May 22, 2015, http://time.com/money /3889400/road-trip-costs-rv-hotel.

11 "The Woman Who Lives on the QE2," BBC, http://news.bbc .co.uk/2/hi/uk_news/england/hampshire/7719605.stm.

12 Lee A. Lindquist and Robert M. Golub, "Cruise Ship Care: A Proposed Alternative to Assisted Living Facilities," *Journal of the American Geriatrics Society* 52 (2004): 1951–1954.

13 Sarah Stevenson, "Is a Cruise Ship Retirement Cheaper Than Assisted Living?" *Senior Living Blog*, February 9, 2015, http://www.aplaceformom.com/blog/2013-2-2-cruise-ship-retirement-assisted-living.

14 http://rlcommunities.com/travel-program; http://www.seniorlivinginstyle.com/senior_travel_programs_hrg; https://www.sunshineretirementliving.com/travel-program.

15 William P. Barrett, "The Best Places to Retire in 2016," *Forbes*, April 4, 2016, http://www.forbes.com/sites/williampbarrett/2016/04/04/the-best-places-to-retire-in-2016/#d15fdd1703ed.

16 Anusuya Chatterjee and Jaque King, "Best Cities for Successful Aging," Milken Institute, 2014, http://assets1c.milkeninstitute.org/assets/Publication/ResearchReport/PDF/BCSA-2014-fnl-pgs.pdf.

17 QuickFacts, United States Census, https://www.census.gov/quickfacts/table/PST045216/4828068,48167.

18 Galveston, Texas, City-Data.com, http://www.city-data.com/city/Galveston-Texas.html.

19 "Caution Against Ranking, Crime in the United States 2011," FBI, Criminal Justice Information Services Division, https://ucr.fbi.gov/crime-in-the-u.s/2011/crime-in-the-u.s.-2011/caution-against-ranking.

20 Moira McGarvey, "Retire on the Gulf Coast of Texas," *Huffington Post*, April 14, 2014, http://www.huffingtonpost.com/moira-mcgarvey-/retire-in-texas_b_5097380.html.

21 FEMA, "How to Prepare for a Hurricane," https://www.fema.gov/media-library-data/1409003345844-0e142725ea3984938c8c6748dd1598cb/How_To_Prepare_Guide_Hurricane.pdf.

22 Gwen W. Morgen, *What if . . . Workbook: Give the Gift of Preparedness to Your Loved Ones* (Seattle: CreateSpace, 2014).

23 Ron Burley, "Prepaid Funerals: A Grave Error?" *AARP the*

Magazine, December 2011–January 2012, http://www.aarp.org
/money/scams-fraud/info-12-2011/prepaid-funerals-grave-error
.html; "Should You Prepay Your Funeral?," *Kiplinger Personal
Finance*, January 2015, http://www.kiplinger.com/article
/retirement/T021-C000-S001-should-you-prepay-your-funeral
.html.

Chapter 13: The End

1 Daniel Schorn, "Kinky's Run For Governor Of Texas." *60
   Minutes*. January 22, 2006, https://www.cbsnews.com/news
   /kinkys-run-for-governor-of-texas/
2 Deuteronomy 30:11-14, "The Jewish Bible: Tanakh: The Holy
   Scriptures–The New JPS Translation According to the
   Traditional Hebrew Text: Torah * Nevi'im * Kethuvim" *Jewish
   Publication Society*, 322–323.

INDEX